Mentoring New Teachers in Post-Compulsory Education

Providing a comprehensive guide to mentoring and professional development in the post-compulsory sector, where educators play a crucial role in shaping the lives of young adult learners, this invaluable resource explores the transformative power of mentoring relationships. It equips mentors and mentees with the tools and techniques necessary to foster growth and unlock their utmost potential.

The book explores the evolving expectations and demands placed on educators in this sector and emphasises the crucial role of mentoring in supporting their professional growth and success. Readers will discover the importance of developing a solid mentoring framework, understanding the needs of mentees, and nurturing effective communication. Through nurturing supportive and dynamic mentoring relationships, educators will learn how to empower new teachers and create an environment of trust, respect, and collaboration. With practical advice, inspiring stories, and step-by-step guidance, this book empowers educators and mentors to navigate the challenging, yet rewarding, journey of professional growth.

It is an invaluable tool for anyone seeking to make a lasting impact on the lives of learners, promote excellence, and cultivate a thriving educational community in the post-compulsory sector.

Paul Euripides Demetriou is an Educational Consultant who has worked for over 35 years with young people and adults in the post-compulsory sector.

Mentoring New Teachers in Post-Compulsory Education

An Evidence-Based Introduction

Paul Euripides Demetriou

LONDON AND NEW YORK

Designed cover image: © Getty Images

First published 2026
by Routledge
4 Park Square, Milton Park, Abingdon, Oxon OX14 4RN

and by Routledge
605 Third Avenue, New York, NY 10158

Routledge is an imprint of the Taylor & Francis Group, an informa business

© 2026 Paul Euripides Demetriou

The right of Paul Euripides Demetriou to be identified as author of this work has been asserted in accordance with sections 77 and 78 of the Copyright, Designs and Patents Act 1988.

All rights reserved. No part of this book may be reprinted or reproduced or utilised in any form or by any electronic, mechanical, or other means, now known or hereafter invented, including photocopying and recording, or in any information storage or retrieval system, without permission in writing from the publishers.

For Product Safety Concerns and Information please contact our EU representative GPSR@taylorandfrancis.com. Taylor & Francis Verlag GmbH, Kaufingerstraße 24, 80331 München, Germany.

Trademark notice: Product or corporate names may be trademarks or registered trademarks, and are used only for identification and explanation without intent to infringe.

British Library Cataloguing-in-Publication Data
A catalogue record for this book is available from the British Library

ISBN: 978-1-032-86401-3 (hbk)
ISBN: 978-1-032-86400-6 (pbk)
ISBN: 978-1-003-52737-4 (ebk)

DOI: 10.4324/9781003527374

Typeset in Galliard
by KnowledgeWorks Global Ltd.

Contents

1 Exploring definitions and categories of mentoring 1

2 Mentoring and new teachers in post-compulsory education 23

3 Finding the right match: Mentors and mentees 38

4 Key models of mentoring and professional learning and development 59

5 Coaching and mentoring 78

6 Mentors and the mentoring relationship 94

7 Supporting planning and observing classroom practice 113

8 Lesson observations and feedback 139

9 Approaches to mentor feedback and maintaining ethical boundaries 170

10 Mentoring and inclusion 199

11 Approaches to failure and repairing mentoring relationships 222

12 Partnership models 239

13 Conclusion 258

Index *267*

Chapter 1

Exploring definitions and categories of mentoring

The concept of mentoring

Mentoring, as a time-honoured practice rooted in the principles of guidance and support, has played a pivotal role in shaping the landscape of education and various professional fields throughout history. With its origins dating back to ancient Greece, where mentor, a character in Homer's Odyssey, provided sage counsel and leadership to Odysseus' son Telemachus, mentoring symbolises a tradition of passing down knowledge, wisdom, and skills from experienced individuals to those seeking growth and development (Ehrich, Hansford and Ehrich, 2011). In the realm of education, mentoring has been instrumental in fostering the professional growth of teachers, administrators, and students alike, nurturing a culture of collaboration, reflection, and continuous improvement (Hackmann and Malin, 2020).

Definitions of mentoring

The notion of mentorship is largely idealised as a positive thing, though original Greek conceptions painted a more complex picture of the relationship between Mentor and Telemachus (Stokes and Garvey, 2017). A mentoring relationship, like any relationship, has good and bad moments – and good and bad outcomes – and mentoring experiences can range from effective to dysfunctional (Sarabipour *et al.* 2021). Mentoring involves both benefits and costs to those engaged in mentoring relationships.

Although there are at least 50 definitions of mentoring, all of which emphasise helping the individual grow and accomplish goals, there appear to be three areas in which many writers are agreed upon, concluding that (Bhopal, 2020):

- A mentoring experience may provide professional and career development support, role modelling, and psychosocial support; mentoring experiences should include planned activities with a mentor.

DOI: 10.4324/9781003527374-1

- Mentoring relationships are personal and reciprocal, though online mentorship options are creating opportunities to build virtual mentoring relationships.

Unlike teaching which has evolved a rich base of pedagogical practices often based on rigorous experimental design, mentoring has usually been based on the individualised practices of mentors (Bova, 2000). Over the past 20 years these notions have been reframed and mentoring is now discussed as a process which involves a set of complex skills that can be taught, practiced, and mastered and accrues measurable benefits for mentees and mentors (Dahlberg and Byars-Winston, 2019).

Mentoring in the workforce as a whole

Mentoring has long served an essential role in developing science, technology, engineering, mathematics, and medicine (professionals). Learning about the current state of knowledge in one's discipline, developing expert skill sets, and becoming familiar with disciplinary culture is a process that occurs gradually over time (Angelique, Kyle and Taylor, 2002). Professionals gather the tacit and disciplinary knowledge needed to work effectively through years of education and training (Dahlberg and Byars-Winston, 2019).

Mentoring is a powerful tool that can be successfully applied in diverse professional settings to facilitate skill development and support career progression. By fostering supportive relationships between experienced mentors and mentees seeking growth, mentoring programmes can significantly impact professional development. One key aspect of successful mentoring is the identification of individual needs and goals, ensuring that the mentorship relationship is aligned with the specific objectives of the mentee (Chaudhuri and Ghosh, 2012). This tailored approach helps in targeting skill gaps and enhancing competencies that are essential for career progression.

Mentoring experiences can be transformative for the people involved. According to research, many mentees form deep, even life-long relationships with their mentors (Woolhouse and Nicholson, 2020).

Effective mentorship provides aspects of both psychosocial and career support and may include role modelling, advising, sponsorship, and helping the mentee develop a supportive network of other mentors and peers. Mentorship, like all working alliances, evolves through stages over time and entails critical and honest self-reflection at multiple stages of the mentorship process (Dahlberg and Byars-Winston, 2019).

Social science research documents the pivotal role of identity in the formation and development of social relationships such as mentorship. Specific dimensions of identity (e.g., science identity, cultural identities) have been linked empirically to academic and career development and to the experience of mentoring relationships (Clutterbuck, 2005).

Furthermore, mentoring provides a platform for knowledge transfer and experiential learning, enabling mentees to gain insights from seasoned professionals and apply this wisdom in their own professional context (Ehrich, Hansford and Ehrich, 2011). Mentors can offer valuable guidance, share industry insights, and provide feedback to mentees, helping them navigate challenges and make informed decisions. This guidance not only accelerates skill development but also fosters a growth-oriented mindset that is vital for long-term career success (Hamlin et al., 2008).

Moreover, mentoring creates a supportive environment that encourages mentees to explore their potential, set challenging goals, and receive constructive feedback on their progress (Dominguez and Hager, 2013). This continuous feedback loop plays a crucial role in skill refinement and empowers mentees to take ownership of their career development. Additionally, mentoring relationships often extend beyond skill development to include aspects such as networking, visibility within the organisation, and career planning, thereby nurturing holistic professional growth (D'Abate, Eddy and Tannenbaum, 2003).

Mentoring encompasses a broad spectrum of interpretations, each reflecting varying perspectives and contexts within which the concept operates (Owusu-Agyeman, 2022). In its traditional sense, it is often defined as a relationship between a more experienced individual (the mentor) and a less experienced individual (the mentee), aimed at providing guidance, support, and opportunities for growth and development. This definition emphasises the transfer of knowledge, skills, and insights from one party to another in a reciprocal and nurturing manner.

Expanding beyond this conventional definition, mentoring is also recognised as a dynamic process that involves mutual learning, exchange of ideas, and collaboration between individuals with diverse backgrounds and experiences (Hamlin and Sage, 2011). In this context, mentoring is viewed as a transformative experience that fosters personal and professional growth, while promoting a culture of reciprocity, trust, and respect (Pottinger, Dyer and Akard, 2019). This broader conception of mentoring highlights the importance of building meaningful connections, fostering inclusivity, and cultivating a supportive environment conducive to individual and collective success (Klasen and Clutterbuck, 2002).

Across diverse professional fields such as business, healthcare, and the arts, mentoring has also demonstrated its enduring value as a means of facilitating career advancement, knowledge transfer, and personal empowerment (Mullen, 2000). Through the establishment of mentor-mentee relationships, experienced practitioners offer guidance, encouragement, and constructive feedback to help mentees navigate challenges, expand their skill sets, and realise their full potential. This reciprocal exchange not only enhances the mentees' professional competencies but also enriches the mentors' leadership skills, emotional intelligence, and sense of fulfilment in supporting others on their journey towards success (Mullen and Klimaitis, 2019).

Throughout history, the concept of mentoring has evolved in response to changing societal norms, technological advancements, and educational paradigms, but its core essence as a transformative process of personal and professional development has remained steadfast (Lord, Atkinson and Mitchell, 2008). By recognising the historical significance of mentoring and its enduring relevance in contemporary contexts, individuals and organisations can harness its power to cultivate talent, build communities, and foster a culture of lifelong learning and achievement (Leonardo, Godshalk and Sosik, 2008).

Mentoring holds particular significance in the field of education due to its profound impact on fostering professional growth and enhancing the learning experience for both educators and students. Within the realm of teaching, mentoring serves as a valuable tool for novice teachers to navigate the complexities of the profession, offering them personalised guidance, practical advice, and emotional support (Kemmis et al., 2013). Through mentorship, educators can gain valuable insights into effective pedagogical practices, classroom management strategies, and professional development opportunities, ultimately enhancing their teaching efficacy and job satisfaction (Higgins and Kram, 2001).

Moreover, mentoring plays a crucial role in promoting collaboration and a sense of community among educators, creating a supportive network where knowledge and expertise can be shared and cultivated (Maxwell et al., 2022). For students, mentoring can provide a personalised and holistic approach to learning, offering individualised support and encouragement to help students reach their full potential academically, socially, and emotionally (Hager and Weitlauf, 2017). By fostering positive relationships between educators and students, mentoring can contribute to a nurturing and inclusive educational environment that promotes student success and well-being (Eklin 2006).

It has been suggested that the central role of a mentor is to help mentees shape their own journeys and find their own voices. Rolfe (2021) points out that there is a wide range of definitions for mentoring. The author points out that the mentor draws on their own insights to help the mentee move forward to achieve their own goals. Clutterbuck (2007 and 2015) defines a mentor as someone with more experience who is able to share his or her knowledge with others in a trusting relationship.

Mentors were originally informally selected for their expertise rather than skills. However, this expectation has since changed, and mentors are perceived as skilled practitioners who support and enable others through their ability to support and also frame conversations through the use of active listening and questioning skills (Baker and Lattuca, 2010).

Mentoring as a journey encompasses both or all parties. It is implied that learning is open-ended, creative, and uncertain, as well as subject to unknowns (Allen, Eby and Lentz, 2006). From this perspective, mentors foster critically supportive, nurturing relationships that actively promote learning, socialisation, and identity transformation within their work environments, organisations, and professions.

Mentoring plays a crucial role in shaping the development and professional growth of teacher trainees. This critical analysis will examine the multifaceted impact of mentoring on teacher trainees, highlighting both the positive and potentially negative aspects of this relationship.

One key benefit of mentoring is the personalised guidance and support provided to trainees, enabling them to navigate the complexities of the teaching profession with greater confidence and competence. Mentors can offer valuable insights, constructive feedback, and practical strategies that help trainees develop their teaching skills and pedagogical knowledge (Woolhouse and Nicholson, 2020).

Moreover, mentoring fosters a sense of belonging and community within the teaching profession, as trainees feel connected to a network of experienced educators who are invested in their success. This sense of support can boost trainees' motivation, resilience, and overall job satisfaction.

Generic benefits of mentoring

According to a study by Nokinto the mentoring of women in HE (2016) some of the main generic benefits include the following:

For mentees:

career advancement, including a higher rate of promotion
increased opportunities and likelihood of staying at the organisation
higher salaries
increased productivity and better time management
personal and professional development, including increased job-related well-being, self-esteem and confidence, and better work-life balance
preparation for the future and heightened career aspirations
developed networking skill

For mentors:

recognised involvement in a programme of strategic importance to your organisation
new perspectives and insights into your organisation or department
potential for networking
additional experience in staff management and development
opportunity for self-reflection and personal satisfaction
career rejuvenation
increased confidence
personal fulfilment, particularly satisfaction from seeing junior staff progress

> **Reflection Task**
>
> According to Hobson et al. (2015), a mentoring scheme can benefit an organisation in numerous ways, including:
>
> Knowledge Transfer: Mentoring facilitates the transfer of knowledge, skills, and experience from seasoned employees to newer or less experienced staff. This helps in ensuring that institutional knowledge is preserved and passed down effectively.
>
> Employee Development: Mentoring supports the professional development of employees by providing them with guidance, advice, and support to navigate their career paths. This can lead to increased job satisfaction, motivation, and retention within the organisation.
>
> Succession Planning: Mentoring helps identify and nurture talented individuals within the college, preparing them for leadership roles in the future. This is crucial for succession planning and ensuring continuity in leadership positions.
>
> Diversity and Inclusion: Mentoring can promote diversity and inclusion by providing support and opportunities for underrepresented groups to thrive and advance in their careers.
>
> Improved Performance: Mentoring can enhance employee performance by providing ongoing feedback, coaching, and guidance. This can lead to increased productivity, efficiency, and overall performance within the organisation.
>
> To what extent do you feel mentoring has had or could have had the same impacts on your college?

Models of mentoring practice

Mentoring approaches are often underpinned by specific theoretical objectives. These may include some of the following.

Mentoring as a psychosocial support system

Applying a theory of psychosocial support will focus mentoring engagement around key developmental roles that support mentees in their growth. It may involve the use of the following techniques:

- Role Modelling
    Mentors should strive to model the norms, behaviours, and attitudes that demonstrate success in their field. Mentees may identify their own best

set of role models in their networks and the broader field (Hager and Weitlauf, 2017).
- Counselling
  Mentors who incorporate counselling into their models may see themselves as friendly and accepting sounding boards for mentees to express their interests and doubts, while directors ensure mentors and mentees are aware of institutional resources for mental well-being concerns.
- Acceptance and Confirmation
  This psychosocial support may be an especially important element of mentoring programmes for marginalised or underrepresented students to help them see their identities represented and feel accepted and confirmed in the organisation or institution. In addition, mentors who are members of underrepresented communities may find that students gravitate to them for their shared experiences, providing valuable support to students.
- Social Integration and Networking
  Mentors may provide opportunities for groups of mentees to collaborate on internal and external shared projects and activities and congregate in shared work and social spaces; celebrating mentees' shared engagement and accomplishments may serve as a reinforcement for those behaviours, further encouraging them to engage and ultimately persist (Tinto, 2012).

Mentoring as a learning partnership

Learning in partnership models helps promote autonomy and self-confidence as mentees approach and achieve their independently or collaboratively designed learning goals, often with the reinforcement of their mentors and communities (Kolb, 2014). This approach may be grounded in theories of adult learning and, therefore, be drawn from the following models:

- Behaviourist
  Mentors may reward mentees for large achievements like successful completion of a big project or incremental achievements like achieving a work target.
- Cognitivist
  Mentors and mentees can design programme materials or activities to enable themselves to reflect upon their current levels of understanding and achievements, along with struggles towards new goals, and to help them process their learning and plan for future achievements (Pottinger, Dyer and Akard, 2019).
- Constructivist
  Mentors create opportunities for mentees to explore their emerging organisational identities and express their creativity as they reflect upon what

they have learnt thus far to create new objectives and construct their identities (Baker and Lattuca, 2010).
- Action and Transformative Learning
  Mentees are supported to be active learners, open to transforming, rather than relying solely upon prior knowledge. According to Mezirow and Taylor (2009), they learn to embrace the new challenges their mentors and programmes introduce as they critically engage their environments to build, expand, and transform their frames of reference.

> Self-Reflection Task for Mentors – Mentoring as a Learning Partnership:
>
> 1 Reflect on how you have approached mentoring as a learning partnership. In what ways have you encouraged active participation and shared responsibility in the learning process with your mentee(s)?
> 2 Think about a recent mentoring session where you collaborated with your mentee as equal partners in the learning journey. What were the key takeaways and insights from that session?
>
> Self-Reflection Task for Mentees – Mentoring as a Learning Partnership:
>
> 1 Reflect on your role as a learner in the mentoring relationship. How have you actively engaged in the learning process and taken ownership of your development with the guidance of your mentor?
> 2 Consider a specific learning goal or skill that you have worked on with your mentor. Reflect on the progress you have made and the contributions of the learning partnership to your growth.

Mentoring with developmental theories

Like learning theories, developmental theories acknowledge that learning and growth occur across time and social contexts. The theories that may contribute to this approach include:

- Levinson's Life Stage Theory (1978)
  Mentors working within this framework support mentees to know that transitions are a natural part of professional life and model how to engage the transitional periods helping them to reflect on how their relationships have changed or are changing as both grow into their newer identities.
- Kegan's Developmental Stages (1982)
  Using the model, mentors provide structures and experiences for mentees to move through key stages. Mentors and mentees may create

developmental learning plans incorporating signals that mentees are preparing to take on greater responsibility. Mutuality and interdependence arise as mentees take on greater responsibilities for their work and career trajectories.

Mentoring underpinned by social theories

- Socialisation

    Mentors can provide self-directed, and co-directed, learning plans as they socialise mentees into the community. Mentors can socialise mentees into an organisation by introducing them to key colleagues and stakeholders, providing insights into the organisation's culture, values, and norms, and offering guidance on navigating internal dynamics and relationships. Mentors can also facilitate networking opportunities, share institutional knowledge, and help mentees understand the organisation's structure and processes. According to Ahn (2010), by acting as a trusted advisor and role model, mentors play a crucial role in helping mentees integrate successfully into the organisational environment.
- Cultural and Social Capital

    Mentors develop their mentees' social and cultural capital by fostering networking opportunities, introducing them to key contacts and resources, and encouraging participation in professional events and activities. Mentors can also provide guidance on building relationships, navigating social dynamics, and understanding cultural nuances within the organisation or industry (Hines, 2014). Facilitating exposure to diverse perspectives and experiences can help mentees expand their networks, enhance their social skills, and develop a deeper understanding of social and cultural contexts that can contribute to their professional growth and success.
- Leader and Members' Social Exchange

    Mentors may provide their mentees access to their networks in exchange for contributing their skills to achieving individual and community goals.

Mentoring with career support theories

- Organisational Learning Supports

    The mentoring programme provides clear individual and big-picture organisational and career-level learning goals, and as a result, mentors and mentees know what goals are expected, how to achieve them, and anticipated job role and developmental outcomes.
- Career Development Functions

    Mentors can play a crucial role in the career development of their mentees by offering guidance, support, and expertise. They can assist in setting goals, creating development plans, and identifying opportunities for growth within the company. Mentors can provide insights into career paths, sharing their own experiences and advice on navigating challenges. They can also offer feedback on performance, help in acquiring new skills, and recommend relevant training or further education. Mentors may advocate for their mentees, connecting them with influential contacts, endorsing them for opportunities, and providing recommendations (Higgins and Kram, 2001). Overall, mentors can help mentees build confidence, resilience, and a strong foundation for long-term career success.

Self-Reflection Exercise – Mentoring Underpinned by Social Theories

Self-Reflection Task for Mentors – Mentoring Underpinned by Social Theories:

1 Reflect on how you have applied social theories in your mentoring approach. How have concepts such as social learning theory or social identity theory influenced your interactions with your mentee(s)?
2 Consider a mentoring session where you consciously incorporated social theories into your practice. How did this influence the dynamics of the relationship and the mentee's development?

Self-Reflection Task for Mentees – Mentoring Underpinned by Social Theories:

1 Reflect on how social theories have impacted your mentoring experience. In what ways have concepts such as social exchange theory or social support theory shaped your interactions with your mentor?
2 Think about a specific mentorship moment where you noticed the application of social theories. How did this contribute to your learning and growth within the mentoring relationship?

Mentoring and coaching

Many people do not distinguish between the relationships and processes of mentoring and other forms of one-to-one developmental learning, such as coaching (Klasen and Clutterbuck, 2002); and questions remain as to the distinction (D'Abate, Eddy and Tannenbaum, 2003). The boundary between the two (coaching and mentoring) is probably more blurred than is sometimes suggested (Beattie *et al.*, 2009; Hamlin *et al.*, 2008).

Definitions for coaching and mentoring are not clear, and the terms are often used interchangeably (According to Oberholzer (2019), mentoring is defined as 'telling' a process by which the mentor guides and provides guidance to help the mentee to progress, whereas coaching is defined as a 'conversation tool' (Van Nieuwenburgh, 2017) to unlock the coachee's potential. While some theorists think of coaching as a type of mentoring, others see the exact reverse – that is, mentoring as a type of coaching.

Arguably, Coaching is an enabling process aiming at enhancing learning and development with the intention of improving the performance in a specific aspect of practice (Lord, Atkinson and Mitchell, 2008) and is the main component of a successful professional development that will become a form of support to reveal a person's potential to maximise their own performance. Mentoring is a dynamic collaborative process where the mentors or coaches demonstrate a range of cognitive coaching competencies that can lead amongst other things to the development of creativity, professional growth, and mastery over problem-solving techniques.

Stages and categories of mentoring

Stages of mentoring

According to Kram (1985), there are four main stages to their relationship, but it is not static, and she recognises that it can move between different stages. These four stages can be seen in terms of an upward spiral, as both parties have the potential to grow and develop because of the relationship. Although the client primarily benefits from the mentoring, there are also opportunities for the mentor to learn. By helping others to analyse their behaviour, mentors too can create a new mindset for themselves, by examining their own skills and working practices and becoming more self-aware (1985).

Initiation

In the initiation stage, two individuals enter into a mentoring relationship. For informal mentoring, the matching process occurs through professional or social interactions between potential mentors and mentees. Potential mentees may search for experienced, successful people whom they admire and perceive as good role models. Potential mentors search for talented people who are 'coachable'. Mentoring research describes this stage as a period when a potential mentee proves him- or herself worthy of a mentor's attention (Lumpkin, 2011). Both parties seek a positive, enjoyable relationship that would justify the extra time and effort required in mentoring.

Formal mentoring programmes manage the matching process instead of letting these relationships emerge on their own. Good matching programmes are sensitive to demographic variables as well as common professional interests. The assignment of a mentee to a mentor varies greatly across formal mentoring programmes. Mentors may review mentee profiles and select their mentees or programme administrators may match mentors and mentees. Regardless of the method, a good formal mentoring programme would require both parties to explore the relationship and evaluate the appropriateness of the mentor–mentee match (Smith and Lynch, 2014).

Cultivation

The cultivation stage is the primary stage of learning and development. Assuming a successful initiation stage, during the cultivation stage, the mentee learns from the mentor. Two broad mentoring functions are at their peak during this stage. The career-related function often emerges first when the mentor coaches the mentee on how to work effectively and efficiently. Coaching may be active within the mentee's organisation when a mentor assigns challenging assignments to the mentee, maximises the mentee's exposure and visibility in the organisation, and actively sponsors the mentee through promotions and recognition (Smith and Lynch, 2014).

Mentors outside of the mentee's organisation can also provide valuable advice on how to thrive and survive, although they may lack organisational power to directly intervene on behalf of the mentee. The psychosocial function emerges after the mentor and mentee have established an interpersonal bond. Within this function, the mentor accepts and confirms the mentee's professional identity and the relationship matures into a strong friendship (Pottinger, Dyer and Akard, 2019).

The cultivation stage is generally a positive one for both mentor and mentee. The mentor teaches the mentee valuable lessons gained from the mentor's experience and expertise. The mentee may also teach the mentor valuable lessons related to new technologies, new methodologies, and emerging issues in the field.

Separation

The separation stage generally describes the end of a mentoring relationship. The relationship may end for a number of reasons. There may be nothing left to learn, the mentee may want to establish an independent identity, or the mentor may send the mentee off on his or her own the way a parent sends off an adult child (Smith and Lynch, 2014).

If the relationship's end is not accepted by both parties, this stage can be stressful with one party unwilling to accept the loss. Problems between the mentor and the mentee can arise when only one party wants to terminate the mentoring relationship (Clutterbuck, 2005). Mentees may feel abandoned, betrayed, or unprepared if they perceive the separation to be premature. Mentors may feel betrayed or used if the mentee no longer seeks their counsel or support.

Redefinition

During the redefinition stage, both mentor and mentee recognise that their relationship can continue but that it will not be the same as their mentoring relationship. If both parties successfully negotiate through the separation stage, the relationship can evolve into a working relationship or social friendship. Unlike the cultivation stage, the focus of the relationship is no longer centred on the mentee's career development (Hamlin and Sage, 2011). The former mentor may establish mentoring relationships with new mentees. Likewise, the former mentee may serve as a mentor to others.

Self-reflective exercise

Complete the table below.

Stages of mentoring	Which skills you will need to manage it effectively
Initiation	
Cultivation	
Separation	
Redefinition	

Categories of mentoring

Previous studies have categorised mentoring into formal and informal types (Bhopal, 2020; Kemmis *et al.*, 2014; Sarabipour *et al.*, 2021). Formal mentoring is organised through a structured programme that involves assigning mentors to protégés to support them, whilst informal mentoring takes the form of an unstructured voluntary relationship (Bhopal, 2020) between an experienced and a novice teacher. Whereas formal and informal mentoring represent the conventional forms of support for novice teachers, emerging literature has revealed other forms of mentoring such as peer mentoring (Sarabipour *et al.*, 2021) and group mentoring (Mullen, Fish and Hutinger, 2010).

Formal mentoring

Formal mentoring programmes differ greatly in nature, focus, and outcomes. For instance, in her extensive review, Jacobi (1991) noted that some programmes train mentors, while others do not; mentors are assigned to mentees, and in other programmes the mentee selects the mentor; some programmes designate the location and frequency of meetings, while others leave it to the participants to decide. This type of one-on-one mentoring pairs a senior staff member with a junior staff mentor, usually from the same department, for a specified time period. This approach assumes mentors accept responsibility for helping mentees grow and develop (Lumpkin, 2011).
 Advantages:

- Formal mentoring increases job performance, enhances confidence, facilitates networking, and decreases turnover, thus positively impacting the entire department (Lumpkin, 2011) and guaranteeing that every junior staff member has a mentor if paired formally (Reimers, 2014) and mentees can receive useful discipline-specific information.

The disadvantages include the following:

- The assigned mentor and mentee may not be a good fit for any number of reasons, such as personalities. To reduce this likelihood, both the mentor and the mentee should have input on who is assigned to them (Allen, Eby and Lentz, 2006).
- Being from the same department, mentees may be reluctant to admit struggles candidly and thus not get the mentoring they need. To address this, expectations for confidentiality should be specified. Additionally, mentees should build a network of mentors – including those from outside the department so they have support to address their full range of needs (Klasen and Clutterbuck, 2002).
- A department may not have enough mentors depending on the ratio of junior staff to senior staff. One way to address this is to engage mentors from a related department.

Informal mentoring

Informal mentoring is defined as voluntary mentoring relationships that are not assigned and lack structure about how mentors work with mentees constituting informal mentoring (Lumpkin, 2011). The advantages are often explained as:

- Informal mentoring tends to be more egalitarian, longer lasting, and occurs with greater frequency than formal mentoring (Ragins and Cotton, 1999).
- Mentees tend to have stronger connections and broader interactions with informal mentors (Sands, Parson and Duane, 1991). In one study, mentees with informal mentors reported higher satisfaction and received greater benefits in most mentoring roles than those with formal mentors (Ragins and Cotton, 1999).
- The voluntary nature can allow for greater flexibility and arguably informal mentoring activities are a sign of a healthy organisational culture (Eklin, 2006).

The disadvantages are often suggested to consist of

- Many departments do not have strong mentoring cultures that naturally lead to informal mentoring. To address this, senior managers can intentionally set up structures and events to nurture informal mentoring relationships, such as workshops and presentations.

- Having a suitable mentor is not guaranteed, and organisation areas most in need of mentoring may be the least likely to find an informal mentor. Furthermore, because mentors tend to gravitate towards younger versions of themselves, groups historically underrepresented in organisations, such as women and minorities, may be informally mentored less frequently, thereby perpetuating inequities (Bova, 2000). As such, informal mentoring is likely best paired with formal mentoring programmes.

Both formal and informal mentoring are normally conducted one-to-one, and as the name suggests, one-to-one mentoring is when a single mentor is paired with a single mentee. This is the most traditional form of mentoring and the most common perception of mentoring as well. This kind of mentoring allows individuals to build stronger personal relationships (Sands, Parson and Duane, 1991). Here, mentors can directly share their knowledge and experience with their mentees over a period of time that suits both parties.

Peer Mentoring

In this category, staff members with equal ranks from either the same or different departments develop supportive networks. They meet regularly to discuss issues and challenges they are facing, as well as share advice, information, and strategies (Angelique, Kyle and Taylor, 2002). It can also effectively address psychosocial needs, increase collaboration, normalise challenges, and reduce isolation (Smith, McAllister and Crawford, 2001). Peer mentoring has shown to be an effective form of mentoring, with positive evaluations of peer mentoring programmes by teachers in educational establishments in the United States and other parts of the globe (Rees and Shaw, 2014; Smith, McAllister and Crawford, 2001; Wasburn, 2007).

Its advantages include:

- Participants are exposed to a range of opinions, advice, and diverse perspectives rather than relying on the sole opinion of one mentor.
- Peers confronting similar challenges/issues may be better suited to give practical advice since they likely have the most recent experience with similar issues.
- Since peer mentoring doesn't rely on being chosen as a mentee, it offers some balance for minorities and women and ensures equal access to mentoring (Wasburn, 2007).

The disadvantages include:

- Since peers may not have experienced all levels of the organisation, this type of mentoring cannot address all aspects of a career (Angelique, Kyle and Taylor, 2002).
- Junior staff may not feel the need to participate in a peer network.

Group and team mentoring

Group mentoring is when a single mentor provides guidance to a group of mentees. This style usually involves more experienced mentors, who have expertise in their field and are also comfortable handling more than one mentee simultaneously. Organisations may use group-based mentoring when mentees on similar career paths require similar training or guidance in a short span of time, and there is a shortage of mentors. Similarly, if several mentees require support on a topic a particular mentor holds expertise in, they may participate in group-based mentoring (Rees and Shaw, 2014).

Team mentoring

Team mentoring is similar to group mentoring but for one difference – it involves more than one mentor. Thus, team mentoring is when a group of mentors, together, mentor a group of mentees. Such a mentoring programme allows individuals with different viewpoints to come together. This kind of mentoring experience is based on the idea of teamwork and collaboration. Juniors and seniors working together on a common/shared goal or project may indulge in team mentoring. Meetings should include both structured discussions and time for informal discussion (Hunt and Weintraub, 2002).

The advantages of both Group and Team mentoring include the following:

- A few mentors can serve many mentees, which can help address the unbalanced numbers of junior and senior staff. It can also maximise the impact of excellent mentors and mentees can learn from each other.
- This format allows for choice of participation and does not force unwilling staff into a mentoring relationship.

The joint disadvantages may include:

- Confidentiality and trust issues may arise. Faculty must be assured that nothing that is said during the mentoring process can be used against them by other members of the group – including senior staff (Hunt and Weintraub, 2002).
- Because of group size, scheduling and having everyone attend all meetings may be difficult, which may cause some mentees to not have the regular contact with mentors and peers that is necessary for effective mentoring. Like other forms of mentoring, this is best paired with different types of mentoring to address the shortcomings of this approach.

Flash mentoring

Mentoring is usually a long-term relationship. But flash mentoring refers to a mentoring style that is short-lived. It's usually a one-time process or event where mentees are mentored on a specific topic in a focused session.

Its advantages include the following:

- It is focused mentoring and therefore has a single shared objective.
- It promotes collaboration and a shared work experience.
- It allows for quick, on-demand access to mentorship, providing flexibility for both mentors and mentees.
- As flash mentoring sessions are shorter in duration, they facilitate rapid knowledge transfer and quick resolution of specific issues or challenges.
- Flash mentoring can connect individuals with a wide range of mentors, enabling exposure to diverse perspectives and expertise (Hackmann and Malin, 2020).

The disadvantages of Flash Mentoring can include:

- Due to the short duration of flash mentoring sessions, there may be limitations in developing deep, long-term relationships or addressing complex professional development needs.
- The transient nature of flash mentoring may result in a lack of continuity in mentorship relationships, impacting the sustainability of learning and growth.
- Given the brief interactions in flash mentoring, there may be challenges in personalising mentorship to individual goals and learning styles.

Reverse mentoring

Reverse mentoring is the opposite of traditional mentoring. In the case of reverse mentoring, junior team members provide guidance to senior professionals who may be unfamiliar with a new technology, product, or idea. This type of knowledge sharing by junior employees enables senior individuals to remain abreast of the latest developments and gain much-needed perspective to develop products for an ever-changing audience.

According to Schunk and Mullen (2013), some of the main advantages include:

- The opportunity it provides for senior employees to gain insights into new technologies, trends, and perspectives that may be more familiar to younger generations. This can help organisations stay relevant and innovative in a rapidly changing business environment. By bridging the generation gap, reverse mentoring can foster a culture of collaboration, diversity, and mutual learning within the organisation.
- It can enhance employee engagement and retention by creating meaningful opportunities for younger employees to contribute to the professional development of their more experienced counterparts.
- It can empower junior employees, boost their confidence, and enable them to showcase their skills and knowledge in a mentorship role. This not only benefits the mentees by providing a platform for growth and recognition but also strengthens the overall talent pipeline within the organisation.

Some of its potential challenges and disadvantages include:

- The need to manage power dynamics and ensure that both mentors and mentees approach the relationship with respect and open-mindedness. Senior professionals may initially find it challenging to accept guidance from younger employees, which could lead to resistance or conflicts in the mentoring relationship.
- There is also the risk of reinforcing stereotypes or assumptions based on age or generational differences. Organisations must actively address biases and promote inclusivity to prevent negative perceptions or misunderstandings from affecting the effectiveness of the mentoring process.
- Managing expectations and setting clear objectives for the reverse mentoring programme is crucial to ensure that the initiative aligns with the organisation's strategic goals and delivers tangible benefits.

Virtual mentoring

As is evident by its name, virtual mentoring refers to a mentoring programme that takes place virtually. It's also referred to as remote mentoring. Individuals can also sign up on mentoring platforms as mentors and share their knowledge or as mentees and find the required support (Leck and Wood, 2013).

Some of the advantages include:

- Because it takes place through video conferencing, it removes the constraints or barriers of location. It also offers flexibility in terms of scheduling and communication, allowing participants to engage in mentoring sessions at their convenience.
- It's also more inclusive in nature since it includes even those employees who may not be able to physically meet each other.
- Individuals can also sign up on mentoring platforms as mentors and share their knowledge or as mentees and find the required support. Virtual mentoring platforms often include interactive features such as chat rooms, discussion forums, and video conferencing, enhancing mentee engagement and participation.
- Virtual mentoring eliminates the need for travel and facilitates cost-effective communication, making it an economical option for organisations with limited resources.
- It can be easily scaled to accommodate a larger number of participants, making it suitable for organisations looking to implement mentoring programmes on a broader scale.

Some of the main disadvantages of Virtual Mentoring include:

- It may lack the personal connection that comes with face-to-face interactions, potentially impacting the quality of the mentoring relationship.

- Because it relies on technology, technical issues such as poor internet connectivity or platform glitches can disrupt mentoring sessions and hinder communication.
- The absence of non-verbal cues in virtual communication can lead to misunderstandings or misinterpretations, potentially affecting the effectiveness of the mentoring relationship.

Self-Reflection Exercises – Skills-Based Mentoring:

1. Describe your current approach to skills-based mentoring. What specific skills do you focus on developing in your mentees?
2. Reflect on a recent mentoring session where you focused on skills development. How effective was your method in helping the mentee improve their skills?
3. What are some areas of improvement you can identify in your skills-based mentoring style? How do you plan to address these areas?
4. Discuss a successful outcome from a skills-based mentoring relationship. How did your guidance contribute to the mentee's skill enhancement?
5. In what ways do you tailor your skills-based mentoring approach to meet individual mentee needs and learning styles?

Self-Reflection Exercises – Career Development Mentoring:

1. Reflect on your approach to career development mentoring. How do you assist mentees in setting and achieving their career goals?
2. Describe a challenging situation you encountered while providing career development mentoring. What strategies did you employ to overcome the challenge?
3. How do you stay updated on industry trends and opportunities to better guide your mentees in career advancement?
4. Discuss a time when you supported a mentee in making a significant career decision. What factors did you consider in offering guidance?
5. What feedback have you received from mentees regarding the impact of your career development mentoring? How do you use this feedback to enhance your mentoring approach?

Self-reflection

> From your perspective, what are the differences between mentoring and coaching, or do you feel that they are the same?

References

Ahn, J. (2010). The Role of Social Network Locations in the College Access Mentoring of Urban Youth. *Education and Urban Society*, 42(7), 839–859. https://doi.org/10.1177/0013124510379825

Allen, T., Eby, L. and Lentz, E. (2006) 'The relationship between formal mentoring program characteristics and perceived program effectiveness', *Personnel Psychology*, 59, pp. 125–153. 10.1111/j.1744-6570.2006.00747.x.

Angelique, H., Kyle, K. and Taylor, E. (2002) 'Mentors and muses: new strategies for academic success', *Innovative Higher Education*, 26, pp. 195–209. 10.1023/A:1017968906264.

Baker, V.L. and Lattuca, L.R. (2010) 'Developmental networks and learning: toward an interdisciplinary perspective on identity development during doctoral study', *Studies in Higher Education*, 35(7), pp. 807–827. https://doi.org/10.1080/03075070903501887

Beattie, R.S., Hamlin, R.G., & Ellinger, A.D. (2009). Toward a profession of coaching? A definitional examination of 'coaching,' 'organization development,' and 'human resource development'. *International Journal of Evidence Based Coaching and Mentoring*, 7(1), 13–38. https://doi.org/10.24384/IJEBCM

Bhopal, K. (2020) 'Success against the odds: the effects of mentoring on the careers of senior Black and Minority Ethnic academics in the UK', *British Journal of Educational Studies*, 68(1), pp. 79–95. https://doi.org/10.1080/00071005.2019.1581127

Bova, B. (2000) 'Mentoring revisited: the Black woman's experience', *Mentoring & Tutoring: Partnership in Learning*, 8, pp. 5–16. 10.1080/713685511.

Dahlberg M.L., Byars-Winston A. (Eds.) (2019). National Academies of Sciences, Engineering, and Medicine; Policy and Global Affairs; Board on Higher Education and Workforce; Committee on Effective Mentoring in STEMM. The Science of Effective Mentoring in STEMM. Washington (DC): National Academies Press (US); 2019 Oct 30. PMID: 31958221.

Chaudhuri, S. and Ghosh, R. (2012) 'Reverse mentoring: a social exchange tool for keeping the boomers engaged and millennials committed', *Human Resource Development Review*, 11(1), pp. 55–76. https://doi.org/10.1177/1534484311417562

Clutterbuck, D. (2005) 'Establishing and maintaining mentoring relationships: an overview of mentor and mentee competencies', *South African Journal of Human Resource Management*, 3. 10.4102/sajhrm.v3i3.70.

D'Abate, C., Eddy, E. and Tannenbaum, S. (2003) 'What's in a name? A literature-based approach to understanding mentoring, coaching, and other constructs that describe developmental interactions', *Human Resource Development Review*, 2, pp. 360–384. 10.1177/1534484303255033.

Dominguez, N. and Hager, M. (2013) 'Mentoring frameworks: synthesis and critique', *International Journal of Mentoring and Coaching in Education*. https://doi.org/10.1108/IJMCE-03-2013-0014

Ehrich, L., Hansford, B. and Ehrich, J.F. (2011) Mentoring across the professions: some issues and challenges 2011, 93–113. https://ro.uow.edu.au/edupapers/1070

Eklin, J. (2006) 'A review of mentoring relationships: formation, function, benefits, and dysfunction', *Otago Management Graduate Review*, 4, pp. 11–23.

Hackmann, D.G. and Malin, J.R. (2020) 'From dyad to network: the evolution of a mentoring relationship', *Mentoring & Tutoring: Partnership in Learning*, 28(4), pp. 498–515.

Hager, M.J. and Weitlauf, J. (2017) 'How can developmental networks change our view of work-life harmony?', *The Chronicle of Mentoring and Coaching*, 1 (Special Issue 10), pp. 894–899.

Hamlin, R., Ellinger, A. and Beattie, R. (2008) 'Toward a profession of coaching? A definitional examination of "coaching," "organization development," and "human resource development"', *International Journal of Evidence Based Coaching and Mentoring*, 7, pp. 13–38.

Hamlin, R. and Sage, L. (2011) 'Behavioural criteria of perceived mentoring effectiveness: an empirical study of effective and ineffective mentor and mentee behaviour within formal mentoring relationships', *Journal of European Industrial Training*, 35, pp. 752–778. 10.1108/03090591111168311.

Higgins, M.C. and Kram, K.E. (2001) 'Reconceptualizing mentoring at work: a developmental network perspective', *Academy of Management Review*, 26(2), pp. 264–288.

Hines, M.E. (2014) 'Social and cultural capitol in formal one-on-one mentoring relationships', Senior Honors Projects, 2010-current. 425. https://commons.lib.jmu.edu/honors201019/425

Hobson, Andrew & Maxwell, Bronwen & Stevens, & Doyle, and Malderez, Angi. (2015). *Mentoring and coaching for teachers in the Further Education and Skills Sector in England: full report.* 10.13140/RG.2.1.4424.9680.

Hunt, J. and Weintraub, J. (2002) 'How coaching can enhance your brand as a manager', *Journal of Organizational Excellence*, 21, pp. 39–44. 10.1002/npr.10018.

Jacobi, M. (1991) 'Mentoring and undergraduate academic success: a literature review', *Review of Educational Research*, 61(4), pp. 505–532. https://doi.org/10.3102/00346543061004505

Kegan, R. (1982) *The evolving self: Problem and process in human development.* Harvard University Press.

Kemmis, S., Heikkinen, H., Fransson, G., Aspfors, J. and Edwards-Groves, C. (2014) 'Mentoring of new teachers as a contested practice: supervision, support and collaborative self-development', *Teaching and Teacher Education*, 43, pp. 154–164. 10.1016/j.tate.2014.07.001.

Klasen, N. and Clutterbuck, D. (2002) *Implementing mentoring schemes, a practical guide to successful programs.* Butterworth-Heinemann.

Kolb, D.A. (2014) *Experiential learning: Experience as the source of learning and development.* FT Press.

Kram, K. (1985) 'Phases of the mentor relationship', *Academy of Management Journal*, 26(4), pp. 608–625.

Leck J.D. and Wood, P.M. (2013) 'Forming Trust in E-Mentoring: A Research Agenda', *American Journal of Industrial and Business Management*, 3(1), pp. 101–109. doi: 10.4236/ajibm.2013.31013.

Leonardo, d, Godshalk, V. and Sosik, J. (2008) 'Mentoring and leadership: Standing at the crossroads of theory, research, and practice', in *The handbook of mentoring at work: Theory, research, and practice.* SAGE Publications, Inc., pp. 149–178. Available at: <https://doi.org/10.4135/9781412976619> [Accessed 11 March 2024].

Lord, P., Atkinson, M. and Mitchell, H. (2008) *Mentoring and coaching for professionals: A study of the research evidence.* National Foundation for Educational Research.

Lumpkin, A. (2011) 'A model for mentoring university faculty', *The Educational Forum*, 75, pp. 357–368.

Mezirow, J. and Taylor, E. (2009) *Transformative learning in practice: Insights from community, workplace, and higher education.* Jossey-Bass.

Mullen, C. and Klimaitis, C. (2019) 'Defining mentoring: a literature review of issues, types, and applications', *Annals of the New York Academy of Sciences*, pp. 1–17. 10.1111/nyas.14176.

Mullen, C.A. (2000) 'Constructing co-mentoring partnerships: walkways we must travel', *Theory Into Practice*, 39(1), pp. 4–11. https://doi.org/10.1207/s15430421tip3901_2

Mullen, C.A., Fish, V.L. and Hutinger, J.L. (2010) 'Mentoring doctoral students through scholastic engagement: Adult learning principles in action', *Journal of Further and Higher Education*, 34(2), pp. 179–197. https://doi.org/10.1080/03098771003695452

Oberholzer, L. 2019. Developing a Culture of Mentoring and Coaching in a Mainstream Secondary Context Through the Use of Lesson Study. *Research in Teacher Education*. 9 (1), pp. 39–44. https://doi.org/10.15123/uel.87649

Owusu-Agyeman, Y. (2022) 'The mentoring experiences of early career and senior academics in a multicampus university in South Africa', *Educational Process: International Journal*, 11(1), pp. 65–85.

Pottinger, E., Dyer, R. and Akard, J. (2019) 'Reflective practice through mentorship: a program reflection', *Journal of Instructional Research*, 8(2), pp 62–69.

Ragins, B.R. and Cotton, J.L. (1999) 'Mentor functions and outcomes: a comparison of men and women in formal and informal mentoring relationships', *Journal of Applied Psychology*, 84(4), pp. 529–550. https://doi.org/10.1037/0021-9010.84.4.529

Rees, A. and Shaw, R. (2014). 'Peer mentoring communities of practice for early and mid-career faculty: broad benefits from a research-oriented female peer mentoring group', *Journal of Faculty Development*, 28(2), pp. 5–17.

Reimers, T. (2014) 'Starting a mentoring initiative', in Reimers, T. (ed.) *Mentoring best practices: A handbook.* University at Albany State University of New York.

Sands, R.H., Parson, L.A. and Duane, J. (1991) 'Faculty mentoring faculty in a public university', *Journal of Higher Education*, 62(2), pp. 174–193.

Sarabipour, S., Hainer, S.J., Arslan, F.N., de Winde, M., Furlong, C., Bielczyk, E., Jadavji, N.M., Shah, A. and Davla, S. (2021) 'Building and sustaining mentor interactions as a mentee', *The FEBS Journal*, 289(2022), pp. 1374–1384.

Schunk, D.H. and Mullen, C.A. (2013) 'Toward a conceptual model of mentoring research: integration with self-regulated learning', *Educational Psychology Review*, 25, pp. 361–389.

Smith, L.S., McAllister, L.E. and Crawford, C.S. (2001) 'Mentoring benefits and issues for public health nurses', *Public Health Nursing*, 18(2). https://onlinelibrary.wiley.com/toc/15251446/2001/18/2

Smith, R. and Lynch, D. (2014) 'Coaching and mentoring: a review of literature as it relates to teacher professional development', *International Journal of Innovation, Creativity and Change*, 4, 67–75.

Stokes, P. and Garvey, R. (2017) *Coaching and mentoring theory & practice.* Sage Publishing.

Tinto, V. (2012) *Leaving college: Rethinking the causes and cures of student attrition.* University of Chicago Press.

Van Nieuwenburgh, C. (2017). *An introduction to coaching skills: A practical guide.* Routledge.

Wasburn, M. (2007) 'Mentoring women faculty: an instrumental case study of strategic collaboration', *Resources*, 15. 10.1080/13611260601037389.

Woolhouse, C. and Nicholson, L. (2020) *Mentoring in higher education: Case studies of peer learning and pedagogical development.* Palgrave Macmillan.

Chapter 2

Mentoring and new teachers in post-compulsory education

Definitions of mentoring in education

Mentoring will be defined as directive practice, providing guidance and advice, and coaching will be defined as non-directive practice, enabling professional learners to find solutions within themselves through the use of learning conversations, frameworks, and questions.

In the realm of education, a mentor plays a pivotal role in supporting and guiding an individual often referred to as a mentee or protégé – on their academic and personal journey. The primary responsibility of a mentor is to provide effective guidance, support, and encouragement to the mentee, with the overarching objective of facilitating their learning and development (Larsen et al., 2023). This role encompasses various key responsibilities that are essential for the mentor-mentee relationship to thrive and yield positive outcomes.

Mentors were informally selected for their expertise rather than skills. In traditional societies and early educational systems, the concept of mentoring and the role of a mentor did not require formal training or professional qualifications. Instead, mentoring was an informal practice based on the principles of apprenticeship, where experienced individuals imparted knowledge and skills to novices in a particular field through a relationship of trust and guidance (Caskey and Weller Swanson, 2020). These mentors were often chosen based on their experience, wisdom, and personal qualities rather than any formal training or certification.

The relationship between mentor and mentee was built on mutual respect, trust, and a shared commitment to learning and growth. Mentors served as role models, advisors, and sources of wisdom, offering guidance and support to help the mentee navigate challenges, acquire new skills, and achieve personal and professional goals (Hobson et al., 2015).

While the informal nature of mentoring in the past allowed for flexibility and personalised guidance, the evolution of education and professional development has led to a growing recognition of the benefits of structured mentoring programmes and trained mentorship professionals (Eleyan and Eleyan, 2011). Many educational institutions, organisations, and industries provide formal mentor training programmes to equip mentors with the necessary skills, knowledge, and tools to effectively support their mentees in achieving success. Despite this shift towards more structured mentorship, the essence of mentoring as a relationship built on support, guidance, and mutual growth remains a timeless and invaluable practice (Duckworth and Maxwell, 2015).

Western (2012, p. 45) refers to a mentor as a 'trained professional helper'. However, this seems to oversimplify a very complex role, where a mentor needs to balance their subject expertise and the support the mentee requires with their responsibility, as seen in particular in teacher education, to assess mentees and their outcomes too (Walters, Robinson and Walters, 2020).

In education, mentoring is more nuanced, depending on where the mentee is at on their mentor journey. In the realm of education, mentoring is a dynamic and nuanced practice that varies depending on the stage of the mentee's journey and their individual needs (Misawa and McClain, 2020). The mentor's role is multifaceted and adaptable, requiring a deep understanding of the mentee's current level of knowledge, skills, and experience to provide tailored support and guidance (Aspfors and Fransson, 2015).

Mentors are perceived as skilled practitioners who support and enable others, through their ability to support, and also frame conversations through the use of active listening and questioning skills (Hobson and Maxwell, 2020).

For mentees at the beginning of their educational journey, mentors often focus on establishing a solid foundation of knowledge, building confidence, and setting clear learning goals (Misawa and McClain, 2020). These mentors may adopt a more directive approach, offering structured guidance, resources, and strategies to help mentees navigate the complexities of their academic pursuits.

As mentees progress in their educational journey and gain more experience and expertise, the mentor's role evolves to one of a facilitator, collaborator, and critical friend (Aderibigbe, Gray and Colucci-Gray, 2018). Mentors at this stage may engage in more in-depth discussions, provide opportunities for reflection and self-assessment, and offer feedback to help mentees refine their skills and enhance their learning outcomes (Cheng and Hackworth, 2021).

As mentees approach key transitions or milestones in their educational trajectory, such as transitioning from one educational level to another or entering the workforce, mentors may serve as coaches, advocates, and connectors. They may assist them in navigating critical decision-making processes, exploring career options, and making informed choices that align with their aspirations and values (Western, 2012).

The mentor needs to understand how to support the mentee accordingly, and the quality of the mentor relationship and the learning conversations are key (Rolfe, Freshwater and Jasper, 2001). Overall, the nuanced nature of mentoring in education underlines the importance of tailoring the mentorship experience to meet the unique needs, goals, and developmental stage of each mentee, ultimately fostering their growth, success, and personal fulfilment (Niklasson, 2018).

Approaches to mentoring

Judgemental mentoring

It involves the mentor observing, evaluating, and giving feedback to the mentee on how to improve their teaching. The underlying purpose of the mentoring is to try to bring about performance improvement through feedback and advice. According to Hobson and Malderez (2013), however, if the mentoring approach is solely or mainly judgemental, it can impact a mentee's self-efficacy and willingness to be autonomous in their approaches to teaching.

Developmental mentoring

Developmental mentoring emerged in Europe in the 1980s as a process for empowering others to take charge of their own professional development and is a flexible and multifaceted approach in which the mentor facilitates growth and learning (Thornton and Beutel, 2024). Some of its main characteristics include the following:

- There is a focus on developing levels of understanding and mutuality of learning for both parties.
- There is no line of accountability, e.g. manager/direct report, supervisor/researcher, so the conversations are more likely to be free from bias.
- The mentor and mentee are able to address difficult issues as they arise due to the significant level of trust built between the two.
- There is an emphasis upon the generosity of time and help by the mentor and the willingness of the mentee to take charge of their learning

(Higgins and Kram, 2001)

Transformational mentoring

The underlying purpose of this approach is to bring about substantial change in an organisation and/or redress systemic inequalities. According to Scandura and Williams (2004), Transformational mentoring includes activities designed to promote long-term, holistic thinking in mentees and will enhance mentees' reputations by emphasising the praiseworthy aspects of their behaviours including experimentation and risk-taking and self-sacrifice.

It will encourage mentee efforts to alter existing organisational practices through the use of critical pedagogies, supporting mentees to experience different cultures and to be an advocate for social justice. Ultimately, it will reduce the level of idealised influence attributed by the mentee to the mentor and impact on their self-efficacy (Wang, 2001).

The Education and Training Foundation framework of mentoring

In order to add clarity and standardisation of their roles, the Education and Training Foundation (ETF) launched a Mentoring Framework as part of its support for mentors and coaches of practitioners in the Further Education (FE) and Training sector in 2021.

The ETF aimed to improve the quality of mentoring and coaching across the sector by offering a range of CPD activities and resources aimed at leaders/managers, mentors, and mentees. The Framework was developed with practitioners and leaders from the sector. It aimed to:

Establish a shared understanding of effective mentoring practice
Enhance the quality of mentoring for practitioners
Ensure that mentoring is supportive and nurturing
Help mentees and mentors to develop teaching, learning, and assessment strategies which meet learners' needs

The Framework sets out a series of practices which it delivers through its website and webinars for leaders/managers, mentors, and mentees to bring about a developmental and nurturing mentoring which supports teachers/trainers with their professional development (ETF, 2021).

The mentoring framework involves a series of relationships between mentor and mentee and which also involves Trainers; Leaders and Mentoring Co-ordinators in a variety of different roles (ETF, 2024).

ONSIDE mentoring

This model has been developed to underpin the mentoring of trainees in post-compulsory education and encompasses six key areas that guide the mentor-mentee relationship towards achieving growth and development (Maxwell et al., 2021).

Mentoring must be:

Offline
The mentee should not be placed in a subordinate position of power in relation to their mentor and should be free to discuss areas of professional

development and to make mistakes without fear of criticism (Brondyk and Searby, 2013). This cautions against the trainee being mentored by their line manager or supervisor. If someone is being mentored by their line manager, there can be a hierarchical association where one person is in a position of power over another which could cause the trainee stress and anxiety about making mistakes (ETF, 2022).

Non-judgemental

Duckworth and Maxwell (2015) recommend that the mentor should be focussing on supporting the mentee with their broader professional development goals. They should not be focussing on evaluations of the performance, and the relationship should be based more broadly on collaborations and professional discussions and founded on an approach that is developmental and collaborative. It should aim to create mutual understanding and help develop strong self-reflection in mentees (Woolhouse and Nicholson, 2020).

Supportive

Mentors play a crucial role in supporting their mentees' psycho-social needs and overall well-being by offering guidance, empathy, and a safe space for the mentee to express their emotions and concerns. Therefore, mentees should be made to feel supported and given the space to discuss their psycho-social needs and well-being and receive the appropriate support (Higgins and Kram, 2001).

Mentoring relationships provide an opportunity for mentees to develop self-awareness, emotional resilience, and coping strategies through the mentor's support and understanding. Additionally, mentors can help mentees develop healthy coping mechanisms, set boundaries, and establish positive relationships, contributing to the mentee's overall well-being and personal growth. By nurturing a supportive and caring mentorship relationship, mentors can positively impact their mentees' mental health and psycho-social development (Mullen and Klimaitis, 2021).

Individualised

Mentors should help to support mentees' psycho-social needs and well-being. They should aim to create a safe and supportive environment, which is crucial in the mentoring relationship, where the mentee feels comfortable to explore challenges, seek guidance, and take risks in their learning journey (Hobson *et al.*, 2015).

Mentors can provide individualised support to their mentees by tailoring their guidance and advice to meet the unique needs, preferences, and goals of each mentee. This personalised approach involves understanding their learning style, strengths, challenges, and aspirations to create a meaningful and effective mentoring relationship (Becher and Orland-Barak, 2018).

They can engage in regular communication and reflection with their mentees to assess progress, provide constructive feedback, and adjust their support as needed. By nurturing a collaborative and responsive mentoring relationship, they can empower them to thrive, overcome obstacles, and achieve their academic and personal goals (Taylor, 2007).

Developmental

Mentors play a critical role in supporting the developmental needs of their mentees by providing guidance, feedback, and opportunities for growth and learning. They can support them by helping them set achievable goals, identify areas for improvement, and develop action plans to enhance their skills and knowledge (West, 2016). The mentor endeavours to empower the mentee by fostering independence, self-efficacy, and confidence, enabling them to take ownership of their learning process and drive their own growth and development (Glover et al., 2021).

They can act as role models, sharing their own experiences, insights, and expertise to inspire and motivate mentees to strive for excellence and continuous improvement. Ultimately by fostering a supportive and empowering environment they can help mentees navigate their developmental journey and unlock their true potential (Swanson and Caskey, 2022).

Empowering

The primary role of a mentor is to empower their mentees by providing them with the confidence, skills, knowledge, and resources to succeed in their personal and professional endeavours. Mentors can act as catalysts for growth and development, guiding mentees to unlock their full potential and achieve their goals (Iredale, 2015).

To empower them, mentors can offer encouragement, motivation, and support, while also challenging them to step out of their comfort zones and take risks, fostering a growth mindset, instilling a sense of self-belief, and promoting resilience in the face of challenges (Orland-Barak and Hasin, 2010).

By providing opportunities for reflection, growth, and self-discovery, mentors enable mentees to build confidence, make informed decisions, and pursue their passions with conviction. In doing so, mentors play a vital role in empowering mentees to reach their fullest potential and thrive in their personal and professional lives (Sempowicz and Hudson, 2012).

They should endeavour to promote mentees' willingness to learn and to provide them with appropriate degrees of challenge. They should also set clear and achievable goals and action plans which help track progress and milestones in the mentee's development, providing structure and direction in their learning journey (Gray, Garvey and Lane, 2016).

Mentor self-reflection exercise using ONSIDE

Complete the table below with two examples of good practice for each category.

Aspects of ONSIDE	Examples of how you could do this
Offline	Discuss with your mentee what approaches they think they will find most helpful
Non-judgemental	Avoid making assumptions: Establish a shared understanding, for example, by asking your mentee to explain their perspective in order to help you understand it clearly
Supportive	Support your mentee to learn from their mistakes, including risks that didn't work out
Individualised	Get to know your mentee and keep getting to know them throughout the mentoring process
Developmental	Collaborate with your mentee, listen to them, and encourage a growing self-reliance
Empowering	Share your teaching experience in order to position them as the lead

Disciplinary issues and mentoring

Trainee teachers on an Initial Teacher Education (ITE) placement can face a variety of disciplinary matters that may arise due to their conduct, performance, or adherence to professional standards. These disciplinary issues can affect their progress in the programme and their future career as educators (Mellor, 2020). Some of the main kinds of disciplinary matters that trainee teachers may include are as follows:

- Professional Conduct
  Where mentees display unprofessional behaviour, such as inappropriate language, gestures, or interactions with students, colleagues, or parents, or sharing confidential or sensitive information about students, staff, or the school environment without proper authorisation (Dominguez and Hager, 2013).
- Attendance and Punctuality
  This can include failing to attend scheduled placements, meetings, or professional development sessions without a valid reason or proper notification and frequently arriving late to school, classes, or other professional commitments.
- Teaching Performance
  There could also be issues with a mentee's teaching competence consistently demonstrating poor teaching practices, such as inadequate lesson planning, ineffective classroom management, or failure to engage students and coming to class unprepared, resulting in poor delivery of lessons and a negative impact on student learning (Ehrich, Hansford and Tennent, 2003).

Role-playing scenarios are an effective way to train ITE mentors on how to handle disciplinary matters involving trainee teachers. These scenarios can help mentors practise their communication, problem-solving, and conflict-resolution skills in a controlled environment. Here are three different role-play scenarios (Nicholls, 2006). You might want to use these role-play scenarios involving potential disciplinary situations to help train new mentors.

Scenario 1: Unprofessional behaviour

Background

A trainee teacher, Abraham, has been observed making sarcastic remarks towards students and colleagues. This behaviour has been reported by several staff members and has also been noticed by the college principal. The mentor needs to address this issue with Alex.

Training objectives

In groups of three, do the following:

Identify the unprofessional behaviour and discuss its impact.
Provide constructive feedback.
Develop a plan for improvement for the mentee.

Play script

Mentor: Good morning, Alex. Thank you for meeting with me today.
Abraham: No problem. Is everything okay?
Mentor: I wanted to discuss some concerns that have been brought to my attention. Several staff members and the principal have noticed that you've been making sarcastic remarks about students and colleagues in your teaching sessions. Can you tell me a bit about what might be happening?
Abraham: I didn't realise it was a big deal. I thought I was just being funny.
Mentor: I understand that you might not have intended to cause any harm, but sarcasm can sometimes be taken the wrong way and can affect the classroom environment and professional relationships. It's important to maintain a positive and professional demeanour at all times. How do you feel about that?
Abraham: I guess I didn't think about it that way. I can see how it might be a problem.
Mentor: I appreciate your understanding. Let's work together on developing strategies to improve this. How about we start with setting a goal to focus on positive communication? I can also

Mentoring and New Teachers in Post-Compulsory Education   31

	observe a few of your classes and give you feedback on your interactions.
Abraham:	That sounds fair. I'll try to be more mindful of my comments.
Mentor:	Great. Let's schedule a follow-up meeting in a couple of weeks to review your progress. Remember, I am here to support you to become the best teacher you can be.

Group question

Which practical tips would you give Abraham in order to improve his positive communication?

Scenario 2: Attendance issues

Background

A trainee teacher, Janelle, has been frequently late to school and has missed several professional development sessions without prior notice. This has raised concerns among the college staff and has affected Janelle's performance and reliability. The mentor needs to address these attendance issues with Jamie.

Training objectives

In groups of three, do the following:

Address the attendance and punctuality issues.
Understand the underlying reasons.
Develop a plan to improve attendance and punctuality.

Role-play script

Mentor:	Hi Janelle, thanks for coming in today. How are you?
Janelle:	I'm okay, just a bit stressed with everything going on.
Mentor:	I understand. I wanted to talk to you about your attendance and punctuality. I've noticed you've been late several times and missed a few professional development sessions. Is everything alright?
Janelle:	I've been having some personal issues with balancing attending college and placement with child care, and it's been hard to manage everything.
Mentor:	I'm sorry to hear that. It sounds like you're dealing with a lot right now. It's important to address these issues because consistent attendance and punctuality are crucial for your development and for maintaining a professional standard. How can we help you manage this better?

Janelle: I could use some help with planning my schedule better. Maybe some tips on time management?

Mentor: Absolutely. Let's work on a plan together. We can start by identifying the main challenges you're facing and then look at some strategies to help you manage your time more effectively. We can also set up regular check-ins to see how you're doing. Does that sound good?

Janelle: Yes, that would be really helpful. Thank you.

Mentor: Great. We'll get through this together. Let's make sure we set some clear goals and take it step by step.

Group task

Design a checklist of different time management strategies that Janelle could use in order to deal with her time management issues

Scenario 3: Inadequate lesson preparation

Background

A trainee teacher, Tayler, has been consistently underprepared for lessons, resulting in poor classroom management and ineffective teaching. This has been observed by both the mentor and the classroom teacher. The mentor needs to address Tayler's lack of preparation and help develop a plan for improvement.

Training objectives

In groups of three, do the following:

- Address the issue of inadequate lesson preparation.
- Provide constructive feedback and support.
- Develop a structured plan to improve lesson planning and delivery.

Role-play script

Mentor: Hi Tayler, thanks for meeting with me. How are you today?

Tayler: I'm doing alright. What's up?

Mentor: I wanted to discuss your lesson preparation. In the last two observations I've done with you, you seem to be having some struggles with this which I feel is impacting your teaching and classroom management. Can you tell me more about your current preparation process?

Tayler: I've been trying to keep up, but I'm finding it hard to stay on top of things and look after two young children under five.

Mentor: This must be overwhelming for you at times. Let's look at how we can make this process more manageable for you. Can you walk me through your typical planning routine?

Tayler: I know this sounds really bad, but I have to put my children to bed first and I usually try to plan the night before, but sometimes I run out of time and end up winging it.

Mentor: Planning last minute must be really stressful for you. Why don't we work on a more structured approach? We can start with creating a weekly planning schedule that allows you to prepare in advance. I can also share some resources and templates that might help streamline your planning process.

Tayler: That sounds helpful.

Mentor: Great. Let's set some specific goals for your lesson planning and have regular check-ins to review your progress and adjust as needed.

Tayler: I appreciate that. I'll definitely do my best to become more organised.

Group question

Design a structured weekly planning schedule for Tayler and provide some ideas for lesson planning that will help them spend less time on planning.

Self-reflection task

Cheng and Hackworth (2021) have identified seven types of mentors which they have presented as the Cs. Rate yourself out of five for each one (Five being excellent) and set targets for how you could improve on these areas.

Types of Mentor	Grade yourself out of Five	How are you going to improve this score?
Content Mentor This is the mentor who is a subject specialist and who can guide the mentee to the most up-to-date research on their subject and their subject specialist pedagogy. A great candidate for a content mentor would be a more senior teacher who has ongoing projects in which the mentee can participate. This could create a mutually beneficial partnership where the mentor's research is furthered while simultaneously enhancing the skills of the mentee – a win-win situation for both parties		

(Continued)

Types of Mentor	Grade yourself out of Five	How are you going to improve this score?
Connecting Mentor This mentor has a vast network and can extend that network to mentees as they seek to get connected both inside and outside of their institutions. These networks and the ability to leverage them are critical to career success as they aid in the development of research collaborations, and expansion of one's own developmental network, and ultimate career success. In addition, the connecting mentor often serves as an advisor and may model techniques for properly interacting with and leveraging one's professional network both in formal and informal settings. The connecting mentor may also function as a sponsor by recommending mentees for important committees and other leadership opportunities		
Coaching Mentor Coaching is thought to be distinct from mentoring in employing 'methods that help the learners gain insights into their own assumptions, clarify meaning about relevant outcomes, and help identify specific actions needed to achieve a desired result'. Coaching is learner-driven in helping mentees gain insight into assumptions, processes, and outcomes of the actions needed to achieve goals. Coaching helps to develop skills, which may include abstract or manuscript writing, presentation skills, grant writing, laboratory techniques, biostatistical analytic skills, or self-monitoring and lifelong learning skills. Coaches help to identify strategies to manage challenges, improve academic performance, and further professional identity development		
Cheerleader Mentor The journey to becoming a successful clinician investigator will have ups and downs. Amid manuscript or grant rejections, failed experiments, and research delays, an encouraging cheerleader mentor is needed to help keep mentees focused on their long-term career goals		

(Continued)

Types of Mentor	Grade yourself out of Five	How are you going to improve this score?
Critiquing, Challenging Mentor Aside from cheerleader mentors, clinician investigators also need mentors who will give critical feedback and will challenge ideas. Mentors are needed to help develop and wordsmith study aims, closely read multiple drafts of manuscripts and grant applications, and offer constructive criticism and ways to improve		
Career Mentor Early-career investigators need mentors who are actively thinking (along with them) about the long-term development of their careers. This could be a division director or department chair. The career mentor will ensure that much-needed discussions about what is needed for promotion, as well as issues of balancing career and personal life, occur on a regular basis		
Colleague Peer Mentor Teaming with colleagues who are in a similar stage of development can enrich early-career investigators' work. Peer mentoring partnerships or groups can provide enhanced engagement, collaboration, social support, and intellectual input. This might include writing accountability groups, writing partners, social groups, or other mechanisms for peer support		

References

Aderibigbe, S., Gray, D.S. and Colucci-Gray, L. (2018) 'Understanding the nature of mentoring experiences between teachers and student teachers', *International Journal of Mentoring and Coaching in Education*, 7(1), pp. 54–71.

Aspfors, J. and Fransson, G. (2015) 'Research on mentor education for mentors of newly qualified teachers: A qualitative meta-synthesis', *Teaching and Teacher Education*, 48, pp. 75–86.

Becher, A. and Orland-Barak, L. (2018) 'Context matters: Contextual factors informing mentoring in art initial teacher education', *Journal of Teacher Education*, 69(5), pp. 477–492.

Brondyk, S. and Searby, L. (2013). 'Best Practices in mentoring: Complexities and possibilities', *International Journal of Mentoring and Coaching in Education*, 2(3), pp. 189–203.

Caskey, M. and Weller Swanson, M. (2020) 'Developing an academic identity using the cognitive apprenticeship model: A kaleidoscopic metaphor', *International Journal of Multidisciplinary Perspectives in Higher Education*, 5(2), pp. 134–139.

Cheng, T.L. and Hackworth, J.M. (2021) 'The "Cs" of mentoring: Using adult learning theory and the right mentors to position early-career investigators for success', *Journal of Pediatrics*, 238, pp. 6–8. doi:https://doi.org/10.1016/j.jpeds.2021.03.023.

Dominguez, N. and Hager, M. (2013) 'Mentoring frameworks: Synthesis and critique', *International Journal of Mentoring and Coaching in Education*, 2(3), pp. 171–188.

Duckworth, V. and Maxwell, B. (2015) 'Extending the mentor role in initial teacher education: Embracing social justice', *International Journal of Mentoring and Coaching in Education*, 4, pp. 4–20. 10.1108/IJMCE-08-2014-0032.

Ehrich, L.C., Hansford, B. and Tennent, L. (2003) 'Educational mentoring: Is it worth the effort?', *Education Research and Perspectives*, 30(1), pp. 42–75.

Eleyan, D., Eleyan, A. (2011) Coaching Tutoring and Mentoring in the Higher Education as a solution to retain students in their major and help them achieve success. May 2011. Conference: The International Arab Conference on Quality Assurance in Higher Education (IACQA), May 10 – 12, 2011, Zarqa University. Jordan.At: Zarqa University, Jordan

Education and Training Foundation (ETF) (2021) FE mentoring framework. https://www.et-foundation.co.uk/professional-development/mentoring/training-hub/

Education and Training Foundation (ETF) (2024) Guide for mentors https://www.et-foundation.co.uk/professional-development/mentoring/training-hub/

Glover, A., Jones, M., Thomas, A. and Worrall, L. (2021) Effective mentoring in Initial Teacher Education. What works and why. The Open University Initial Teacher Education Partnership PGCE Programme. Final PRAXIS funded project report (PRAXIS 2021/22 21 AG. July 2022.

Gray, D.E., Lane, D.A. and Garvey, R., (2016). A critical introduction to coaching and mentoring: Debates, dialogues and discourses. Sage.

Higgins, M.C. and Kram, K.E. (2001) 'Reconceptualizing mentoring at work: A developmental network perspective', *The Academy of Management Review*, 26(2), pp. 264–288. https://doi.org/10.2307/259122

Hobson, A. and Malderez, A. (2013) 'Judgementoring and other threats to realizing the potential of school-based mentoring in teacher education', *International Journal of Mentoring and Coaching in Education*, 2, pp. 89–108. 10.1108/IJMCE-03-2013-0019.

Hobson, A.J. and Maxwell, B. (2020) Mentoring substructures and superstructures: An extension and reconceptualisation of the architecture for teacher mentoring. *Journal of Education for Teaching*, 46(2), pp. 99–112.

Hobson, A.J., Maxwell, B., Stevens, A., Doyle, K. and Malderez, A. (2015) Mentoring and coaching for teachers in the further education and skills sector in England full report. Education Research Centre, University of Brighton Centre for Education and Inclusion Research, Sheffield Hallam University.

Iredale, A. (2015) In Pursuit of Professional Knowledge and Practice: Some Experiences of Lifelong Learning Sector Trainee Teachers in England 2008 - 10. Doctoral thesis, University of Huddersfield. available at http://eprints.hud.ac.uk/id/eprint/26227

Larsen, E., Jensen-Clayton, C., Curtis, E., Loughland, T. and Nguyen, H.T. (2023) 'Re-imagining teacher mentoring for the future', *Professional Development in Education*, 6, pp. 1–15.

Maxwell, B., Hobson, A. and Manning, C., (2021). Mentoring and coaching- trainee and early career teachers: Conceptual review.

Mellor, P., (2020). Working with your mentor. In *A practical guide to teaching physical education in the secondary school* (pp. 287–304). Routledge.

Misawa, M. and McClain, A., (2020). 'A mentoring approach: Fostering transformative learning in adult graduate education', *Journal of Transformative Learning*, 6(2), p. 52.

Mullen, C.A. and Klimaitis, C.C. (2021) 'Defining mentoring: A literature review of issues, types, and applications', *Annals of the New York Academy of Sciences*, 1483(1), pp. 19–35.

Nicholls, G. (2006) Mentoring: The art of teaching and learning. In *The theory and practice of teaching* (pp. 157–168). Routledge.

Niklasson, L. (2018) 'Mentors in initial teacher education – initiatives for professional development', *Journal of Arts and Humanities*, 07(8), pp. 11–22.

Orland-Barak, L. and Hasin, R. (2010) 'Exemplary mentors' perspectives towards mentoring across mentoring contexts: Lessons from collective case studies', *Teaching and Teacher Education*, 26(3), pp. 427–437.

Rolfe, G., Freshwater, D. and Jasper, M. (2001) *Critical reflection for nursing and the helping professions: A user's guide*. Palgrave Macmillan.

Scandura, T.A. and Williams, E.A., 2004. 'Mentoring and transformational leadership: The role of supervisory career mentoring', *Journal of Vocational Behavior*, 65(3), pp. 448–468.

Sempowicz, T. and Hudson, P. (2012). 'Mentoring preservice teachers' reflective practices to produce teaching outcomes', *International Journal of Evidence Based Coaching and Mentoring*, 10(2), pp. 52–64.

Swanson, K.W. and Caskey, M.M. (2022) 'Mentoring dialogue and practice: A transformative experience', *Journal of Transformative Learning*, 9(1), 195–217.

Taylor, E.W. 2007. 'An update of transformative learning theory: A critical review of the empirical research (1999–2005)', *International Journal of Lifelong Education*, 26, pp. 173–191.

Thornton, K. and Beutel, D. (2024) 'Guest editorial: Mentoring and coaching preparation and training in professional contexts', *International Journal of Mentoring and Coaching in Education*, 13(4), pp. 417–421.

Walters, W., Robinson, D.B. and Walters, J. (2020) 'Mentoring as meaningful professional development: The influence of mentoring on in-service teachers' identity and practice', *International Journal of Mentoring and Coaching in Education*, 9(1), pp. 21–36.

Wang, J. (2001) 'Contexts of mentoring and opportunities for learning to teach: A comparative study of mentoring practice', *Teaching and teacher education*, 17(1), pp. 51–73.

West, A. (2016) 'A framework for conceptualizing models of mentoring in educational settings', *International Journal of Leadership and Change*, 4(1), p. 11.

Western, S. (2012) 'Coaching and mentoring: A critical text', *Human Resource Management International Digest*, 21(2), 55–66.

Woolhouse, C. and Nicholson, L. (2020) *Mentoring in higher education case studies of peer learning and pedagogical development: Case studies of peer learning and pedagogical development*. Palgrave Macmillan.

Chapter 3

Finding the right match

Mentors and mentees

> **Self-reflection activity**
>
> Some questions:
>
> - When you were a trainee/new teacher or if you are one now, how did you obtain a mentor?
> - What were the strengths and the weaknesses of the way this happened?
> - In your current institution, how are mentors recruited and selected?
> - What are the strengths and weaknesses of this process?

Recruitment and selection of mentors and mentees

Mentor recruitment

Recruiting mentors in Further Education is a crucial process to ensure that mentees receive the support they need to succeed academically, socially, and emotionally. There are various methods and strategies employed to attract and engage mentors in educational settings:

- In-house recruitment
    In-house mentor selection in education refers to the practice of recruiting mentors from within the organisation, such as experienced teachers or staff members, to support and guide less experienced colleagues (De Rosa et al., 2023). This is the method most commonly used in institutions in the UK. This approach has its own set of strengths and weaknesses that can impact the effectiveness of the mentoring programme.

DOI: 10.4324/9781003527374-3

Strengths

FAMILIARITY WITH INSTITUTIONAL CULTURE

In-house mentors are already familiar with the institutional culture, policies, and procedures, which enables them to provide more targeted and relevant support to mentees.

ESTABLISHED RELATIONSHIPS

In-house mentors may already have established relationships with mentees, creating a foundation of trust and rapport that can enhance the mentoring relationship.

ACCESS TO RESOURCES

They may have access to educational resources, professional development opportunities, and support networks within the school, which can benefit mentees in their professional growth.

COST-EFFECTIVE

It can be a cost-effective option for institutions as they do not need to allocate additional resources for external mentor recruitment and training (De Rosa et al., 2023).

Weaknesses

LIMITED DIVERSITY

This type of recruitment may result in a lack of diversity in perspectives and experiences, potentially limiting the range of support and guidance available to mentees.

POTENTIAL FOR CONFLICT OF INTEREST

Mentors may face challenges in providing unbiased feedback and guidance to mentees, especially if they have personal or professional relationships with them.

LIMITED AVAILABILITY

Mentors may already have full workloads and responsibilities, making it challenging for them to dedicate sufficient time and energy to mentoring activities.

SKILL AND TRAINING GAPS

They may not possess the necessary mentoring skills and training required to effectively support mentees, leading to inconsistencies in the quality of mentoring experiences (Achinstein and Athanases, 2006).

- External Partnerships

   External mentoring is common in cases where mentees in placement teaching in areas of shortage, such as Maths, are by necessity frequently mentored by nonspecialists who in many cases may not possess an adequate grasp of relevant subject content and subject pedagogy (Hobson *et al.*, 2012). It can be provided in three different ways: As subject mentoring, where one mentor supports a small number of mentees through termly face-to-face meetings and online support; as e-mentoring, where after an initial meeting one mentor supports around ten mentees, largely online; and as network mentoring, where one mentor supports a larger number of mentees (2012). This approach also has strengths and weaknesses which can affect its impact on mentoring.

Strengths of using external partnerships in mentor recruitment in education

DIVERSE EXPERTISE

They can bring a wealth of diverse expertise from professionals with different backgrounds and experiences, providing a broader range of knowledge and skills to support mentees in their educational goals and also provide fresh perspectives and innovative approaches that may not be readily available within the organisation. This can help mentees gain new insights and develop creative problem-solving skills.

NETWORKING OPPORTUNITIES

Collaborating with external partners can expand the networking opportunities for mentees, connecting them with professionals with different approaches to teaching and strengthening their professional relationships beyond the institutional environment (AIR, 2019).

Specialised training

External mentors may have specific training or certifications in mentoring practices, providing mentees with access to specialised knowledge and resources to support their growth and development (Hobson *et al.*, 2015).

Weaknesses of using external partnerships in mentor recruitment in education

LIMITED UNDERSTANDING OF THE INDIVIDUAL INSTITUTIONAL CULTURE

They may lack familiarity with the specific culture and dynamics of the educational institution, which could hinder their ability to effectively support mentees in navigating the institutional environment and hinder their assimilation into the institution. There may be a risk of misalignment between the goals and values of external partners and the educational institution, leading to conflicting priorities and challenges in establishing a cohesive mentoring programme.

LIMITED AVAILABILITY

External mentors may have limited availability or conflicting commitments, making it challenging to establish consistent and long-term mentoring relationships with mentees.

COST CONSIDERATIONS

Collaborating with external partners may involve financial costs, such as fees for mentoring services or professional development resources, which could be a barrier for educational institutions with limited budgets (McIntyre and Hobson, 2016).

- Collaboration
  The concept of the collaborative models of mentoring shifts the focus of mentoring from the top-down approach of institutions assigning mentors to mentees to a more independent approach with the focus on the mentee. Mentees can also develop their own relationship networks in relation to their particular needs and often have a variety of different mentors fulfilling different roles or purposes of development (Bung, 2015). This approach also has many strengths and weaknesses.

Strengths of using collaborative approaches in mentor recruitment in education

SHARED DECISION-MAKING

Collaborative approaches promote shared decision-making and diverse perspectives and experiences to support mentees and where multiple voices are heard and considered in the mentor selection process. This can lead to more inclusive and equitable selection criteria that reflect the needs and goals of mentees (Mackintosh, 2022).

PROFESSIONAL GROWTH

Collaborative mentor selection processes provide opportunities for professional growth and development among all stakeholders involved. Mentors selected through a collaborative approach may benefit from diverse perspectives and feedback, leading to enhanced mentoring skills and practices (Bung, 2015).

Weaknesses of using collaborative approaches in mentor recruitment in education

TIME-CONSUMING

Collaborative mentor selection processes can be time-consuming due to the need to coordinate schedules, gather input from multiple stakeholders, and reach consensus on selection criteria. This may result in delays in appointing mentors and initiating the mentoring relationship.

POTENTIAL CONFLICTS

Collaborative approaches may lead to conflicts or disagreements among stakeholders regarding mentor selection criteria, preferences, or biases. Resolving conflicts and reaching consensus in a collaborative setting can be challenging and may impact the effectiveness of the mentor selection process (Seeliger, 2009).

- Selection by mentee

  Within this approach, mentees are given the opportunity to find placements and mentors that support their requirements. These choices may be influenced by subject specialism, proximity to home, or familiarity with an institution or simply by preference (Glover *et al.*, 2022). This approach has also strengths and limitations.

Strengths of mentees finding their own mentors

PERSONAL CONNECTION

When mentees have the freedom to choose their own mentors, they may be more likely to find someone with whom they have a strong personal connection. This can create a more comfortable and supportive mentoring relationship (Kochan *et al.*, 2015).

MOTIVATION AND ENGAGEMENT

By allowing mentees to find their own mentors, they are empowered to take an active role in their own personal and professional development. This can increase motivation and engagement in the mentoring process, and they may have specific needs or goals that they want to work on with a mentor. This can enable them to find someone who can provide tailored support and guidance in areas that are important to them (Manthiram and Edwards, 2021).

Weaknesses of mentees finding their own mentors

LACK OF EXPERIENCE

Some mentees may not have a good understanding of what makes a successful mentor or may not know how to identify a mentor who can best support their needs. This could result in them choosing a mentor who may not be the most effective match. In addition, mentees who lack access to a wide network of potential mentors may struggle to find a suitable mentor on their own. This could result in them not having the support they need to reach their full potential (Glover *et al.*, 2022).

BIAS OR PREJUDICE

Mentees may subconsciously select mentors based on bias or prejudice, such as choosing someone who is more similar to them or holds similar opinions. This may limit the diversity of perspectives and experiences that can be gained from a mentoring relationship (Kochan *et al.*, 2015).

Research suggests that an effective recruitment campaign which attracts a healthy number of applicants helps to increase selectivity and maximise selected participants' commitment to mentoring programmes and relationships (Morales, Ambrose-Roman and Perez-Maldonado, 2015). Some programmes usefully use testimonials from existing or previous satisfied mentors and/or mentees to increase interest. It is important, in recruiting, to be as clear as possible about what participation would entail, including time commitments required (Manthiram and Edwards, 2021).

- Three ways in which colleges can recruit potential mentors. Add some of your own suggestions to this list

Networking events and workshops

Host networking events and workshops specifically for experienced teachers to connect with trainee teachers and learn about mentorship opportunities. Provide a platform for experienced teachers to share their knowledge and experiences with trainee teachers, showcasing the benefits of becoming a mentor. By fostering a supportive and collaborative environment, colleges can attract experienced teachers who are passionate about mentoring and helping others succeed in the field of education.

Incentives and recognition

Offer incentives and recognition to experienced teachers who take on mentorship roles at the college. This could include financial incentives, professional development opportunities, or public recognition for their contributions to the development of future educators. By acknowledging the valuable role that mentors play in supporting trainee teachers and the overall success of the college's education programmes, colleges can attract experienced teachers who are motivated to share their expertise and mentorship skills.

Alumni visits

Invite ex-students from your teaching programmes to discuss with staff members their experiences of being mentored and how they benefited from the support given. If this is difficult to do in person, ask them to present this online.

Mentor selection

Research suggests that a key variable influencing the quality of mentoring programmes is the extent to which rigorous processes of mentor selection are employed (Hobson *et al.*, 2015; Hobson and Maxwell, 2020). Generally, such criteria include mentors' possession of relevant knowledge and experience. This might include, for example, the ability to scaffold professional tasks (Kramer-Simpson, 2018) and some of the following criteria:

- Have at least one year of experience
- Have at least three years of managerial experience
- Have preferably undertaken different duties
- Have strong communication skills
- Be good at providing feedback
- Be flexible
- Have strong managerial skills, able to work with different people
- Be able to spare time
- Give emphasis to personal development
- Want to improve themselves in mentoring
- Volunteering to be mentors

This may also include having received an appropriate report from an internal or external teaching inspection and a higher-level teaching qualification, normally at Master's level. If applicants meet the criteria, they are often given a place in a mentor pool, before checks are undertaken to establish whether they could become programme mentors (Hobson *et al.*, 2015). Prospective mentors may also be invited to attend an induction mentor training session, at which their suitability for the role is usually but not always confirmed (2015). Some mentoring schemes take up references (Beltman and Schaeben, 2012) and/or interview applicants for the mentor role.

The American Institute for Research select mentors according to five categories: Critical elements of effective mentoring, attitude and dispositions, professional competence and experience, communication skills, and interpersonal skills (AIR, 2019). They also place emphasis on the prioritising of knowledge of student assessment (formative and summative) and standards (learning and teaching) which they argue are critical elements for successful mentoring.

- Critical elements of effective mentoring
    Within this criterion would include the answers to questions such as:

    Does the prospective mentor use formative assessments effectively to gauge student learning and adjust their teaching strategies?
    Do they use summative data to reflect on their practices to improve student learning over time?
    Do they have a range of teaching strategies to effectively meet the needs of diverse learners?
    Does the mentor candidate effectively understand and use teaching and professional standards to improve achievement?

- Mentor attitudes and dispositions
    This category would include answers to questions like:

    Is the mentor strongly committed to the teaching profession?
    Are they willing to serve as a role model for other teachers?
    Are they eager to collaborate and share information and ideas with colleagues?
    Are they reflective and able to learn from mistakes?
    Can they accept feedback willingly and make changes to their practice based upon it?
    Are they willing to advocate on behalf of colleagues?
    Are they flexible, persistent, resilient, and open-minded?
    Are they calm and resourceful under pressure?
    Are they willing to participate in training to improve their mentoring skills?

- Professional competence and experience
    This category would include answers to questions like:

    Does the mentor have sufficient subject specialist knowledge and experience at working across several different levels to support a mentee?
    Is the mentor regarded by the institution and peers as an outstanding teacher?
    Do they demonstrate excellent classroom management skills?

Does the mentor have a good knowledge of the institutional policies and procedures?
Does the mentor candidate collaborate well with teachers and support staff?
Does the mentor feel comfortable being observed?
Are they willing to learn new teaching strategies from and with beginning teachers?
Do they have a strong understanding of evidence-based practices?
Do they collect and use data to monitor their students' formative progress and modify their teaching accordingly?
Is the mentor able to support learning for a wide range of diverse students?

- Communication skills
    This category would require answers to questions like:

    Is the mentor able to break down and explain effective teaching strategies with clarity?
    Do they use active listening skills attentively?
    Can they ask questions that prompt reflection and understanding?
    Does the mentor candidate understand how to scaffold support and offer feedback in positive and productive ways?
    Are they discreet and able to maintain confidentiality?

- Interpersonal skills
    Questions related to this category would include the following:

    Is the mentor able to maintain a trusting professional relationship?
    Are they able to support a mentee's professional and emotional needs?
    Do they work well with individuals from different cultural backgrounds?
    Are they approachable, patient, and able to easily establish rapport with others?
    Can they provide constructive feedback in a manner that would encourage mentees to be open, reflective, and responsive?

Self-reflection activity

Work through each question of the selection categories and grade yourself in each out of five (five is outstanding) and then note down which areas you need to work upon as a mentor.

Selection categories	Personal rating out of five	Areas you need to improve upon
Critical elements of effective mentoring		
Mentor attitudes and dispositions		
Professional competence and experience		
Communication skills		
Interpersonal skills		
Any other areas not mentioned		

Barriers to the effective recruitment and selection of mentors

The effective recruitment and selection of mentors in education play a crucial role in providing quality mentorship to support the growth and development of mentees. However, there are several barriers that can hinder this process, impacting the success of mentoring programmes. One of the main barriers to effective recruitment and selection of mentors in education is the limited awareness and outreach efforts. This can result in a lack of visibility of mentorship opportunities, leading to difficulty in attracting qualified candidates to serve as mentors.

Mentoring in education requires a significant time commitment, both in terms of the recruitment process itself and the ongoing mentorship responsibilities. Many potential mentors may be hesitant to commit to this level of time and energy, especially if they already have demanding professional or personal obligations.

Another barrier is the lack of sufficient incentives. Without adequate recognition, support, or compensation for their efforts, potential mentors may be less motivated to participate in mentorship programmes, impacting the overall quality of mentorship (Heider, 2005).

Ensuring that mentors have the necessary qualifications, skills, and training to effectively support mentees is essential for successful mentorship. However, a lack of clear guidelines for mentor qualification and training can be a significant barrier to effective recruitment and selection of mentors in education (Bradbury and Kaballa, 2012).

In some cases, cultural or diversity considerations may pose barriers to the recruitment and selection of mentors in education. It is important to ensure that mentors reflect the diversity of the student population to provide meaningful and relevant support to all mentees. Failure to address these considerations can result in mismatches between mentors and mentees, compromising the effectiveness of mentorship relationships (Bowman, 2014).

Lack of time and lack of incentives are also issues which deter potential mentors. It has been suggested that mentor training currently provided by the centres of ITE in the UK places too much emphasis on completion of documentation rather than developing the skills, knowledge, and understanding required to mentor successfully (Estyn, 2018).

According to a study by Fisher-Ari, Eaton and Dantzler (2009), gaps in communication often made vetting, developing, and supporting the initiation of meaningful partnerships challenging. Their participants discussed the persistent challenges of mentors who neither volunteered nor knew about their mentees until they showed up in their classroom on the first day. Also, there were conversations about mentor teachers who did not begin their mentoring endeavours with a clear understanding of the purposes and complex opportunities and responsibilities of their role (2009).

Line managers as mentors

A further issue highlighted in the ITT mentoring literature is the deployment of line managers as mentors. This can create tensions between the non-judgemental support advocated in most models of mentoring and organisational performance requirements (Cullimore and Simmons, 2008; Tedder and Lawy, 2009). Mentors with direct management responsibilities may approach what are intended by ITT providers to be supportive and developmental observations of teaching as they would observations conducted to monitor teacher performance (Hobson, Maxwell and Káplár-Kodácsy, 2021).

Although the expertise of an experienced teacher is important in mentoring student teachers, it may have been a long time since they were a student teacher themself. It has also been suggested the other responsibilities and demands on the time of heads of department or those in more senior positions could impact how much time they would actually be able to offer the student. A teacher more recently qualified can potentially empathise with the student teacher better as less time has elapsed since they were in the same situation (Glover *et al.*, 2022).

Appointed mentors

According to Fletcher, Astall and Everatt (2021), one of their research respondents commented that in their experience when mentors were appointed, as opposed to volunteering for the role, this can make them as a student feel awkward because they were being a burden to them. Some of their respondents also commented that they can tell the difference between the mentors who have been volunteered to be a mentor and those who had volunteered because the former mentors often lacked motivation. Others reported on mentors being allocated to the role due to their senior position, and therefore, the passion to mentor student teachers can be lacking (2021).

Three types of mentoring relationships

According to Wang and Fulton (2012), there are three types of mentoring relationships:

- The Responsive mentoring relationship
  In this relationship, the mentor acts as an instructor or supervisor by observing the new teacher. This reflects the competency model in which the mentee is given systematic feedback about performance and progress (Wong and Premkumar, 2007).

- The Interactive relationship

    Mentors and mentees would recognise each other as peers, bring to the relationship their own contributions, develop, and adjust the action agenda jointly in response to the interests and desires of both. The mentor in this relationship was characterised as a friend, colleague, and trusted advisor. This model mainly draws upon the concepts of the reflective model in which the mentor's role is to support the development of the mentee as a reflective practitioner. The reflective model is also known as educational mentorship (Anderson and Shannon, 1988), whereby mentoring takes on many different roles and functions such as mentoring as teaching, sponsoring, encouraging, counselling, and befriending (Hellsten, Prytula and Ebanks, 2009).

- The Directive mentoring relationship

    The mentor would take charge, set the action agenda, develop a clear expectation for the novice's performance, guide novices towards the expected performance through modelling, and offer feedback and direct suggestions. In this relationship, the mentor assumed a role as a master teacher, guide, and coach. This draws upon the apprentice model, where the mentee observes and learns from the mentor. Many mentorship models utilise the apprenticeship mode (Hellsten, Prytula and Ebanks, 2009).

    The critique of this approach is that the relationship is very top-down or hierarchical in nature, where the 'expert' mentor passes on knowledge and skills to the less-experienced mentee (Hellsten, Prytula and Ebanks, 2009). Thus, the apprenticeship model of mentorship does not honour or recognise the early-career teacher's previous or existing experiences; instead, the mentee is expected to default to the mentor's knowledge and experience. This encourages replication or conformity to the mentor's teaching practices while dismissing the development of new approaches to teaching and learning for both the mentor and the mentee (Rippon and Martin, 2006).

Self-reflection exercise

What are the strengths and weaknesses of the following models of mentoring? Which one do you practice or desire to practice as a mentor?

Models of mentoring relationships	Strengths	Weaknesses
The Responsive mentoring relationship		
The Interactive relationship		
The Directive mentoring relationship		

Matching mentor and mentee

Matching criteria

It is possible that there are underlying characteristics (i.e. responsive listening, trustworthiness, strong and effective communication skills, mutual respect, refraining from passing judgement, and holding a growth-mindset) that are important for all mentors (Deng, Gulseren and Turner, 2022). However, some research has shown that successful mentoring is based on matching the mentee and mentor according to personal and attitudinal similarities (Fisher-Ari, Eaton and Dantzler, 2019). When establishing a mentorship programme, defining clear matching criteria is essential. The criteria can vary depending on the goals of the mentoring programme. Here are a few common factors programmes may consider when matching them.

- Expertise and experience

    Experience level is an important factor to consider in mentor-mentee matching. A mentee just starting out in their career may benefit from a mentor with several years of experience in their field. On the other hand, a more experienced mentee may benefit from a mentor with a wealth of knowledge and experience in another specific but related area. Or, in a reverse mentoring relationship, having a mentor who is new to the team, organisation, or sector can help the mentee greatly. Fresh eyes and outside perspective have great value in mentoring relationships too (Bradbury and Koballa, 2008).

Goals and objectives

It's important for mentors and mentees to have some alignment on their goals and objectives to ensure a mutually beneficial relationship. If a mentee has a specific career goal in mind, for instance, becoming a Curriculum Manager, an excellent match for them might be a mentor who has already achieved that goal. This means the mentor could be in a strong position to provide valuable insight and guidance to the mentee (De Rosa *et al.*, 2023).

Availability and commitment

It is important to make sure that both parties have enough time to commit to the mentoring relationship. If the mentor is too busy with other commitments, they may not be able to provide the support and guidance that the mentee needs. Similarly, if the mentee is not able to commit enough time to the relationship because they are bogged down with coursework, for instance, they may not be able to fully benefit from the mentor's expertise (Kramer-Simpson, 2018).

- Diversity and inclusion

    A well-rounded and inclusive mentorship programme should be founded upon consideration of diversity and inclusion factors such as gender,

ethnicity, and background (Mackintosh, 2022). Both mentor and mentor will benefit from an environment and a relationship where there is a wealth of perspectives and experiences.
- Participant involvement
  It can be good practice to involve mentors and mentees in the matching process by asking them to express their preferences, expectations, and concerns. Give them the opportunity to review and accept or decline potential matches and encourage them to meet and get to know each other before committing to a mentoring relationship. By involving the participants, you can increase their engagement, motivation, and ownership of the mentoring relationship (Wang and Fulton, 2012).
- Compatibility and communication style
  Ideally, the mentor and mentee should have compatible personalities and communication styles (Seeliger, 2009). Some people prefer a more formal approach, while others thrive in a casual setting, and thus understanding these preferences can ensure a comfortable and effective pairing.
- Co-development of practice
  Another key criterion for meaningful partnership is a commitment to the simultaneous development of their mentee and to a mentor's own continued development, learning, and progress (Bowman, 2014).

Mismatches between mentor and mentee

These can occur and can be the result of a variety of different influences, including the following:

- Clashes with professional culture
  Through their research in the United States, Kardos *et al.* (2001) characterised three types of professional cultures or subcultures within schools: Veteran-oriented cultures, novice-oriented cultures, and integrated cultures. In Veteran-oriented cultures, new teachers described norms of professional interaction determined, in large part, by the veterans, with little attention to the particular needs of beginning teachers.
  In Novice-oriented cultures, on the other hand, new teachers described norms of professional interaction determined by novices, thus leaving them with little experienced guidance about how to teach(Hobson et. al 2012).
  However, in Integrated professional cultures, new teachers described being provided with sustained support and having frequent exchanges with colleagues across experience levels.
- Weak friendship and lack of trust
  Results from the research of Beyene *et al.* (2002) suggested that neither race nor gender was perceived as a critical influence on the mentoring process, but that friendship, nurturance, open-mindedness, and trustworthiness were key to mentoring relationships.

- Impact of unequal power relationships

  Unequal power relationships can have a significant impact on mentor and mentee relationships in colleges, affecting the quality of support, communication, and overall effectiveness of the mentoring process (Wang and Fulton, 2012). Here are some ways in which unequal power dynamics can influence mentor and mentee relationships in colleges:
- Lack of trust

  When there is a significant power differential between the mentor and mentee, the mentee may feel hesitant to share their thoughts, concerns, or challenges openly. This can lead to a lack of trust in the relationship, hindering their ability to seek guidance and support from the mentor (Bradbury and Koballa, 2018).
- Imbalance of influence

  Unequal power relationships can create an imbalance of influence, where the mentor's authority and expertise can overshadow the mentee's opinions and perspectives. This imbalance can result in them feeling disempowered and lacking agency in decision-making and goal-setting processes (Kramer-Simpson, 2018).
- Limited opportunities for development in mentees

  In an environment where power dynamics are skewed, mentees may be less likely to take risks, voice their ideas, or challenge the status quo. This can limit their growth opportunities and hinder their ability to develop independent critical thinking, problem-solving skills, and self-confidence (Norman and Feiman-Nemser, 2005).
- Potential for exploitation

  In extreme cases, unequal power relationships in mentor and mentee interactions can lead to exploitation, where the mentor may misuse their authority to manipulate, control, or take advantage of the mentee. Such situations can have lasting negative effects on the mentee's well-being and professional development (Wong and Premkumar, 2007).

Self-reflection activity

How will you manage issues related to power relationships between you and your mentee?

Issues related to power relationships	Your approach
Lack of Trust	
Imbalance of Influence	
Limited Growth Opportunities	
Potential for Exploitation	

- Incompatible personal history and dispositions

  Incompatible personal histories and dispositions can have a profound impact on mentor and mentee relationships in colleges, influencing the effectiveness of the mentorship, communication, and overall support provided (Bjorklund, 2023). Here are some ways in which they can impact their relationships:

- Communication challenges

  Differences in personal histories and dispositions can lead to miscommunications and misunderstandings between them. These disparities may affect how information is conveyed, interpreted, and understood, hindering effective communication within the mentorship relationship (Beyene *et al.*, 2002).

- Lack of connection

  They can result in a lack of connection or rapport between them. When mentees and mentors have divergent backgrounds or outlooks, it may be challenging to establish a meaningful connection that supports effective mentorship (Norman and Feiman-Nemser, 2005). A sense of shared experiences, values, or perspectives is essential for building trust and a strong mentoring bond.

- Mismatched expectations

  Differences can lead to mismatched expectations regarding the mentorship relationship. Mentors and mentees may have contrasting ideas or goals for what they hope to achieve through the mentoring process. This misalignment can create tension, frustration, or disappointment if the mentorship does not meet the expectations of either party (Daly, 2017).

- Conflict resolution

  They can pose challenges in resolving conflicts or disagreements within the mentorship relationship. Divergent approaches to problem-solving, communication styles, or conflict resolution strategies can impede their abilities to address issues effectively and maintain a positive mentoring dynamic (Norman and Feiman-Nemser, 2005).

- Different conceptions of mentoring

  Different conceptions of mentoring can significantly impact mentor and mentee relationships in colleges, influencing the dynamics, expectations, and outcomes of the mentoring process. When individuals hold varying beliefs and understandings about mentoring, it can lead to misunderstandings, conflicts, and ineffective support (Estyn, 2018). For example:

- Expectations misalignment

  If the mentor and mentee have divergent views on what mentoring entails, there can be a mismatch in expectations. For example, if the mentor sees mentoring as primarily providing advice and guidance, while the mentee expects emotional support and encouragement, it can lead to frustration and disappointment on both sides (Bjorklund, 2023).

- Role clarity

  In addition, different conceptions of practical mentoring can create confusion around roles and responsibilities within the mentor-mentee relationship. If one party views the mentor as a hands-on coach, while the other

sees them as a passive observer, it can lead to uncertainty about how to interact and engage effectively (Bradbury and Koballa, 2018).
- Relationship dynamics

   They can influence the dynamics of the mentor-mentee relationship. For instance, if the mentor believes in a directive, top-down approach, while the mentee prefers a more collaborative, equal partnership, it can create power struggles and hinder the establishment of trust and mutual understanding (Fletcher, Astall and Everatt, 2021).
- Feedback and Evaluation

   Dissimilar views on mentoring can impact how feedback and evaluation are perceived and utilised within the mentor-mentee relationship. If the mentor values constructive criticism and objective assessments, but the mentee prefers positive reinforcement and validation, it can hinder communication and growth opportunities (Bradbury and Koballa, 2008).
- Misalignment of Goals

   Different conceptions of teaching and supporting learners can result in misaligned goals between them. If a mentor focuses on promoting independence and self-directed learning, while the mentee values direct instruction and guidance, it can lead to disagreements on the desired outcomes of the mentoring process. This can hinder the mentee's growth and development if their goals are not effectively supported (Kardos *et al.*, 2001).

Self-reflection task

If there are disagreements over your mentoring and teaching approaches, how will you deal with some of the main issues?

Some of the main issues	Your approaches
Expectations Misalignment	
Role Clarity	
Relationship Dynamics	
Feedback and Evaluation	
Varying Expectations	
Misalignment of Goals	
Communication Challenges	

Mentees transitioning

Transitioning from an adult professional to a trainee teacher can have a significant impact on the mentor and mentee relationship in educational settings, affecting the dynamics, expectations, and overall effectiveness of the mentoring process. When a mentee makes the shift from being an experienced adult professional to a trainee teacher, several challenges and opportunities may arise that influence their interactions with their mentor (Fletcher, Astall and Everatt, 2021). Here are some examples:

Shift in roles and power dynamics

As a trainee teacher, the mentee may experience a shift in roles and power dynamics within the mentorship relationship. While in their previous professional role, the mentee may have been accustomed to being seen as an expert, the transition to a trainee teacher position may require them to adopt a more receptive and learning-oriented stance towards their mentor (Deng, Gulseren and Turner, 2022). This change in roles can influence the mentor's approach and the mentee's willingness to seek guidance and support.

Adjustment to new expectations and responsibilities

Moving from an adult professional to a trainee teacher often involves adapting to a new set of expectations, responsibilities, and challenges in the academic environment. The mentee may need to learn new teaching strategies, classroom management techniques, and assessment practices, which can create a sense of vulnerability and uncertainty. This adjustment period can impact the mentor and mentee relationship, as the mentor may need to provide additional support and guidance to help the mentee navigate these new demands (Anderson and Shannon, 1988).

Development of teaching identity and pedagogical philosophy

Transitioning may also involve the development of a teaching identity and pedagogical philosophy. The mentee may need to reflect on their beliefs about teaching and learning, classroom management, and student engagement and integrate these principles into their practice (Bradbury and Koballa, 2008). This process of self-discovery and growth can impact the mentor and mentee relationship, as the mentor plays a crucial role in guiding the mentee's exploration of teaching approaches and values.

Self-reflection task

How will you support your mentee whilst they encounter these challenges in their placement

Challenges for mentee	How will you support them?
Shift in roles and power dynamics	
Adjustment to new expectations and responsibilities	
Development of teaching identity and pedagogical philosophy	

References

Achinstein, B. and Athanases, S.Z. (2006) *Mentors in the making: Developing new leaders for new teachers*. Teachers College Press.

Anderson, E.M. and Shannon, A.L. (1988) 'Toward a conceptualization of mentoring', *Journal of Teacher Education*, 39, pp. 38–42. http://dx.doi.org/10.1177/002248718803900109

Beltman, S. and Schaeben, M. (2012) 'Institution-wide peer mentoring: benefits for mentors', *The International Journal of the First Year in Higher Education*, 2, pp. 33–44. 10.5204/intjfyhe.v3i2.124.

Beyene, T., Anglin, M., Sanchez and Ballou, M. (2002) 'Mentoring and relational mutuality: protégés' perspectives', *The Journal of Humanistic Counseling, Education and Development*, 41(1), pp. 87–102.

Bjorklund Jr., P. (2023). '"I kind of have that place to sit.": Exploring first-year teachers' experiences of belonging', *Teaching and Teacher Education*, 131, 1–10.

Bowman, M. (2014) 'Teacher mentoring as a means to improve schools', *BU Journal of Graduate Studies in Education*, 6(1), 47–50.

Bradbury, L.U. and Koballa, T.R (2012). Mentoring in Support of Reform-Based Science Teaching. In: Fraser, B., Tobin, K., McRobbie, C. (eds) Second International Handbook of Science Education. *Springer International Handbooks of Education*, vol 24, pg. 7–25

Bradbury, L.U. and Koballa, T.R. (2018) 'Borders to cross: identifying sources of tension in mentor–intern relationships', *Teaching and Teacher Education*, 24(8), pp. 2132–2145.

Bung, P. (2015) 'Collaborative mentoring models in higher educational Institutions: a win-win-win strategy for mentor, mentee, and the Institutions', *Journal of Advances in Business Management*, (3), pp. 197–203. ttps://www.academia.edu/34392981/Collaborative_mentoring_models_in_higher_educational_institutions_A_win_win_win_strategy_for_mentor_mentee_and_the_Instituion

Cullimore, S. and Simmons, J. (2008) The emerging dilemmas for mentors and mentees in the new context for training in-service teachers in the learning and skills sector. Paper presented at the BERA Annual Conference, September 3–6, Herriot-Watt University, Edinburgh, UK.

Daly, C. (2017) External mentoring for new teachers: mentor learning for a change agenda. https://discovery.ucl.ac.uk/id/eprint/1560487/1/Daly_RV34%20CLEAN%20VERSION.pdf

Deng, C., Gulseren, D. and Turner, N. (2022) 'How to match mentors and protégés for successful mentorship programs: a review of the evidence and recommendations for practitioners', *Leadership & Organization Development Journal*. 10.1108/LODJ-01-2021-0032.

De Rosa, S., Battaglini, D., Bennett, V. et al. (2023) 'Key steps and suggestions for a promising approach to a critical care mentoring program', *Journal of Anesthesia, Analgesia, Critical Care*, 3, p. 30. https://doi.org/10.1186/s44158-023-00116-4

Estyn (2018) The professional learning continuum: mentoring in initial teacher education. https://www.estyn.gov.wales/thematic-report/professional-learning-continuum-mentoring-initial-teacher-education

Fisher-Ari, T.R., Eaton, A. and Dantzler, M. (2019) 'Mentor matching: innovations in clinical practice across PDS networks', *School-University Partnerships*, 12(2), pp. 94–100.

Fletcher, J., Astall, C. and Everatt, J. (2021) 'Initial teacher education students' perceptions during a practicum in primary schools: a New Zealand experience', *International Journal of Mentoring and Coaching in Education*. 10.1108/IJMCE-10-2020-0069.

Glover, A., Jones, M., Thomas, A. and Worrall, L. (2022) Effective mentoring in Initial Teacher Education. What works and why. The Open University Initial Teacher Education Partnership PGCE Programme. https://oro.open.ac.uk/85130/

Heider, K.L. (2005) 'Teacher isolation: How mentoring programs can help', *Current Issues in Education*, 8(14). Retrieved September 1, 2009, from http://cie.ed.asu.edu/volume8/number14/

Hellsten, L., Prytula, M., Ebanks, A., & Lai, H. (2010). 'Teacher induction: Exploring beginning teacher mentorship', *Canadian Journal of Education Revue Canadienne De l'éducation*, 32(4), 703–733. Retrieved from https://journals.sfu.ca/cje/index.php/cje-rce/article/view/3057

Hobson, A., Maxwell, B. and Káplár-Kodácsy, K. (2021) The role of the mentoring programme coordinator: a rapid evidence review. *Education and Training Foundation*. https://www.et-foundation.co.uk/wp-content/uploads/2021/05/ETF_MCoord_Report_UoB_SHU_29_April_2021_Final.pdf

Hobson, A., Maxwell, B., Stevens, A., Doyle, K., & Malderez, A. (2015). Mentoring and coaching for teachers in the Further Education and Skills Sector in England: full report. https://10.13140/RG.2.1.4424.9680

Hobson, A., McIntyre, J., Ashby, P., Hayward, V., Stevens, A. and Malderez, A. (2012) The nature, impact and potential of external mentoring for teachers of physics and other subjects in England. https://www.gatsby.org.uk/uploads/education/reports/pdf/gatsby-impact-of-mentoring.pdf

Hobson, A.J. and Maxwell, B. (2020) 'Mentoring substructures and superstructures: an extension and reconceptualisation of the architecture for teacher mentoring', *Journal of Education for Teaching*, 46(2), 184–206

Hobson, A.J. and Mullen, C.A. (2023) 'Co-mentoring amongst teachers and leaders in transnational schooling contexts', in Craig, C.J., Mena, J. and Kane, R.G. (eds.) *Studying teaching and teacher education: Advances in research on teaching*, 44(2), pp. 193–212. Emerald Publishing Limited.

Kardos, S.M., Johnson, S.M., Peske, H.G., Kauffman, D. and Liu, E. (2001) 'Counting on colleagues: new teachers encounter the professional cultures of their schools', *Educational Administration Quarterly*, 37(2), pp. 250–290. https://doi.org/10.1177/00131610121969316

Kochan, F., Searby, L., George, M.P. and Edge, J.M. (2015) 'Cultural influences in mentoring endeavors: applying the cultural framework analysis process', *International Journal of Mentoring and Coaching in Education*, 4(2), pp. 86–106. http://dx.doi.org/10.1108/IJMCE-03-2015-0010

Kramer-Simpson, E. (2018) 'Feedback from internship mentors in technical communication internships', *Journal of Technical Writing and Communication*, 48, pp. 359–378. https://doi.org/10.1177/0047281617728362

Mackintosh, J. (2022) 'Educative mentoring', *Link*, 6(1). https://www.herts.ac.uk/link/volume-4,-issue-1/educative-mentoring

Manthiram, K. and Edwards, K.M. (2021) 'Reflections on the mentor-mentee relationship', *Journal of Pediatric Infectious Diseases Society*, 26, piab 025.

McIntyre, J. and Hobson, A. (2016) 'Supporting beginner teacher identity development: external mentors and the third space', *Research Papers in Education*, 31(2), pp. 133–158.

Morales, E., Ambrose-Roman, S. and Perez-Maldonado, R. (2015) 'Transmitting success: comprehensive peer mentoring for at-risk students in developmental math', *Innovative Higher Education*, 41. 10.1007/s10755-015-9335-6.

Norman, P. and Feiman-Nemser, S. (2005) 'Mind activity in teaching and mentoring', *Teaching and Teacher Education*, 21, pp. 679–697. 10.1016/j.tate.2005.05.006.

Rippon, J.H. and Martin, M. (2006) 'What makes a good induction supporter?', *Teaching and Teacher Education*, 22(1), pp. 84–99. doi:10.1016/j.tate.2005.07.004.

Seeliger, C. (2009) The perfect match: the impact of mentor and mentee similarity in formal alumni-student mentoring. https://openlibrary.org/books/OL53410382M/The_perfect_match

Tedder, M. and Lawy, R. (2009) 'The pursuit of "excellence": mentoring in further education initial teacher training in England', *Journal of Vocational Education & Training*, 61, pp. 413–429. 10.1080/13636820903363634.

Ughasoro, M.D., Musa, A., Yakubu, A., Adefuye, BO, Folahanmi, AT, Isah, A, Onyemocho, A, Chukwu, EE; Chukwudi, CU, Dadi Mamud, JN, Effa, E, Egharevba, HO, Etokidem, A, Mbachu, AN, Njokanma, AR, Ogunfowokan, AA, Ohihoin, NE, Onwuamah, C, Orunmuyi, TA, Salako, AO, Yusuf, AA, Okubadejo, N, Anepo-Okopi, J, Ezechi, O, Salako, BL (2022) 'Barriers and solutions to effective mentorship in health research and training institutions in Nigeria: mentors, mentees, and organizational perspectives', *Nigerian Journal of Clinical Practice*, 25(3), pp. 215–225. doi:10.4103/njcp.njcp_154_20.

van Nieuwerburgh, C. and Barr, M. (2016) 'Coaching in education', in Bachkirova, T., Spence, G. and Drake, D. (eds.) *The SAGE handbook of coaching*. Sage. https://au.sagepub.com/en-gb/oce/the-sage-handbook-of-coaching/book245418

Wang, J. and Fulton, L.A. (2012) 'Mentor-novice relationships and learning to teach in teacher induction: A critical review of research',. *Multidisciplinary Journal of Educational Research*, 2(1), pp. 56–104.

Wong, A. and Premkumar, K. (2007) 'An introduction to mentoring principles, processes, and strategies for facilitating mentoring relationships at a distance', *MedEdPORTAL*, 6. 10.15766/mep_2374-8265.3148.

Chapter 4

Key models of mentoring and professional learning and development

The apprenticeship model of mentoring

The apprenticeship model of mentoring in education has been a long-standing framework for professional development and skill acquisition, particularly in teacher training programmes. This pedagogical approach emphasises the transmission of knowledge and skills from experienced educators to novice teachers through hands-on experience and guided practice. The apprenticeship model has a particularly strong foothold within vocational pedagogy (Lawrence, 2019). As a metaphor, it refers to an asymmetrical relationship between two individuals, one who has mastered the skills of the trade (the master) and another who has not (the apprentice). Similar to a traditional teacher-student relationship, this model is based on one-way communication. During the process, the apprentice acquires tacit knowledge through observing the master as she uses her skills (Polanyi, 1958). This perspective can also be used to analyse the interplay between parent and child. Through participation in daily activities, children learn skills by observing their parents (Rogoff, 1990). This kind of learning is sometimes described as observational learning (Bandura and Walters, 1977).

Nielsen and Kvale (1999, p. 19) mention four characteristics of the apprenticeship model as a pedagogical idea.

Participation in a community of practice

The apprenticeship takes place in a social organisation, for instance, a community of craftsmen. The apprentice learns by participating in a group of competent practitioners of a craft. The novice advances from 'peripheral legitimate participation' to 'full participation' and gradually becomes a more competent member of the professional culture. Mentoring is done all the time in these communities, but it is not considered a separate activity. Reflection and action take place side by side. Mentoring does not follow a universal formula, but is adapted to the specific situation (Furlong and Maynard, 1995).

Professional identity

The apprentice learns by completing practical assignments that gradually become more difficult. The professional identity is developed through the process of mastering new skills. A reflective conversation should take place soon after the assignment in order to help reinforce cognitive and skills development (Eberle, 2018).

Learning through imitation of the master

The novice observes and imitates the work of the master or other skilled workers in a community. The mentoring process follows a traditional pattern, starting with the master demonstrating the correct execution of an assignment. The apprentice then starts to practice and is corrected by the master until she is proficient at the skill. The master will often give more in the beginning of the process and gradually less.

The quality of the work is evaluated through practice

The quality of a product is judged on its functionality and the customers' feedback. The master governs the accumulated knowledge of the particular craft and has developed subtle and complex criteria for the evaluation of craftsmanship. These criteria, however, are often characterised by tacit knowledge and are therefore not articulated (Hargreaves, 2002).

The apprenticeship model assumes that competence cannot be acquired through verbal communication alone. Competence is partly situational and improvisational. Visualisation, demonstration, observation, and imitation are principal techniques (Billett, 2016).

Self-reflective scenario exercise

Shamala is a trainee Maths teacher on a placement in the West Midlands. She is happy working with her mentor as a person but feels that her 'autonomy' and 'natural creativity' are being strangled by her mentor's 'micromanagement' of her teaching as she provides her with her own lesson plans, power points, and resources. She has discussed this with her mentor several times but says that her mentor says she is 'not ready' to teach independently yet.

How would you handle this situation?
What would you say to the mentee?
What would you say to the mentor? (If anything)

The collaborative or peer model of mentoring

Peer Collaborative Mentoring (PCM) has the elements of friendship, empathy, and mutual interest along with the characteristics of peer assistance and collaboration. At the heart of this approach are three elements: (1) mutual aspirations and a common purpose, (2) trust and fairness, and (3) interaction which is shared. The notions of common interest and mutual benefit are clearly understood in this type of relationship. There are, however, three additional elements which are seen as essential to the peer collaborative mentoring concept: (1) parity; (2) reciprocal interaction; and (3) shared interest or mutuality (Carvalho and Santos, 2022). Mentees have the opportunity to converse with a mentor or mentors and peers, present and defend ideas, exchange knowledge and experience, question other conceptual frameworks, and be actively engaged.

Kilburg (1992) defines this model as a nurturing process in which both parties (a more experienced and skilled person and a less experienced person) serve as equal partners, role models, teachers, sponsors, encouragers, and friends and professionally support one another. Both parties act as resources for one another and help each other accomplish professional and/or personal goals. Mentoring functions are carried out within the context of an ongoing caring relationship. This model fosters a sense of community, promotes reflective practice, and encourages the exchange of innovative ideas.

Mentoring and relationships

Positive interpersonal relationships can help pre-service teachers manage their negative emotions and deepen their understanding of how best they learn. Lejonberg *et al.* (2018) suggest that pre-service teachers' perception of a safe relationship is a prerequisite for the success of pre-service teacher learning. While people tend to operate differently, hold different beliefs, and work within different power structures, a commitment to collaboration and reciprocity can help them achieve common goals in mentoring (Nielsen and Kvale, 1999). Research also shows that pre-service teachers' self-regulation can be facilitated and boosted through intervention and instruction (Fonagy and Target, 2002).

Co-regulation plays a significant role in self-regulation. Self-regulated individuals can manage their behaviour well irrespective of the environmental circumstances and experiences they encounter, and they make informed proactive decisions where necessary (Gunawardena, 2023). Co-regulation, according to Hadwin, Järvelä and Miller (2018), stimulates appropriation of strategic planning, enactment, reflection, and adaptation, which can happen through interpersonal interactions and exchanges. Therefore, co-regulation creates opportunities for self-regulated learning, and these interactions can help trainees reflect on their feelings, perceptions, and emotions. Mentors as co-regulators can provide useful feedback for pre-service teachers to perform roles that Saariaho et al. (2019) explained as strategies for self-regulation, which include goal setting and task analysing at the preparatory stage, strategy use and monitoring at the performing stage, and reflection at the appraisal stage.

Peer mentoring support

In this model, mentors also collaborate with other mentors to provide extra support for mentees in support groups or Action Learning Sets, where they can come together to explore, discuss, and reflect on their practice (Whitmore, 2009). The Peer Mentor support group serves three functions: Developmental, resourcing, and qualitative. The developmental function supports the building of knowledge, skills, and understanding in the context of mentoring theory and practice. The resourcing function provides a supportive space, whereby mentors can share their mentoring experiences and develop insight through reflection and dialogue. The qualitative function provides the space to support the quality and robustness of mentoring practice through dynamic inquiry (Whitworth, Kimsey-House and Sandahl, 2007).

Through Action Learning Sets, mentors are able to engage in questioning insight, focusing on development and understanding; the learning is holistic, integrating learning from mentoring practice and the dynamic enquiry of peers. As mentors grow and develop their experience, the commitment is heightened (Whitmore, 2009).

The wider purpose of collaborative mentoring support is to build a Community of Practice (COP), creating a network of mentors who are keen to share practice, learn from each other through ongoing interaction, and provide peer support. The concept of the COP was derived from a sociocultural model which was designated as legitimate peripheral participation in the work of Lave and Wenger (1991). The role of the mentor is to assist the mentee within a COP in their movement from 'legitimate peripheral' to full 'participation'. Central to this are conversations with the mentee, which provide the ideal context for developing the practice of informed reflection 'on-action' and increase the likelihood of more appropriate intuitive responses 'in-action' (Schön, 1987).

One of the key strengths of the collaborative or peer model is its emphasis on collegiality and collaboration, which can lead to a more supportive and nurturing professional environment for both mentors and mentees (Revans, 1982). This reciprocal exchange of knowledge and skills can enhance professional growth and contribute to continuous improvement in teaching practices.

Research suggests that collaborative mentoring has a positive impact on both mentor's and mentees' metacognitive development as the act of explaining to others gives mentors opportunities to hone the process of reflective knowledge building and to deepen their own learning if metacognitive activity is stimulated (Kilburg, 1992). Therefore, mentees can be encouraged to assess their own knowledge and check whether their explanations make sense (Carvalho and Santos, 2022).

The collaborative model of mentoring in education, while lauded for its emphasis on peer-to-peer support and shared learning experiences, is not without its shortcomings. One of the primary challenges of this model is the potential lack of structured guidance and expertise that may be present in more traditional, hierarchical mentoring relationships. Without a clear delineation of roles and responsibilities, mentees may struggle to receive the targeted feedback and direction needed to develop their skills effectively (Wenger, 1998).

Additionally, the collaborative model of mentoring may inadvertently perpetuate the reproduction of existing norms and practices within a school or educational institution. Peer mentors, while well-intentioned, may not possess the breadth of experience or knowledge required to challenge entrenched ideas or suggest innovative approaches to teaching and learning. This can result in a perpetuation of the status quo, stifling opportunities for growth, creativity, and outside-the-box thinking (Wenger, McDermott and Snyder, 2002).

In addition, the collaborative model of mentoring may lack the formal structures and accountability mechanisms that are present in more traditional mentoring models. Without clear expectations, evaluation criteria, and opportunities for ongoing assessment and feedback, the effectiveness of the mentoring relationship may be compromised. This can lead to a lack of consistency in the support provided to novice teachers, making it difficult to track progress and ensure that developmental goals are being met (Carvalho and Santos, 2022).

Collaborative mentoring workshop exercise

Here is a plan of a workshop that I held to equip potential mentors with the skills and strategies needed to effectively implement the collaborative mentoring approach with trainee teachers.

Duration: 60 minutes

Materials Needed

- Presentation materials
- Whiteboard or flip chart
- Sticky notes
- Markers

Steps

1. Introduction (5 minutes):
    - Welcome participants and provide an overview of the workshop objectives.

- Discuss the importance of collaborative mentoring in supporting the professional growth of trainee teachers.

2. Understanding Collaborative Mentoring (10 minutes):
   - Present key concepts and principles of the collaborative mentoring approach.
   - Highlight the benefits of collaborative mentoring for both mentors and mentees.

3. Role-Playing Scenarios (20 minutes):
   - Divide participants into pairs, with one playing the role of the mentor and the other as the trainee teacher.
   - Provide each pair with a scenario involving a mentoring session and ask them to practice applying collaborative mentoring techniques.
   - Encourage participants to focus on active listening, asking open-ended questions, and fostering a non-judgemental, supportive environment.

4. Group Discussion (15 minutes):
   - Regroup and facilitate a discussion on the challenges and successes encountered during the role-playing exercise.
   - Encourage participants to share strategies for overcoming obstacles and enhancing the collaborative mentoring experience.

5. Action Planning (10 minutes):
   - Ask participants to reflect on their learnings and identify specific action steps they can take to integrate collaborative mentoring practices into their mentoring relationships with trainee teachers.
   - Have participants write down their action plans on sticky notes and share them with the group.

6. Closing (5 minutes):
   - Summarise key takeaways from the workshop.
   - Encourage participants to continue practising and refining their collaborative mentoring skills.

The action reflection model

The model was developed during a time in the 1980s when mentors were facing criticism for taking too much control over the student teachers' practicum. It was assumed that the student teachers had to follow the mentor's wishes, since the final certification of teacher candidates was ultimately the mentor's decision (Tonna, Bjerkholt and Holland, 2017). As a result, some critics argued that teacher education primarily produced dependent teachers (Kamarudin et al., 2020).

Arguably, the action-reflection model is humanistic and dialectic and influenced by Rogers' ideas of self-realisation and personal growth (Rogers, 1961) and Schön's emphasis on the teacher's capability to reflect on their own actions (Schon, 1987).

Originally, the model was geared towards the mentoring of student teachers regarding topics related to teaching. Today, the model is also used in the mentoring of experienced teachers, and the mentoring varies depending on how long the teacher has been teaching. Newly qualified teachers, for instance, might need mentoring to acquire a clearer professional identity and more experienced professionals might use mentoring to avoid stagnation and burnout (Pedler, Burgoyne and Brook, 2005).

Mentoring and reflection

Mentoring aligns with the idea of reflection, which in a way shapes teachers' perceptions of professionalism, eventually leading paths for creating teacher agency. The concepts underlying reflective practice date back to the 1900s, when reflective practice was seen as a way of exploring individual and collective experiences through interaction and reflection (Hargreaves, 2002). In the 1980s, Schön introduced the idea of Reflective Practice in order to explain how professionals meet the challenges of their work in a professional manner through improving practices. Reflective practices were categorised as follows (Schön, 1987): Self-Reflection, Peer Reflection, Group Reflection, and School-wide Reflection.

Through these processes, teachers can play the role of a mentor or a mentee by taking turns. Furlong and Maynard (1995) note that as a co-enquirer, mentors and mentees interact and shoulder responsibilities for their own learning. According to Hargreaves (2002), mentors or mentees in a reflective practice could share their experiences and their feelings, and therefore, professional dialogues could be seen as ripples creating waves for learning.

This constant reflective practice is vital to understanding their own teaching. Although this skill of reflecting often is initially at a surface level, noting if it was a good or bad lesson, and either feeling positive or negative about teaching abilities (Pottinger, Dyer and Akard, 2019).

By modelling best practice, mentors can encourage mentees to dive deeper and learn from experiences and lessons, whether good or bad, which will allow for growth and future teaching success. Within the process participants develop awareness of their own learning path as teacher, mentor and a mentee (Tutunis and Ozge, 2018). Consequently, through active interaction and cooperation, teachers develop a sense of belonging to the practice and learn new ways to collaborate and reify their identities as learners and practitioners (Wenger, 1998; Wenger, McDermott and Snyder, 2002).

Practice theory is an important term in the action-reflection model. It can be defined as the values, experiences, and knowledge that underpin a person's actions or plan of action. It refers to every person's subjective notion of practice and preparedness for practice (Orem, Blinkert and Clancy, 2007). The term is also ever changing, often incoherent and largely unconscious and difficult to formulate. McDermott and Snyder (2002) suggest that every person has a personal, cognitive action strategy which builds on knowledge and experience with other people. These strategies and ideas are arranged according to the values that they consider relevant.

According to them, mentoring should be based upon developing the mentee's own practice theory, and thus mentoring focuses on the theory behind the practice (2000). The goal is to create awareness about core values that direct their actions. The mentee can achieve an increased understanding of these core values when asked to justify and explain their own actions. This will make it possible for the mentee to expand their repertoire of actions. Since the core values in practice theory are often contradictory, it is essential to help the mentee develop self-awareness. Professional and authentic conversations are the most effective ways to achieve this. Weasmer and Woods (2003) suggest that authentic dialogues enable us to articulate our own experiences, implicit hopes, and fears in the intellectual and emotional company of others whom we trust.

In the action-reflection model, the focus is on planned, formalised mentor-mentee meetings, as opposed to the apprenticeship model, where the focus is rather on informal mentoring in the ongoing daily interaction (Poortman, Illeris and Nieuwenhuis 2014). The mentoring is based on the mentee's expressed needs, and the mentee is usually asked to develop a mentorship plan for the practicum. This is a document that will help both the mentor and the mentee prepare for the mentoring (Wijoyo, Rahayu and Dwiprahasto, 2016).

Here are two basic ways this model can be applied:

1 Enhancing Teaching Practices

   Action: A mentor observes a mentee's teaching session and notes specific areas for improvement, such as classroom management or engagement strategies.

   Reflection: Both discuss the observed session, reflecting on what went well and what could be improved. The mentor encourages the mentee to consider the impact of their teaching methods on student learning outcomes.

   Outcome: The mentee gains insights into their teaching practices, leading to actionable steps for improvement. For example, they might plan to incorporate more interactive activities to increase student engagement (Revans, 1982).

2 Professional Development

   Action: The mentor and mentee set professional development goals, such as completing a course on differentiated instruction or attending a workshop on educational technology.

Reflection: Throughout the process, the mentor and mentee reflect on the progress towards these goals. They evaluate the effectiveness of the new knowledge and skills in the mentee's teaching practice.

Outcome: The mentee not only achieves the set goals but also integrates the new skills into their daily teaching routine, enhancing their overall professional competence. This reflective practice helps in continuous professional growth and the adaptation of best practices in education. By utilising the model, mentoring becomes a dynamic and continuous process of professional growth and improvement for both mentors and mentees (Pedler, Burgoyne and Brook, 2005).

Criticism

The Action-Reflection model has been criticised for several reasons. Firstly, some believe that the model serves to weaken the mentor's professional authority because of the focus on dialogue (Whittington, 2020). Secondly, some question whether there is too much emphasis on individual differences and preferences, and not enough emphasis on the ability to adapt to the specific mentoring tasks (Pedler, Burgoyne and Brook, 2005). Thirdly, some suggest that the theoretical basis for the model is unclear. By emphasising reflection, we might lose the focus on proper actions, and whilst developing the mentee's ability to reflect, the purpose of reflection might be forgotten (Tonna, Bjerkholt and Holland, 2017).

> **Self-reflection and peer reflection exercise**
>
> Write a short evaluation of a mentoring session in which you participated as either a mentor or a mentee. Note down your thoughts, feelings, and observations. Compare notes with either your mentee or your mentee.

Systemic mentoring (SM)

Characteristics

Systemic mentoring is a mentoring approach designed to create awareness in the mentee of how people influence and are influenced by their environment. The mentoring approach is based on ideas proposed by Bateson (2002) and Bronfenbrenner (1977), among others, whose works focused on social systems and interpersonal relationships. Central concepts in the systems theory are wholeness, human relations, and circularity.

The term wholeness is used to emphasise that phenomena are connected to each other. As a consequence, people will always influence each other mutually in human relations. For instance, in an educational institution, there will be relations between mentors, between management and the mentor, and between mentor and mentee. Even though not all these parties participate directly in the mentoring, they can all influence how the mentoring is organised Additionally, on the organisational level, there are relations between institutions involved in mentoring (Bronfenbrenner, 1977), for example, the teacher training provider and the teaching placement. Thus, when the mentee tries to solve a problem, this may also involve parties which are directly involved in mentoring (Hawkins and Turner, 2019).

Systemic mentoring and questioning

In systemic mentoring, exclusive why-questions are viewed as unproductive as they imply the existence of a single cause and one effect (i.e. 'Why did you do that?') (Whitmore, 2009). In contrast, systemic mentoring uses a more circular explanation model where all parties will always contribute to the interaction and in a process known as punctuating. The term punctuation refers to the concept that there are always alternative ways to understand an incident. If a person punctuates the interaction differently, they will have a different understanding of the interaction (Whittington, 2020).

SM draws clearly from the notions of Systemic Coaching (SC), and while the processes vary, there are common elements that exist across this type of coaching. For example, the Coach and Coachee also apply a systemic viewpoint to the process, and there is also a focus in SC on recognising and integrating the needs of different participants within the system (Hawkins and Turner, 2019).

Lawrence (2015) suggests that SC is not about a particular set of skills or techniques; rather, it is a mindset that includes a belief in the significance of 'authentic reflective dialogue'. It is suggested that only through dialogue and questioning can the Coachee stand 'outside' the system and develop a thorough understanding of the problems they are encountering and find solutions (Hawkins and Smith, 2006)". This notion has also been applied to Systemic Mentoring and in developing its approaches to questioning, which include:

- Questions that explore differences
    These questions assume that people react differently to a situation. The intention is to increase the awareness of how people react differently in a situation (MCLeod, 2003).
- Those that explore differences on a relational level
    These questions explore differences in interpersonal relations. The mentee is asked to describe different relationships and explain how they are different (Weinstein, 2013).

- Questions that explore differences in opinions, ideas, values, and motives
  These questions focus on how a person imagines other people perceive the situation. The aim is to stimulate the person to think empathically about the situation.
- Questions that explore differences between the present and the future
  The focus is on the involved parties' reaction in previous situations, and how they might have reacted differently. All these questions can give the mentee a wider and more complex picture of an experienced situation (Lawrence, 2015).
- Questions that explore behavioural effect
  These questions try to make the mentee more aware of the mutual influence people have on each other. They focus on how the mentee experienced other people's behaviour and how we experienced other people's behavior. The ability to understand the other person's perspective is essential to empathy (Gilbert and Whittleworth, 2009).
- Triadic questions
  The purpose of triadic questions is to create awareness of the third party's experience of the interaction. These questions also attempt to create awareness of the reciprocal relationship between people (Whitney and Amanda, 2003). The mentor should help the mentee to develop an ability to observe themselves from the outside (Boyle and Boice, 1998).
- Hypothetical questions
  By asking questions about different future scenarios, the mentee is encouraged to reflect on alternative options.
- If you were successful in making changes, what would the situation be like?
- What is hampering such a change? (Boyle and Boice, 1998)
  Such hypothetical questions may help them look for an alternative course of action. It's also important to be stimulated to reflect upon how the situation might look if the problem was solved (Lewis, Passmore and Cantore, 2016).

A training exercise in how to develop approaches to systemic mentoring

Objective: To allow mentors to practice and develop their systematic mentoring abilities through a simulated mentoring scenario.
Duration: 90 minutes

Materials Needed:

- Simulation scenario briefing document, Role-play materials (name tags, scenario description cards), Observation rubric, and Debriefing question prompts

Steps:

1. Briefing (10 minutes):
   - Provide mentors with the simulation scenario details, including the roles they will play and the objectives they need to achieve during the activity.

Scenario Description:

Your mentee is Anja, a trainee teacher who is struggling with classroom management and lesson planning. Your task is to apply systemic mentoring techniques to support her in improving her teaching practice.

Key Objectives:

1. Identify the specific needs and challenges of the mentee, Anja.
2. Develop a systemic mentoring plan that addresses Anja's needs and meets with the goals of the mentoring programme.
3. Implement the mentoring plan by setting clear objectives, establishing regular check-ins, and providing constructive feedback to support Sarah's professional growth.
4. Reflect on the effectiveness of the mentoring process and adjust as needed.

This simulation scenario aims to give mentors hands-on experience in applying systemic mentoring strategies and techniques in a realistic mentoring context, fostering their development as effective mentors in the educational setting.

2. Role-play (60 minutes):
   - Divide mentors into pairs, with one assuming the role of the mentor and the other as the mentee.
   - Implement the simulation scenario, giving mentors the opportunity to engage in systemic mentoring practices such as goal setting, action planning, feedback provision, and progress monitoring.
   - Encourage mentors to take notes and observations during the role-play.

3. Debrief (20 minutes):
   - Gather mentors together for a debriefing session.
   - Use an observation rubric to facilitate a structured discussion on the systematic mentoring practices demonstrated during the simulation.
   - Encourage mentors to reflect on their strengths and areas for improvement in their systematic mentoring approach.
   - Discuss how mentors can apply the lessons learned from the simulation to their real mentoring interactions.

4. Reflection (10 minutes):
   - Provide groups with reflective prompts to encourage them to think about how they can further develop their systematic mentoring abilities.

- Encourage groups to set specific goals for improving their systematic mentoring practices moving forward.

Appreciative inquiry

Appreciative inquiry (AI) is a mentoring approach that seeks to identify and foster the best in people and organisations. AI, as a participatory approach, aims to explore ideas that people have about what is valuable in what they do (Boyd and Bright, 2007; Reed, 2007). It has slowly been growing in popularity over the past decades (Cooperrider and Srivastva, 1987; Cooperrider and Whitney, 2005). Since the inception of this model, AI approaches have been used in a variety of contexts, including business, military, and educational settings. They have also been adapted to individual improvement initiatives, including professional coaching and academic advising (Mather *et al.*, 2024).

AI aims to build on the strengths of what people have achieved in their organisation, rather than concentrating on their problems. By focusing on the shared strengths and achievements of the organisation, the AI framework posits that the individual within the organisation will come to realise what has been achieved and their role in these achievements and will build on these achievements rather than becoming bogged down in perceived problems and failures (McNamee, 2003).

When undertaking an Appreciative Inquiry, aspects of the person's life they find meaningful and productive are examined, and by deliberately connecting mentees' past successes to their futures as trainee teachers, they are more likely to have a sense of agency and promise in their pursuits (Cooperrider and Whitney, 2005). This approach is done on the assumption that people will achieve transformative goals quickly by strengthening their pre-existing resources (Bridges and Bridges 2017).

According to Cooperrider and Srivastva (1987), Appreciative Inquiry builds on the following assumptions:

- All organisations and all individuals have success stories to show that can contribute to positive development.
- All development is based on experience. And when the process is started with positive experiences, the road to development becomes more meaningful, and thus positive experiences should be made visible and active in the organisation.
- Inquiry and change stand in a dialectic relationship to each other. By starting an inquiry, a change process is simultaneously started.

According to Ludema *et al.* (2006), when making these changes, employees may understand what is important in the organisation, what creates a good life, happiness, development, and freedom. Arguably, people who are recognised for their strengths and qualities are willing to give more (Cooperrider and Whitney, 2005). In order to understand what is working, it is necessary to reflect on the characteristics of good experiences and achievements.

AI is seen as social construction in action (McNamee, 2003), and this is enacted by bringing participants together to share what has worked with each other to develop knowledge that can shape social interactions in the organisation in the future (Fynn, 2014). This approach could be useful when mentees are dealing with challenges where positively focused creative thinking could be helpful, for example, where a challenge has been around for some time, or where they are feeling hopeless about a situation. It could also be used with groups of trainees who could explore something together and can empower individuals, teams, and institutions to make sustainable positive change (Dreyfus and Dreyfus 1986).

According to Orem, Blinkert and Clancy (2007), AI works on the premise that notions of realities are constructed on five principles:

- The Positive Principle

  Positive questions amplify the positive core, and momentum for change requires positive affect and social bonding. The positive principle proposes that momentum and sustainable change require positive affect and social bonding. Sentiments like hope, excitement, inspiration, camaraderie, and joy increase creativity, openness to new ideas and people, and cognitive flexibility Bachkirova (2022).

- The Constructionist Principle

  This includes the power of language and social context in which individuals and groups create their perceived reality. The constructionist principle proposes that what people believe to be true determines what they do and think and action emerges from relationships (Bushe, 2007). Through the language and discourse of daily interactions, people co-construct the organisations they inhabit. The purpose of inquiry is to stimulate new ideas, stories, and images that generate new possibilities for action (Orem, Blinkert and Clancy, 2007).

- The Principle of Simultaneity

  This proposes that as people inquire into human systems, they change them. QLuestions are never neutral; they are fateful, and social systems move in the direction of the questions they most persistently and passionately discuss. The moment a question is asked is the moment change can occur as inquiry is an intervention (Cooperrider and Srivastva, 1987).

- The Poetic Principle

  This principle acknowledges that reality is fluid and that the same event or story can have endless interpretive possibilities. The poetic principle proposes that organisational life is expressed in the stories people tell each other every day, and the story of the organisation is constantly being co-authored. The words and topics chosen for the inquiry have an impact far beyond just the words themselves (Cooperrider and Whitney, 2000).

- The Anticipatory Principle
  People move in the direction of their future images. Human systems are forever projecting ahead of themselves a horizon of expectation that brings the future powerfully into the present as a mobilising agent. Appreciative inquiry uses the creation of positive imagery on a collective basis to refashion anticipatory reality (Cooperrider and Srivastva, 1987).

The four phases of appreciative inquiry

An appreciative inquiry is traditionally implemented in four phases (Cooperrider and Srivastva, 1987; Cooperrider and Whitney, 2005; Ludema *et al.*, 2006;). This is also referred to as the 4D cycle: Discovery, Dream, Design, and Destiny:

- Discovery
  The purpose of the discovery phase is to identify situations where an organisation or an individual's performance is at its best. The discovery is done through systematic charting, for instance, by qualitative data collection methods such as interviews (Clouder and King, 2015). The idea is that by telling stories, people reveal how they perceive and experience their lives. And by bringing these stories forward, it can be possible to create a common experience base around what they value and what energises them in their daily lives (Cooperrider and Whitney, 2000). During interviews, the following positively formed questions could be posed:

  - What makes us happy?
  - What contributes to making us happy?
  - What helps us bring forward the positive?

  When listening to employees during this process, energising aspects of the stories are explored to uncover and understand the areas that give vitality to individuals and organisations.

- Dream
  After charting valuable experiences, future dreams and visions are formulated based on shared participatory notions MCLeod (2003).
- Design
  In the design phase, employees formulate precise goals and create an action plan for the way ahead. In this phase, the organisation's employees try to create relations and systems that can support the desired development. The purpose of this phase is to define a vision and what is needed to realise this vision (Cooperrider and Srivastva, 1987).
- Destiny
  During the destiny phase, the employees adopt initiatives in order to realise the goals that were developed in the design phase. This requires a specific action plan describing what needs to be done when and by whom. The employees reinforce positive experiences from the past and attempt

new measures. The learning process continues with adjustments and experimentation (Fynn, 2014).

The Appreciative Advising model developed by Bloom, Hutson and Ye (2008) added two D's to Cooperrider's original 4D scheme and renamed the Destiny phase to Deliver. These extra D's are:

- Disarm

  During this stage the aim is to establish rapport and comfort within the relationship between mentor and mentee, and by developing this rapport, the mentee feels valued and heard (Bloom, Hutson and Ye, 2008). Mentors need to ensure that mentees understand their presence and potential for success are validated and affirmed by tutors and staff. The mentor can foster this mindset by first demonstrating authentic interest in the mentee and their experience and then presenting themselves as co-learners (Mather *et al.*, 2024). The mentor should approach the entire relationship, and most certainly the initial meetings, with curiosity and openness to their experiences, knowledge, and goals, and value their questions and responses (2024).

- Deliver and don't settle

  One of the central roles of the mentor is to highlight aspects of the mentee's work that demonstrate growth and success. The mentor should also provide feedback on those aspects of the work that might be experienced as challenging and enable the mentee to address those challenges by drawing on personal strengths, supportive networks, and resources (Cooperrider and Whitney, 2005).

Self-reflective task

Think of a trainee who you think could benefit from making a change.

1. What questions could you ask them using the 6D's approach?
2. How could you use this approach with groups or teams?

4D stages	Your questions
Disarm	
Discovery	
Dream	
Design	
Deliver	
Don't Settle	

References

Bachkirova, T. (2022) *Developmental coaching: working with the self.* McGraw-Hill Education.

Bandura, A. and Walters, R.H. (1977) *Social learning theory.* Vol. 1. Prentice Hall.

Bateson, G. (2002) [1979] *Mind and nature: a necessary unity*. Hampton Press.

Billett, S. (2016) 'Apprenticeship as a mode of learning and model of education', *Education + Training*, 58(6), pp. 613–628.

Bloom, J., Hutson, B. and Ye, H. (2008) *The appreciative advising revolution*. Stipes Publishing.

Boyd, N.M. and Bright, D.S. (2007) 'Appreciative inquiry as a mode of action research for community psychology', *Journal of Community Psychology*, 35, pp. 1019–1036.

Boyle, P. and Boice, B. (1998) 'Systematic mentoring for new faculty teachers and graduate teaching assistants', *Innovative Higher Education*, 22, pp. 157–179. doi: 10.1023/A:1025183225886.

Bridges, W. and Bridges, S. (2017) *Managing transitions: making the most of change*. Revised 4th edn. Nicholas Brealey Publishing.

Bronfenbrenner, U. (1977) 'Toward an experimental ecology of human development', *American Psychologist*, 32(7), p. 513.

Bushe, G.R. (2007) 'Appreciative inquiry is not (just) about the positive', *OD Practitioner*, 39(4), pp. 30–35.

Carvalho, A.R. and Santos, C. (2022) 'Developing peer mentors' collaborative and metacognitive skills with a technology-enhanced peer learning program', *Computers and Education Open*, 3, p. 100070. doi:10.1016/j.caeo.2021.100070.

Clouder, D.L. and King, V. (2015) 'What works? A critique of appreciative inquiry as a research methodology', in Huisman, J. and Tight, M. (eds) *Theory and method in higher education research, vol. 1: theory and method in higher education research II*. Vol. 10. Emerald Group Publishing Limited, pp. 169–190. doi:10.1108/S2056-375220150000001008.

Cooperrider, D.L. and Srivastva, S. (1987) 'Appreciative inquiry in organizational life', in Pasmore, W. and Woodman, R. (eds) *Research in organizational change and development*, Vol. 1. JAI Press, pp. 129–169.

Cooperrider, D. and Whitney, D. (2000) 'Appreciative inquiry: A positive revolution in change. Berrett-Koehler.

Dreyfus, H. and Dreyfus, S.E. (1986) *Mind over machine*. Simon and Schuster.

Dunphy, L., Proctor, G., Bartlett, R., Haslam, M. and Wood, C. (2010) 'Reflections and learning from using action learning sets in a healthcare education setting', *Action Learning: Research and Practice*, 7(3), pp. 303–314.

Eberle, J. (2018) 'Apprenticeship learning', in *International handbook of the learning sciences*. Routledge, pp. 44–53.

Fonagy, P. and Target, M. (2002) 'Early intervention and the development of self-regulation', *Psychoanalytic Inquiry*, 22(3), pp. 307–335.

Furlong, J. and Maynard, T. (1995) *Mentoring student teachers*. Routledge.

Fynn, A. (2014) 'Appreciative Inquiry of a Mentoring Programme in Soweto', *New Voices in Psychology*, 10(1), pp. 84–95.

Gilbert, A. and Whittleworth, K. (2009) *OSCAR coaching model: simplifying workplace coaching*. 1st revised ed. Worth Consulting Ltd.

Gunawardena, M. (2023) 'Mentoring pre-service teachers: the THIINK4 reflective cycle', *Australian Journal of Teacher Education*, 48(4), pp. 76–94.

Hadwin, A., Järvelä, S. and Miller, M. (2018) 'Self-regulation, co-regulation, and shared regulation in collaborative learning environments', in *Handbook of self-regulation of learning and performance*. Routledge, pp. 83–106.

Hargreaves, A. (2002) 'Teaching and betrayal', *Teachers and Teaching: Theory and Practice*, 8(3/4), pp. 393–407. doi:10.1080/135406002100000521.

Hawkins, P. and Smith, N. (2006) *Coaching, mentoring and organizational consultancy: supervision and development*. McGraw-Hill Education.

Hawkins, P., and Turner, E. (2020). *Systemic coaching: delivering value beyond the individual*. Routledge/Taylor & Francis Group.

Kamarudin, M., Kamarudin, A.Y., Darmi, R. and Saad, N.S.M. (2020) 'A review of coaching and mentoring theories and models', *International Journal of Academic Research in Progressive Education and Development*, 9(2), pp. 289–298.

Kilburg, G. (1992) A Study of Peer Collaborative Mentoring for the Professional Development of International Graduate Teaching Assistants. A Thesis submitted to Oregon State University in partial fulfillment of the requirements for the degree of Doctor of Philosophy Completed April 23, 1992 Commencement June 1992. file:///C:/Users/44798/Downloads/KilburgGaryM1992.pdf. Accessed on April 6th 2024.

Lave, J. and Wenger, E. (1991) *Situated learning: legitimate peripheral participation*. Cambridge University Press.

Lawrence, P. (2015) 'What is systemic coaching?', *Philosophy of Coaching: An International Journal*, 4, pp. 35–52. doi:10.22316/poc/04.2.03.

Lawrence, P. (2021) Coaching Systematically. Five ways of thinking about Systems. Routledge.

Lejonberg, E., Elstad, E., Sandvik, L.V., Solhaug, T. and Christophersen, K.A. (2018) 'Developmental relationships in schools: pre-service teachers' perceptions of mentors' effort, self-development orientation, and use of theory', *Mentoring & Tutoring: Partnership in Learning*, 26(5), pp. 524–541.

Lewis, S., Passmore, J. and Cantore, S. (2016) *Appreciative inquiry for change management: using AI to facilitate organizational development*. 2nd edn. Kogan Page Ltd.

Ludema, J., Cooperrider, D. and Barrett, F. (2006). In Reason, P and. Bradbury, H. Sage, Appreciative inquiry: The power of the unconditional positive question. *Handbook of action research*. pp. 189–199.

Mather, P.C., Gut-Zippert, D.M., Robinson, D., VanDerveer, B.J. and Balarabe, O.A. (2024) 'Mentoring new faculty: an appreciative approach', *Journal of Appreciative Education*, 11, pp. 1–11.

MCLeod, A. (2003) *Performance coaching: the handbook for managers, HR professionals and coaches*. Crown House Publishing.

McNamee, S. (2003) 'Appreciative evaluation within a conflicted educational context', *New Directions for Evaluation*, 2003, pp. 23–40. doi:10.1002/ev.97.

Nielsen, K. and Kvale, S. (1999) *Mastery: learning as social practice*. Ad Notam Gyldendal.

Orem, S.L., Blinkert, J. and Clancy, A.L. (2007) *Appreciative coaching: a positive process for change*. Jossey-Bass.

Pedler, M., Burgoyne, J. and Brook, C. (2005) 'What has action learning learned to become?', *Action Learning: Research and Practice*, 2, pp. 49–68. doi:10.1080/14767330500041251.

Polanyi, M. (1958) *Personal knowledge*. Routledge and Kegan Paul.

Poortman, C.L., Illeris, K. and Nieuwenhuis, L. (2014) 'Apprenticeship: from learning theory to practice', in *Contemporary apprenticeship*. Routledge, pp. 11–31.

Pottinger, E., Dyer, R. and Akard, J. (2019) Reflective practice through mentorship: a program reflection. *Journal of Instructional Research*, 8(2), 98–118.

Reed, J. (2007) *Appreciative inquiry: research for change*. Sage.

Revans, R.W. (1982) 'What is action learning?', *Journal of Management Development*, 1(3), pp. 64–75.

Rogers, C.R. (1961) *On becoming a person: a therapist's view of psychotherapy*. Houghton Mifflin.

Rogoff, B. (1990) *Apprenticeship in thinking: cognitive development in social context*. Oxford University Press.

Saariaho, E., Toom, A., Soini, T., Pietarinen, J. and Pyhältö, K. (2019) 'Student teachers' and pupils' co-regulated learning behaviours in authentic classroom situations in teaching practicums', *Teaching and Teacher Education*, 85, pp. 92–104. doi:10.1016/j.tate.2019.06.003.

Schön, D.A. (1987) *Educating the reflective practitioner.* Jossey-Bass.
Tonna, M.A., Bjerkholt, E. and Holland, E. (2017) 'Teacher mentoring and the reflective practitioner approach', *International Journal of Mentoring and Coaching in Education,* 6(3), pp. 210–227.
Tutunis, B. and Ozge, H. (2018) 'The impact of reflective practices of English language teachers on the development of a sense of agency', *Journal of Education and Training Studies,* 6, p. 107. doi:10.11114/jets.v6i10.3409.
Weasmer, J. and Woods, A.M. (2003) 'Mentoring: professional development through reflection', *The Teacher Educator,* 39(1), pp. 65–77.
Weinstein, A. (2013) *Executive coaching and the process of change: a practioner's guide.* CreateSpace Independent Publishing Platform.
Wenger, E. (1998) *Communities of practice: learning, meaning, and identity.* Cambridge University Press. doi:10.1017/CBO9780511803932.
Wenger, E., McDermott, R. and Snyder, W.M. (2002) *Cultivating communities of practice.* Harvard Business School Press.
Whitmore, J. (2009) *Coaching for performance: growing human potential and purpose—The principles and practice of coaching and leadership.* 4th edn. Nicholas Brealey Publishing.
Whittington, J. (2020) *Systemic coaching and constellations: an introduction to the principles, practices and application.* Kogan Page.
Whitworth, L., Kimsey-House, H. and Sandahl, P. (2007) *Co-active coaching.* Davies Blade Publishing
Wijoyo, Y., Rahayu, G.R. and Dwiprahasto, I. (2016) 'Evaluation on teaching mentoring program based on reflective pedagogy paradigm', *Indian Journal of Pharmaceutical Education and Research,* 50(2), pp. S180–S187.

Chapter 5

Coaching and mentoring

Coaching

The term coaching originates from the word 'coach', a medium of transport. In 19th century England, the word 'coach' came to be used to describe a private teacher who assisted students preparing for exams. The transposition of a word for transport to a name for a teacher came about for these 19th century exam preparation teachers due to the students' conception that they were being driven through the examinations or were able to ride through the examinations on a coach with the help of their prep teachers. In some recent conceptions of mentoring, the word 'coach' is used metaphorically as the guide who assists the mentee on her inner journey. The coach assists the mentee to improve her own abilities by developing mental or practical skills (Bloom, Hutson and Ye, 2008). Additionally, several other types of coaching have emerged. The term is today normally used as a reflective and conversational method whereby one person assists another to realise the maximum potential of their abilities in a particular area.

Coaching and mentoring model

Differences between mentoring and coaching

Coaching and mentoring are increasingly popular processes where individuals receive guidance in order to develop their skills, knowledge, and experience or meet their goals or objectives. It is increasingly accepted that both coaching and mentoring may, in specific contexts (Allison and Harbour, 2009)

- Be relatively directive or non-directive
- Require and draw upon the helper's experience
- Be of long or short duration
- Involve giving advice
- Work with goals set by the learner or for the learner
- Deal with significant transitions the learner wishes to make
- Address broad personal growth ambitions

DOI: 10.4324/9781003527374-5

Overall it has been suggested that coaching in most applications addresses performance in some aspect of an individual's work or life, while mentoring is more often associated with much broader, holistic development and with career progress.

Coaching aims to produce optimal performance and improvement at work. It focuses on specific skills and goals and may also have an impact on an individual's personal attributes, such as social interaction or confidence. The process typically lasts for a defined period of time or forms the basis of an ongoing management style (Hamlin, Ellinger and Beattie, 2006).

Although there's a variety of definitions, there are some generally agreed principles of coaching in organisations. It's essentially a non-directive form of development focusing on improving performance and developing an individual. Personal factors may be included, but the emphasis is on performance at work. Coaching activities have both organisational and individual goals for individuals to assess their strengths and development areas. It is a skilled activity which should be delivered by those trained in coaching skills. The coach does not need to be a more experienced person in comparison to the coachee in regard to the matter to be coached; instead, their skills in listening and questioning are crucial to establishing the relationship (Jones, Woods and Guillaume, 2016).

The critical components of coaching models include many of the following coach–coachee relationship, problem identification and goal setting, problem solving, transformational process, and mechanisms by which the model achieves outcomes. It has been suggested that some of the central factors which impact positive coaching outcomes include the coach's role and attributes, selection of coaching candidates and coach attributes, obstacles and facilitators to the coaching process, benefits and drawbacks of external versus internal coaches, and organisational support (McDonald Connor, 2017).

Mentoring in the workplace describes a relationship in which a more experienced colleague shares their greater knowledge to support the development of an inexperienced individual. It calls on the skills of questioning, listening, clarifying, and reframing that are associated with coaching (Kamarudin *et al.*, 2020).

One key distinction is that mentoring relationships tend to be longer term than coaching arrangements. An effective mentoring relationship is one where there are learning opportunities for both participants, encouraging joint sharing and learning. Coaching focuses on performance improvement, with the learner having primary ownership of their goals and the coach having ownership of the process. Mentoring, on the other hand, primarily fulfils the need to upskill new teachers to ensure that internal professional growth is provided for new teachers (Nuis, Segers and Beausaert, 2023).

Combining mentoring and coaching

Coaching and mentoring are two distinct support models that are often seen as complementary approaches to professional development. While coaching primarily focuses on skill-building, goal setting, and performance improvement, mentoring emphasises relationship-building, knowledge-sharing, and career development. By fusing these models together, a more comprehensive and effective support system can be created to meet the diverse needs of individuals seeking guidance and growth in their professional endeavours (McDonald Connor, 2017).

Integrating coaching and mentoring involves combining the structured and goal-oriented nature of coaching with the relational and developmental aspects of mentoring. This fusion allows for a more holistic approach to supporting individuals as they navigate their career paths, overcome challenges, and achieve their goals. By incorporating coaching techniques such as active listening, questioning, and feedback into mentoring relationships, mentors can provide targeted support that is tailored to the specific needs and aspirations of their mentees (2017).

Furthermore, blending coaching and mentoring models encourages a collaborative and dynamic learning environment, where mentors can serve as both guides and facilitators of growth. This approach enables mentees to not only receive expert advice and guidance but also actively engage in reflective practice, goal setting, and action planning. By leveraging the strengths of both coaching and mentoring, individuals can benefit from a dual support system that fosters personal and professional development in a more holistic and sustainable manner (Fynn, 2014).

Through a process combining similar elements of encouragement, self-management, support, and evaluation, both coaching and mentoring are learner-centred with learning at their core. In addition, they utilise conversation processes such as questioning, reforming statements, summarising, listening reflectively, and personal reflection in order to evoke learning (Griffiths, 2015).

It is also emphasised within coaching literature that the reciprocal relationship between mentor and mentee is key in both areas and suggested that learning is reciprocal as a result of this (Hawkins and Turner, 2019). Coaching also has a similar end goal to that of mentoring, which is the internalising of the training as the learner becomes their own teacher (Lawrence, 2019).

Thus, despite the potential hierarchical differences in the learning relationship of mentoring and the commitment of coaching to goal-directed action, mentoring theory can provide a basis for understanding the coaching process and how it creates, reciprocates, and supports learning for the long run (Griffiths, 2015). Central to overcoming the relationship problems is the establishment of open, trusting, non-judgemental, and supportive environments for effective coaching (Weinstein, 2013).

Integrating different coaching models into mentoring

There are many different types of coaching, such as Behaviourist, Humanist, Positive Psychology, Cognitive coaching, Systematic coaching, Instructional coaching, and Goal setting coaching (Whittington, 2020). All of these can be integrated into mentoring approaches in order to define the relationship and to provide it with greater structure and clarify its approaches to outcomes. These types of coaching can be found in the following main coaching models:

- GROW

   According to Whitmore (2009), the GROW model helps to solve problems and achieve goals because it is a solution-focused model. There are four stages in the model, which require the coach to captivate the coacher's interest. It is grounded on the belief that individuals have the most appropriate solutions to their problems, while the coach, on the other hand, will succeed with some proven techniques, practice, and even instincts (Kamarudin *et al.*, 2020). Each of the four distinct stages can be represented by a simple question, or a series of questions to help develop people and discover their potential. It has been suggested to be an ideal model for setting goals, solving problems, preserving personal achievement, and efficiency (Leedham and Parsloe, 2016).

   Goal

   According to Whitmore (2009), setting goals before exploring reality helps to develop goals which are not influenced by an individual's current situation. At the same time, the goals must be SMART: Specific, Measurable, Acceptable, Realistic, and Timely (Bianco-Mathis, Nabors and Roman, 2002). The main question to be addressed when setting goals is whether or not they fit the overall objectives. It is essential to set a goal that is clear and specific. Starr (2021) argues that the idea of setting goals is strongly related to the goal-setting theory, which advocates the setting of clear, specific, and challenging goals as this leads to clear direction and motivation. The second stage is the reality in which the coachee will explain the current reality and what is wrong to help them to see why change is necessary (Weinstein, 2013).
   Reality

   It is essential for both parties to know the current situation because the argument is that it is difficult for them to solve the problem if they do not have a clear picture of the anticipated destination (Whitworth, Kimsey-House and Sandahl, 2007). According to Bridges and Bridges (2017), people cannot solve problems they do not understand or reach goals without considering the starting point. It is vital for the coach and the coachee to keep focus and become aware of the situation. The crucial coaching role is to stimulate the coachees' self-evaluation and identify the obstacles that have been holding them back. This is the crucial part where the coach need to summarise and repeat what he or she understands with regard to the actual situation of the coachee. At this phase, it often reveals the fundamental fears and beliefs that can be worked on during or in between coaching sessions (Hamlin, Ellinger and Beattie, 2006).

Option

The option stage is to generate ideas that can contribute to the solution of the problem. It involves exploring various options and focusing not only on the right answers but also on several alternatives to have as many options as possible so that specific action steps can be selected (Griffiths, 2015). The solutions need to be structured, and then every option needs to be evaluated by creatively brainstorming the process. A coach has to create an environment in which the coachee feels safe to express his or her ideas and thoughts without fear of being judged. The last step of the GROW coaching model is the choice of one option from the various options stated. Then, the choice is transformed into a more concrete plan. After a well-planned strategy, the coachee's motivation to follow this plan is maximised (Hobson *et al.*, 2009).

Will

The Will stage is aimed to empower the coachee to choose a course This is in accordance with the opinion that in coaching, the coach should help individuals to move from their current positions towards greater effectiveness and fulfilment (Leedham and Parsloe, 2016). The assumption is that, if questions in each stage are properly dealt with, obstacles that may negatively impact the individual's performance will be reduced and they will agree to implement with the aim of achieving their goal, allowing them to control their actions and self-determination (Ryan and Deci, 2017).

Limitations

While the GROW model can be highly effective in helping individuals achieve their goals, it has a variety of limitations (Mogonea, 2022):

- It follows a structured framework, which may not always be suitable for every situation or individual. Some people may require a more flexible or tailored approach to address their specialised and unique challenges and needs.
- The GROW model places a strong emphasis on goal setting, which may not always be the most appropriate approach, especially for individuals dealing with complex or multifaceted problems.
- It focusses primarily on cognitive processes and does not explicitly address the emotional aspects of goal achievement, which can play a significant role in an individual's success.
- There is also a lack of process for transitioning from intention to action, and thus it may not adequately support coaches in moving from the intention to change to taking actionable steps that result in behavioural change.
- It does not proactively address potential obstacles or setbacks that coachees might encounter, nor does it provide strategies for overcoming these challenges.

There is also a limited integration of self-efficacy as the model does not explicitly incorporate elements that enhance self-efficacy, which is crucial for maintaining new behaviours and recovering from setbacks (Kamarudin *et al.*, 2020).

Research also suggests that sometimes options are rushed through during GROW sessions without thoroughly exploring the thinking behind them, leading to less effective outcomes (Panchal and Riddell, 2020).

A checklist of guide questions when using GROW

- 1. Establish the Goal
    When doing this, it's useful to ask questions like:

    How will you know that your mentee has achieved this goal? How will you know that the problem or issue is solved?
    Does this goal fit with their overall career objectives? And does it fit with the institutions?

- 2. Examine the Current Reality
    Next, ask your mentee to describe their current reality.
    Useful coaching questions in this step include the following:

    What is happening now (what, who, when, and how often)? What is the effect or result of this?
    Have you already taken any steps towards your goal?
    Does this goal conflict with any other goals or objectives?

- 3. Explore the Options
    Once you and your mentee have explored the current reality, it's time to determine what is possible – meaning all of the possible options for reaching their objective.

    Help your mentee thought shower as many good options as possible. Then, discuss these and help them decide on the best ones.

    Typical questions that you can use to explore options are as follows:

    What else could you do?
    What if this or that constraint were removed? Would that change things?
    What are the advantages and disadvantages of each option?
    What factors or considerations will you use to weigh the options?
    What do you need to stop doing in order to achieve this goal?
    What obstacles stand in your way?

- 4. Establish the Will
    Useful questions to ask here include:

    So, what will you do now, and after that? When? What else will you do?
    What could stop you moving forward? How will you overcome this?
    How can you keep yourself motivated?
    When do you need to review progress? Daily, weekly, monthly?

- **GROWS**

    The GROWS model incorporates phases of initiation, maintenance, and recovery, focusing on self-efficacy to overcome obstacles and setbacks. It was designed by Panchal and Riddell by integrating elements from the Health Action Process Approach (HAPA) into the GROW model to address gaps in GROW such as transitioning and lack of coachee self-efficacy (Panchal and Riddell, 2020). GROWS incorporates phases of initiation, maintenance, and recovery, focusing on self-efficacy to overcome obstacles and setbacks.

    The Grows model drawing from HARPA breaks behavioural change into two stages: Initiation of change and maintenance of new behaviours. It proactively focuses on developing strategies which increase self-efficacy for maintaining new behaviours by overcoming obstacles and recovering from setbacks. GROWS questions were designed to encourage reflection on initiating new behaviours, maintaining new behaviours, and assessing the participants' perceived self-belief, motivation, commitment, and competency in developing the new behaviours (Panchal and Riddell, 2020).

- How successful were you in initiating and maintaining the actions you agreed to in the previous session on a scale from zero to ten? Why did you choose these numbers?

    Results from their work indicated that the GROWS model was more effective in helping participants identify strategies, understand obstacles, and maintain behavioural change and that participants found the GROWS model's questions more challenging but beneficial, leading to deeper reflection and more tangible action plans (2020).

Limitations

Some of the limitations associated with the GROWS model include the following:

Oversimplification:
    While the GROWS model offers a structured approach, it may sometimes oversimplify complex issues.

Dependence on self-awareness:
    The effectiveness of the GROWS model relies on the employee's ability to self-assess accurately.

Time-consuming:
    Thoroughly exploring each step – particularly in the options and reality phases – can be time-consuming (Whittington, 2020).

Some examples of GROWS questions to be used in mentor training role-plays include:

- What will you do to initiate and maintain the new behaviour?
- What obstacles might you encounter, and what will you do to overcome them?
- How confident are you in your ability to commit to the actions you've agreed to on a scale from zero to ten?
- What have you learned about changing your own behaviour from using this model?

- **OSCAR Model**

   The OSCAR coaching model was originally designed by Gilbert and Whittleworth, with the aim of building on the 1990s GROW coaching model, focusing on solutions rather than problems (2009). The OSCAR model proposes that if the five elements, Outcome, Situation, Choices and Consequences, Action, and Review, are understood and applied by the coach, then the long-term result of the mentoring relationship will achieve the desired outcomes (2009).

Outcome

During this phase, the mentor helps the mentee to clarify the outcomes (for the short term and longer term) around issues raised.

Situation

The mentor will help the mentee to clarify where they are to raise awareness of their situation, their feelings, and how these may be impacting their life and those of their peers.

Choices and consequences

The mentor will encourage the mentee to generate as many alternative courses of action as possible and facilitate their awareness about the consequences of each choice.

Action

During this phase, a plan of action will be negotiated using SMART targets.

Review

Both parties develop a review plan that will enable the mentee to track their progress and make changes if necessary.

The model can help the mentor to align their coaching conversations with the desired outcomes and the criteria for success and also encourages both mentor and mentee to review the progress and the results regularly. The OSCAR model can be beneficial because it helps to define measurable and realistic outcomes, track the impact of the coaching, and celebrate the achievements learning from the feedback and reflection (Gilbert and Whittleworth, 2009).

Limitations

Some of the shortcomings of this model may include the following:

It can be somewhat formulaic and rigid, potentially stifling creativity and flexibility in the coaching process.
Complex scenarios requiring a multifaceted understanding might not be effectively addressed with this model.
It might not be suitable for those opposed to self-guided learning.
Coaches might become overly focused on following the steps rather than adapting to the unique needs of the coachee.
The model places significant emphasis on achieving specific outcomes, which can sometimes lead to a narrow focus on short-term goals rather than fostering long-term development and learning (Weinstein, 2013).

Self-reflection task

Think about a student you are currently mentoring, have mentored, or are thinking about mentoring. Complete this table by devising some of the questions you would like to ask them.

Stages of OSCAR and sample questions	*Your questions*
Outcome: What is it you would like to achieve from this discussion? What is your long-term goal? Once you have reached your goal – what does it look like? What does it feel like?	
How do you currently feel about your situation? Where are you at now in terms of your goals? What has been happening in your work and life recently? How do you think others feel about your current situation?	
Consequences: What current options for action are available to you? What are the consequences of any potential choices? What would be the impacts on other people? Which of your options has the best consequences for you and for others?	

(Continued)

Stages of OSCAR and sample questions	Your questions
Actions: What immediate actions will you take? When are you going to take those actions? Who is going to provide the support for you throughout the process? How motivated are you to take these actions?	
Review: How do you plan to review your progress? When is it suitable for us to review progress? Have your actions been moving you towards your goal? Are you still motivated to take the agreed actions?	

- **CLEAR model**

  The CLEAR model is another variation of the GROW model, and it stands for Contracting, Listening, Exploring, Action, and Review (Hawkins and Smith, 2006).
- Contracting

  During this phase, the scope of the issue and the desired outcomes and the ground rules are established. This contracting process is one of the differences which the model has from some of the other models. This enables the mentee to decide how they would like to be supported (Hawkins and Smith, 2006).
- Listening

  The issue is explored through active listening and catalytic interventions, which can help the mentee to develop an understanding of the situation and generate personal insight. Listening is also given greater priority here as when a mentee feels they are being heard, they are more likely to feel valued, and when they feel valued, their self-confidence rises, and they are more likely to commit to change (2006).
- Exploring

  During the exploring phase, the mentee is supported to understand the personal impact the situation is having on the self and is challenged to think through possibilities for future action in resolving the situation.
- Action

  Here, the mentee is supported in establishing a way forward which leads to the next stage.
- Review

  The review stage involves reviewing outcomes and also prompts feedback on the effectiveness of the process. The latter is regarded as crucial to changes in support that can be made and prompts reflection in both mentor and mentee (Hawkins and Smith, 2006).

Limitations

Some disadvantages of this approach can include:

If there is vague contracting, the outcomes will be more unclear to achieve.
If the coach lacks expertise in areas like the use of active listening or experience in action planning, this can also affect the outcomes.
If the feedback is unclear during the review stage, this can result in weak reflection.
It can also be time-consuming, particularly during the contracting and listening stages, which are crucial for establishing trust and understanding, but they may slow down the progress, especially if the coaching sessions are limited in number.
The model relies heavily on the skill and experience of the coach in facilitating deep exploration and active listening, which can vary significantly and impact the effectiveness of the coaching (Leedham and Parsloe, 2016).

Active listening teaching activities

Mindful listening group practice

In many ways, active listening is a mindfulness practice. The listener is trying to stay focused on the present, with what is being shared. And they are working to accomplish this without judgement.

Here is an excellent activity to practice mindful listening in a group.

1. Have the group sit in a circle.
2. Offer an ice breaker question or prompt, such as something they are grateful for today.
3. Rather than go around the circle, ask participants to share spontaneously when they feel ready.
4. Invite them to notice if they are thinking about their answer, rather than listening.
5. Ask them to be present with the person who is sharing.
6. Challenge them to notice if they are uncomfortable with the silences.

Mindful listening alone

At any moment, you can drop in and practice mindful listening. Simply stop what you are doing, close your eyes, and try to see how many sounds you can hear around you and within you. Notice if there are judgements arising and try not to attach to them. Stay with the flow of sounds for as long as you can.

Listening accurately

1 Step In Their Shoes and select someone that you would like to work on your relationship with. When you talk, try your best to take their point of view. For instance, try picturing that you are them, going about their day. Does your capacity to feel empathy change by taking their perspective?
2 Fact-Check Your Interpretations Reflect on the dialogues you and that person have had. Make a conscious effort to fact-check your interpretations and assumptions regarding what they said.
3 Give Your Full Attention during a conversation, start by giving your full attention to the other person. Before you move on to other things, consider what might occur if you asked: 'I would like to clarify that I've understood you correctly. May I?' Almost every time, you'll get a positive response.
4 Try to clarify what you think you have heard – identify and reflect their emotions. If you are unsure whether you've understood correctly, just ask.
5 Clarify What You've Said During conversations. You might try asking the speaker if they could share what they've heard from you. How would you clear up any misunderstandings if they arose?

- **COACH Model**

  The COACH model, which stands for Care, Observe, Ask, Challenge, and Honour, is argued to be a holistic coaching model (Bachkirova, 2022). The model aims to facilitate mentors to establish rapport with their mentees on a professional and personal level, help them to evaluate their strengths, clarify the desired outcomes, raise awareness of their current situation and options, agree on a course of action, and reinforce the key learnings and commitments (Moyes, 2009). It aims to promote a collaborative and supportive relationship between mentor and mentee. It stands for Connect, Outcome, Awareness, Course, and Highlights.

Connect

During the Connect step, mentors can ask questions such as 'How are you feeling today?' or 'What is on your mind?'.

Outcome

The Outcome step helps the mentee define and refine their goal for the session.

Awareness

Awareness step helps them explore their current reality and identify obstacles or gaps.

Course

In the Course step, coaches help the mentee decide on a specific and realistic action plan to achieve their goal.

Highlights

Finally, in the Highlights step, both review and summarise key points and commitments from the session. Questions such as 'What are you most proud of or excited about?' or 'How will you hold yourself accountable?' can be asked to help the mentee reflect on their progress (Grant, 2020).

Limitations

The COACH model has several shortcomings that may limit its effectiveness in certain coaching scenarios. One significant limitation is its relatively rigid structure. While the sequence of steps can provide a useful framework, it may not be flexible enough to address the unique and dynamic needs of every coachee (Grant, 2020). This rigidity can sometimes lead to a one-size-fits-all approach, which may not be suitable for all individuals or situations.

Another drawback is that the model places a strong emphasis on the coach's role in guiding the coachee. This can sometimes result in a more directive style of coaching, which may not be appropriate for all coachees, particularly those who respond better to a more collaborative or non-directive approach. The balance between providing guidance and allowing the coachee to find their own solutions can be delicate, and the COACH model may not always facilitate this balance effectively.

The model also assumes that the coach has a deep understanding of the coachee's context and challenges. Without this understanding, the coach may struggle to ask the right questions or provide meaningful challenges. This can hinder the development of trust and rapport, which are crucial components of a successful coaching relationship (Kamarudin *et al.*, 2020).

Additionally, the COACH model may not adequately address the emotional and psychological aspects of coaching. While it includes elements of care and honour, it may not fully account for the complexities of human emotions and the impact they have on personal and professional development. Coaches using this model may therefore need to supplement it with other techniques and approaches to effectively address these aspects (McDonald Connor, 2017).

COACH self-reflection activity for a mentor

In a reflective journal or worksheet, reflect on a previous meeting with your mentee or one you hope to have and write down your thoughts and observations for each component of the COACH model:

- Connect: How did you establish a connection with their mentee during the session?
- Outcome: What specific goals or outcomes were discussed or achieved during the session?
- Awareness: How did the mentor help your mentee gain awareness of their strengths, areas for growth, or blind spots?
- Course: What actions or plans were identified to help your mentee move forward in their development?
- Highlights: What were the key highlights or insights from the mentoring session?

Provide your mentee with a reflective journal or worksheet that outlines each component of the COACH model. Encourage the mentee to reflect individually on their mentoring experience and jot down their thoughts, feelings, and insights under each category. Prompt them to consider questions such as:

- Connect: How has the mentor-mentee relationship evolved over time? What connections have you established with your mentor?
- Outcome: What specific goals or outcomes have you achieved through the mentoring relationship? How have these impacted your personal and professional development?
- Awareness: What new insights or self-awareness have you gained through the mentoring process? How has this awareness influenced your actions and decisions?
- Course: What strategies or actions have you implemented based on your mentor's guidance? How have these actions shaped your growth and progress?
- Highlights: What are the key highlights or memorable moments of your mentoring journey? How have these moments influenced your learning and development?

Ask your mentee to identify specific action steps or goals based on their reflections and discussions and encourage them to create a personal development plan that integrates the insights gained from the reflective exercise.

References

Allison, S. and Harbour, M. (2009) *The coaching toolkit: a practical guide for your school*. Sage Publications.

Bachkirova, T. (2022) *Developmental coaching: working with the self, - Second edition*. McGraw-Hill Education.

Bianco-Mathis, V.E., Nabors, L.K. and Roman, C.H. (2002) *Leading from the inside out: a coaching model*. Sage.

Bloom, J., Hutson, B. and Ye, H. (2008) *The appreciative advising revolution*. Stipes Publishing.

Bridges, W. and Bridges, S. (2017) *Managing transitions: making the most of change*. John Murray Business Books.

Fynn, A. (2014) 'Appreciative inquiry of a mentoring programme in Soweto', *New Voices in Psychology*, 10(1), pp. 84–95.

Gilbert, A. and Whittleworth, K. (2009) *The OSCAR coaching model*. Worth Consulting.

Grant, A.M. (2020) 'An integrated model of goal-focused coaching: an evidence-based framework for teaching and practice', in *Coaching researched: A coaching psychology reader*, John Wiley, pp. 115–139.

Grant, A.M. (2022). 'Reflection, note-taking and coaching: if it ain't written, it ain't coaching!' in Tee, D and Passmore, J. (eds.) *Coaching Practiced*. John Wiley and Sons.

Griffiths, K. (2015) 'Personal coaching: a model for effective learning', *Journal of Learning Design*, 8(3).

Hamlin, R., Ellinger, A. and Beattie, R. (2006) 'Coaching at the heart of managerial effectiveness: a cross-cultural study of managerial behaviours', *Human Resource Development International*, 9. doi:10.1080/13678860600893524.

Hawkins, P. and Smith, N. (2006) *Coaching, mentoring and organizational consultancy: supervision and development*. McGraw-Hill Education.

Hawkins, P. and Turner, E. (2019) *Systemic coaching: delivering value beyond the individual*. Taylor Francis.

Hobson, A., Ashby, P., Malderez, A. and Tomlinson, P. (2009) 'Mentoring beginning teachers: what we know and what we don't', *Teaching and Teacher Education*, 25, pp. 207–216. doi:10.1016/j.tate.2008.09.001.

Jones, R.J., Woods, S.A. and Guillaume, Y.R.F. (2016) 'The effectiveness of workplace coaching: a meta-analysis of learning and performance outcomes from coaching', *Journal of Occupational and Organizational Psychology*, 89(2), pp. 249–277. doi:10.1111/joop.12119.

Kamarudin, M., Kamarudin, A.Y., Darmi, R. and Saad, N.S.M. (2020) 'A review of coaching and mentoring theories and models', *International Journal of Academic Research in Progressive Education and Development*, 9(2), pp. 289–298.

Lawrence, P. (2019) 'What is systemic coaching?', *Philosophy of Coaching: An International Journal*, 4, pp. 35–52. doi:10.22316/poc/04.2.03.

Leedham, M. and Parsloe, E. (2016) *Coaching and mentoring*. 3rd edn. Kogan Page.

McDonald Connor, C. (2017) 'Commentary on the special issue on instructional coaching models: common elements of effective coaching models', *Theory Into Practice*, 56(1), pp. 78–83. doi:10.1080/00405841.2016.1274575.

Mogonea, F. (2022). A possible mentoring model: the GROW model. *Analele Universității din Craiova seria Psihologie-Pedagogie/Annals of the University of Craiova Series Psychology-Pedagogy*, 44, pp. 60–70. doi:10.52846/AUCPP.2022.2.05.

Moyes, B. 2009. 'Literature review of coaching supervision.' *International Coaching Psychology Review*, 4(2), pp. 162–173.

Nuis, W., Segers, M. and Beausaert, S. (2023) 'Conceptualizing mentoring in higher education: a systematic literature review', *Educational Research Review*, 41, p. 100565. doi:10.1016/j.edurev.2023.100565.

Panchal, S. and Riddell, P. 2020. 'The GROWS model: extending the GROW coaching model to support behavioural change', *The Coaching Psychologist* 16(2), pp. 12–25.

Ryan, R.M. and Deci, E.L. (2017) *Self-determination theory: basic psychological needs in motivation, development, and wellness.* Guilford Press. doi:10.1521/978.14625/28806.

Starr, J. (2021) *The coaching manual: the definitive guide to the process, principles and skills of personal coaching.* Pearson Business.

Weinstein, A. (2013) *Executive coaching and the process of change: a practitioner's guide.* CreateSpace Independent Publishing Platform.

Whitmore, J. (2009) *Coaching for performance: growing human potential and purpose—the principles and practice of coaching and leadership.* 4th edn. Nicholas Brealey Publishing.

Whittington, J. (2020) *Systemic coaching and constellations: an introduction to the principles, Practices and Applications.* Kogan Page.

Whitworth, L., Kimsey-House, H. and Sandahl, P. (2007) *Co-active coaching.* Davies Blade Publishing.

Chapter 6

Mentors and the mentoring relationship

Mentoring skills and attributes

Research has highlighted that there is a considerable overlap between the skills required to be an effective mentor and educational coach (Hargreaves, 2010). These include an ability to establish rapport and trust with their mentee or coachee, the ability to listen for meaning in the conversation, their skill in questioning for understanding, their influence in prompting action, reflection, and learning in the mentee/coachee, and their ability to develop confidence including celebrating success. Evidence further suggests that their ages, level of education, and work experience do influence the perception of their quality and influence their credibility and the likelihood that mentees/coachees will be open to being supported by them (Feldman and Lankau, 2005). Other skills and qualities include:

Building rapport – Lai and McDowall (2014) identify the relationship between mentor/coach and trainee as being key to successful training outcomes, with the mentor/coach having the responsibility for initiating a comfortable and positive development experience. For example, listening, understanding, and encouragement all contribute to a deeper and more successful experience for both parties (O'Broin and Palmer, 2010).
Being present – Effective training starts with being as present and available to the trainee as possible, responding to the needs of that person and being aware of things that might make this challenging, and ensuring the time and place are conducive to being present.
Effective communication skills – Lai and McDowall (2014) also emphasise the benefits of actively listening and reflecting back; using powerful questioning techniques; supplying and seeking feedback; allowing space for story sharing; and using appropriate verbal and body language.
Demonstrating empathy – Cox and Bachkirova (2007) stress the need for the trainer to acknowledge and understand emotion as normal, working to understand the trainee's emotional reactions and difficulties, rather than ignoring or trying to change or control them (i.e. displaying emotional intelligence).

Collaboration and facilitation – Mentoring and coaching is a reflective and collaborative process, with continuous discussion and negotiation between trainer and trainee, facilitating positive changes in behaviour to meet their mutual goals (Lai and McDowall, 2014). The OSCAR model which we discussed in the previous chapter will help to structure this process.

Qualities and attitudes – Lai and McDowall (2014) looked across several studies and found that the most highlighted qualities for a trainer were:

Openness/honesty/authenticity
Integrity/confidentiality
Non-judgemental/objective
Enthusiasm/passion
Commitment/motivation to help

McHenry (2018) suggests it is possible to increase Unconditional Positive Regard (UPR) by reflecting on what might make this challenging (conflicting values, attitudes, personal preferences, political affiliation, religious beliefs, etc.). In addition, finding out where a trainee's views have come from may make it easier to empathise.

Trust is crucial to engaging trainees and establishing a positive and effective training relationship. Having a clear, upfront contract and a transparent process will help, such as agreeing accountabilities, evaluation methods, confidentiality and discussing any coaching models or theories being used (O'Broin and Palmer, 2010). Demonstrating the qualities and behaviour listed above all benefit trust.

Most people with some experience of working with others already have many of these skills and qualities. Others can be developed with a little bit of patience and practice (e.g. actively listening, demonstrating empathy). However, the best way to use these skills can be to use a structured coaching model, such as the OSCAR or COACH models (as discussed in the previous chapter), to help the flow of coaching conversations.

The mentoring relationships

Mentoring and Coaching emphasise and prioritise the personal relationship (Hargreaves, 2010). Some research suggests that educators are more resistant to professional learning that tackles something new in their pedagogy, more than professionals outside of education, and this is vital to overcoming the challenge of forming significant relationships, which is key (2010). Supportive relationships can play a central role in the capacity building of teachers. Teachers who lack these types of relationships and who encounter a particularly challenging aspect of their role may see seeking assistance from a mentor as a sign of incompetence (Knight, 2009).

Central to this is the partnership philosophy based on principles of equality, choice, voice, dialogue, reflection, praxis, and reciprocity. Some research suggests that mentees are four times more likely to implement teaching practices in a partnership approach than those learnt during traditional professional learning sessions (Knight, 2009). Key to this is trust and research suggests that it is crucial that a culture of trust between the coach and teacher is present and within the organisation, and time must be given to establish trust between them (Wenger, McDermott and Snyder, 2002).

According to research by Guedes (2021), the selection and allocation of trainers based on their subject matter expertise makes a difference in the relationship between them and the trainee. The evidence suggests that their age, level of education, and work experience can influence perceptions of their quality and credibility and impact trainee likelihood to be open to training (Feldman and Lankau, 2005). Subject matter expertise was a further aspect crucial to the relationship and how they were seen by their trainees (2005).

From their research, they also concluded that participants valued trainers who could empathise with them regarding the subject matter taught and their classroom contexts and therefore were more likely to establish the necessary relationship connection. In addition, they argued that the participants who were more open and trusting with their pedagogical challenges based this openness on the empathy and expertise of their trainers who had context/subject experience over just coaching process knowledge alone (Feldman and Lankau, 2005).

The trainer's way of being encompassing their approach and mannerisms, these affect efforts and the quality of the relationship they establish with their trainee, supporting the view that what training involves is just as important as how it is done (van Nieuwerburgh, 2017; Whitmore, 2009).

Stages of mentoring

Kram first conceptualised four sequential stages through which mentoring relationships evolve based on qualitative research in organisational settings (1985). These were:

- Initiation, when mentors and mentees form expectations and get to know one another.
- Cultivation, when the relationship matures, and mentors typically provide the greatest degree of psychosocial and career support.
- Separation, when mentees seek autonomy and more independence from mentors.
- Redefinition, this occurs when mentors and mentees transition into a different form of relationship characterised by more peer-like interactions or terminate the relationship.
    Building upon this, Clutterbuck (2008) explained the development of the mentoring relationship in five phases:
    - Phase 1: Rapport-building
        In this phase, mentor and mentee decide whether they want to work together and negotiate what each expects of the other.

- Phase 2: Direction-setting
  During this phase, they achieve clarity about what each aims to achieve from the relationship and how.
- Phase 3: Progress-making
  Having helped the mentee define and commit to personal change, the mentor must guide and support them as needed.
- Phase 4: Winding down
  This occurs when the relationship has helped to deliver the desired outcomes, or the mentee outgrows the mentor.
- Phase 5: Moving on/professional friendship
  This phase can occur if the formal mentoring relationship evolves into a less committed, more casual one.

Over the course of their academic and career pursuits, mentees' expectations and needs are likely to change; as such, the type of support needed from and provided by mentors will vary across different mentorship stages. Because mentors and mentees have various expectations of one another based on their own needs, which can change over time, challenges may arise from misaligned expectations in their relationship across mentorship stages (Hudson, 2013).

Mentoring relationship theories

Ecological systems theory

According to the ecological systems theory framework, individuals participating in mentorship bring to a mentoring relationship various behaviours, personal factors, and environmental variables that shape their mentorship needs and expectations and their responses to mentorship. While a mentoring relationship develops among individuals, it also occurs in the context of a department, college, and university, each with policies and practices that influence the success of both the mentee and the mentoring relationship. In addition, the success of the mentoring relationship depends at least in part on the cultural and social attitudes and practices of the individuals in that relationship (Bronfenbrenner, 1993).

Social cognitive career theory (SCCT)

SCCT is used to explain individuals' motivation, goal setting, and persistence in achieving a desired academic outcome and career path (Lent, Brown and Hackett, 1994). Self-efficacy beliefs and outcome expectations are argued to be two primary factors influencing individuals' choices and actions. The mentoring relationship is suggested to be a key influence on mentees' self-efficacy beliefs and outcome expectations (Byars-Winston et al., 2010).

Social exchange theory

Social exchange theory presents that people are self-interested actors who engage in reciprocal relationships to reach their goals and objectives by obtaining valued resources or benefits in exchange for providing something of value to the other participants in the relationship (Blau, 1964). It provides a means for understanding the potential benefits and costs of mentorship for both mentors and mentees, thereby enabling institutions to create structures and put policies in place to maximise the benefits and minimise or mitigate the costs to both parties.

> **Self-reflection activity**
>
> As a mentor, reflecting on how they engage in social exchanges with their mentee can deepen their understanding of the factors at play in your mentoring relationship. The following self-reflective activity is designed to help you explore and evaluate your mentoring practices through the lens of Blau's Social Exchange Theory.
> Some self-reflective questions:
>
> 1 What resources, support, or knowledge do I offer to my mentee in our mentoring relationship?
> 2 How do I communicate my expectations for reciprocity and mutual benefit in the mentoring exchange?
> 3 What are the perceived costs and rewards for both me as a mentor and my mentee in our interactions?
> 4 How do I foster a sense of trust, commitment, and mutual obligation in our mentoring relationship?
> 5 In what ways do I navigate potential conflicts of interest or power differentials based on the social exchanges occurring within our mentoring dynamic?
> 6 How do I recognise and address imbalances or disparities in the social exchanges between me and my mentee?
> 7 What strategies can I implement to enhance the quality and effectiveness of the social exchanges within our mentoring partnership?
> 8 How do I monitor and evaluate the impact of social exchange dynamics on the overall development and outcomes of our mentoring relationship?

Social capital theory

Social capital theory examines the social reproduction of inequality, looking at how the powerful take advantage of their social networks and connections to transfer power from one generation to the next (Bourdieu, 1977). Social capital exists in the relationships among people (i.e. mentors and mentees), in their exchange of information, and in the changes in the relationships among them. Using this model can help mentors understand the power relationships of a mentoring relationship by looking at things like trust, expectations, and obligations, access to information, rewards and sanctions, and funds of knowledge and experience, and how these influence the development of a relationship.

Self-reflection activity

As a mentor, reflecting on how you leverage social capital in your mentoring relationships can enhance your understanding of power dynamics, influence, and access to valuable resources that can benefit your mentees.

Some self-reflection questions:

1 Who are the key individuals or groups in my professional network that I can tap into to support my mentees' growth and development?
2 How do I navigate power dynamics within my mentoring relationships to ensure equitable access to resources and opportunities for my mentees?
3 In what ways do I facilitate introductions and connections for my mentees to expand their social networks and access new opportunities?
4 How do I model effective networking and relationship-building behaviours to empower my mentees to cultivate their social capital?
5 What steps can I take to address any disparities in social capital that exist between my mentees and their peers to promote equal access to resources and opportunities?
6 How do I recognise and challenge implicit biases or stereotypes that may influence the way I perceive and engage with individuals from diverse backgrounds in terms of social capital?
7 What strategies can I implement to increase my own social capital and expand my network to benefit both myself and my mentees?

Self-reflection exercise

Look at the descriptions below and decide which of Clutterbuck's five phases of mentoring each pair are currently in.

a Nick has a mentor called Alison. She is in a very senior role and hardly ever available. He finds this frustrating and doesn't feel like he's had a chance to get to know her or talk about his development.

> b Opie is very happy to have Louise as a mentor. They get on well and meet regularly. Although they are very clear on what they expect from each other in terms of the relationship, Sue feels she needs help to set some goals and progress.
> c Parminder has been working with her mentor, Andrew, for 12 months. She has really progressed during their time as mentor and mentee but often feels like she knows what he's going to say.
>
> Once you've chosen what phase they are in, consider what you would do next if you were in the mentee's position.

Mentor and mentee roles

A recurring issue in mentoring is confusion and uncertainty about the nature and purpose of mentors' and mentees' roles and the boundaries of these roles (Duckworth and Maxwell, 2015). This has a variety of different dimensions which include the following.

Lack of understanding of programme content

Mentors and mentees may have differing understandings of coaching and mentoring (Colley, 2003; Tedder and Lawy, 2009). In addition, ITT mentors often lack understanding of the aims and content of the training programme that their mentee is undertaking. The latter point can impact the effectiveness of the relationship in several different ways (Ingleby, 2010).

When mentors lack understanding of the aims and content of the training programme that their mentee is undertaking, the mentoring relationship can be negatively impacted in several ways:

- Mentors may struggle to provide relevant guidance and support to their mentees, and mentees may feel lost or confused without proper direction from their mentors, affecting their learning experience and growth.
- They may have different expectations regarding the mentoring process, such as the amount of time they should meet, how often they should be observed, due to the mentor's lack of understanding of the training programme. This can lead to misunderstandings, frustration, and a lack of alignment in terms of goals and desired outcomes (2010).
- In addition, mentors who do not understand the content of the training programme may provide ineffective or irrelevant feedback to their mentees which may not meet its requirements in terms of depth or methods. This can hinder the mentee's progress and development, as they may not receive sufficient feedback or effective feedback that is tailored to their specific needs and learning objectives (Kochan and Pascarelli, 2012).

- This lack of understanding on the mentor's part can create a barrier in the mentor-mentee relationship, causing tension and communication gaps. Therefore, the mentee may feel unsupported and undervalued, leading to a breakdown in trust and rapport between them (van Ginkel, van Drie and Verloop, 2018).

Tedder and Lawy (2009) found that even trained and experienced mentors were uncertain about their role. It therefore appears that role descriptors and mentor training in many institutions, while important, have not to date satisfactorily addressed or resolved the issue, leaving many mentors and mentees still uncertain about their roles (Hardman and Hardman, 2010).

Confusion of differing models and responsibilities of mentoring

Ingleby (2010) claims that role confusion arises because mentor roles are aligned with bureaucratic tasks and mentoring is not characterised as professional expertise. Tedder and Lawy (2009) suggest that uncertainty arises in the ITE mentor role due to the differing models of mentoring implemented in the FE and Skills sector and because it is trying to address and support different types of transition. These include induction into the organisation in the subject area and the teaching profession.

Developing their explanation for role confusion, Tedder and Lawy (2009) go on to argue that the diverse purposes and processes of ITT mentoring are mediated by the mentors' past experiences, the diverse needs and expectations of trainee teachers, and the learning culture. Mediation of mentoring purposes and processes by mentors, mentees, and the learning culture is to be expected across all types of mentoring in the sector, even when purposes may be more clearly defined.

Managerialism, judgements, and mentoring

There are consistent criticisms about 'confusion' of assessment roles, 'failure' by teacher trainers (Office of Standards in Education, Ofsted, 2007) and mentors (Office of Standards in Education, Ofsted, 2008) to define pass or fail boundaries, and insufficient attention to action planning and setting targets. Rather than engaging in a professional discussion with trainees in a way that recognises the problematic character of teacher practices, the role of mentors and teacher trainers has shifted to one where they are required to ensure that the trainees write action plans to set targets (Tedder and Lawy, 2009).

Critical friend versus pastoral supporter

Cullimore and Simmons's (2010) research uncovered tensions between different aspects of mentors' roles, particularly between being a critical friend who provides constructive criticism and being a role model for good practice in teaching and learning. Further tensions were found between being a critical friend and being a listener, counsellor, and friend. Some of these may include the following:

- Critical Friend vs. Listener
   The mentor may struggle to strike a balance between providing critical feedback and actively listening to the mentee's concerns without judgement.
- Counsellor vs. Friend
   The mentor may face challenges in providing counselling and guidance while maintaining a professional distance to avoid becoming too emotionally involved.
- Balancing Roles
   They may find it difficult to transition between being a critical friend, a listener, a counsellor, and a friend, leading to role confusion and blurred boundaries.

Self-reflective question

How would you advise a fellow newly appointed mentor who is being asked to mentor a former student from a course that they taught?

Self-reflection task

The relationship tensions	The main issues related to them	How I will manage them
Critical friend versus listener		
Counsellor versus friend		
Balancing roles		

Relationships and reflection

Self-reflection and the mentoring relationship

Self-reflection is a vital component of the mentoring relationship for both mentors and mentees, as it allows individuals to gain deeper insights into their beliefs, actions, strengths, and areas for growth. Through the process of self-reflection, mentors and mentees can enhance their self-awareness, improve their communication skills, and foster personal and professional development (Hargreaves, 2010).

For mentors, it is crucial to understand their own biases, assumptions, and limitations that may impact their mentoring approach. By taking the time to reflect on their experiences, they can evaluate their mentoring practices, identify areas for improvement, and enhance their ability to support and guide their mentees effectively. Self-reflection enables them to develop a deeper understanding of their mentees' needs, challenges, and learning styles, allowing them to tailor their mentoring strategies accordingly. Additionally, self-reflection helps mentors cultivate empathy, patience, and emotional intelligence, which are essential qualities for building a trusting and supportive mentoring relationship (Cullimore and Simmons, 2010).

Similarly, for mentees, self-reflection is a transformative process that promotes personal growth, critical thinking, and self-discovery. By engaging in self-reflection, they can assess their goals, values, strengths, and areas for development, leading to increased self-awareness and self-confidence. They can also reflect on their achievements, setbacks, and learning experiences during the mentoring relationship, enabling them to set meaningful goals, overcome challenges, and make informed decisions about their academic and professional paths. Self-reflection empowers them to take ownership of their learning journey, seek feedback from their mentors, and continuously strive for personal and professional excellence (Hudson, 2013).

> 'I was encouraged by my mentor to reflect on my teaching after every session. I bought a notebook to record my thoughts and feelings after every session and supplemented it with student feedback which I took from post it notes which I gave to my class at the end of the session. I then used to set myself targets for improvements which I used to discuss with my mentor each week. The whole self-reflective process really developed my self-confidence and made me feel I was in control of my own learning.

Power relationships and mentoring

Some commentators have defined the mentoring relationship as one that is a socially constructed power relationship, and suggested the power that mentors have and exercise within mentoring relationships can be helpful or hurtful to the mentee (Hudson, 2013; Stevenson *et al.*, 2023).

They also note that it can assist mentees' psychosocial development and that mentoring relationships can be powerful and life-changing events in people's lives (Hudson, 2013) and can have a variety of impacts which include:

- providing a safe and supportive space for mentees to express their feelings, concerns, and emotions and, therefore, navigate challenges, build resilience, and develop coping strategies.
- building self-confidence and encouraging and empowering mentees to set goals, take risks, and believe in their abilities (Straw, Walker and Binfield, 2020).

- providing mentees with opportunities to develop and practice essential social skills, such as effective communication, conflict resolution, and teamwork, which can be enhanced when mentors model positive social behaviours and provide guidance on building and maintaining relationships.
- challenging mentees to explore their values, beliefs, and aspirations, fostering personal growth and self-awareness through offering perspective, insights, and encouragement to help mentees journey into personal and professional development (Wenger, McDermott and Snyder, 2002).

Mentoring outcomes

One central expectation is support by mentors for mentees to make the transition between a student teacher and a trainee teacher in a teaching placement. According to Tedder and Lawy (2009), there are three types of transitions and different kinds of transitions make different kinds of demands on mentoring:

- Induction into an organisation or institution
  Mentoring would enable a trainee to become familiar with the resources that are available, the customs and practices of particular locations, and with the range of staff who are colleagues.
- Induction into a subject
  Induction into becoming a subject specialist and mentoring that supports a novice in meeting the specific demands of a particular subject area.
- Induction into the teaching profession
  Mentoring which supports someone becoming a member of the profession, in developing the knowledge, skills, and values appropriate for a teacher in the learning and skills sector.

Mentors' attitudes about their mentees

Mentors are expected to attend to the different and individual needs of their mentees which may derive from their different learning preferences, teaching concerns, stages of development, readiness levels regarding various teaching competencies, tensions in professional identity formation, images and beliefs about teaching, and goals and expectations concerning the mentoring relationship (van Ginkel, van Drie and Verloop, 2018).

Research seems to suggest that mentees are judged by mentors in two particular domains of development. Firstly, in terms of personal attributes such as patience, honesty, initiative, a willingness to learn, being knowledgeable and creative, and having a positive influence on the institution. Secondly, they are judged within the professional domain, regarding the professional practices and norms of professional conduct, such as planning, assessing, and managing behaviour in classrooms (2018).

There are also domains related to social judgement which impact the way mentors see their mentees. These are sometimes called Social Utility and Social Desirability. The former relates to traits such as perseverance, conscientiousness and hardworking, competence/capability, problem-solving capacities, and drive and commitment. The latter comprises the properties of being friendly, kind, engaging, and being honest, responsible, and sincere (Kochan and Pascarelli, 2012).

Some research suggests that mentors describing attributes of their mentee teachers' learning in terms of internal traits or dispositions use three social explanatory styles: Dispositions, Self-Control and Historicism (van Ginkel, van Drie and Verloop, 2018).

What are the strengths and weaknesses of using each style of social explanatory model to judge your mentees?

Social explanatory models	Strengths	Weaknesses
Dispositional explanations focus on the internal, stable traits and attributes of the mentee, such as their personality, attitudes, and values		
Control explanations focus on internal and malleable factors such as resilience, self-confidence, determination, and commitment		
Historicist explanations tend to focus on external and formative influences, such as family background, previous educational experiences, to explain why they have become the person they are		

Self-reflective activity

What are the central characteristics of a mentee who evidences to you a 'mentoring mindset'? Complete the table

Features of a 'mentoring mindset'	How would they evidence this to you?
For example. Passion for subject specialism	
Or. Responds well to feedback	

According to Colley (2003), mentoring involves two types of outcomes: 'soft' and 'hard' outcomes.

Key differences between soft and hard outcomes (Colley, 2003)

Aspect	Soft outcomes	Hard outcomes
Nature	Subjective and qualitative	Objective and measurable
Focus	Personal growth and interpersonal skills	Professional performance and technical skills
Measurement	Observed indirectly or through reflection	Assessed using specific criteria or metrics
Examples	Confidence, empathy, self-awareness	Lesson plans, assessments, teaching standards
Timeline	Develop over time	Achieved at specific milestones
Evaluation	Requires discussion and observation	Can be assessed through tangible evidence

Training exercise for mentors and mentees

Training objective

To assess the soft and hard outcomes of a mentoring relationship based on Colley's (2003) framework.

Instructions

1 Soft Outcome Reflection

- Ask the mentor and mentee to individually reflect on the personal growth, confidence, communication skills, and emotional support gained from the mentoring relationship.
- Have a discussion where they share their reflections and insights on how the soft outcomes have impacted their personal and professional development.

2 Hard Outcome Assessment

- Provide a checklist of specific goals, skills development, knowledge acquisition, and career advancements that were set at the beginning of the mentoring relationship.
- Ask the mentor and mentee to evaluate and rate their progress towards achieving these goals, highlighting any measurable outcomes achieved.

3 Comparison and Discussion
- Facilitate a discussion where they compare the soft and hard outcomes experienced in the mentoring relationship.
- Encourage them to discuss the interplay between personal growth and measurable achievements, and how both types of outcomes contribute to the overall success of the mentoring relationship.

Factors which may impact the mentoring relationship:

- In the case of the mentor, they should be motivated to undertake a positive attitude towards the mentor role. They should have strong teaching skills and subject knowledge and also have a progressive mindset, open to new ideas about learning, teaching, and mentoring and in particular, committed to own learning, development and growth, as well as that of mentee (Straw, Walker and Binfield, 2020).
- The mentee should have a mentoring mindset which encompasses a willingness and motivation to be mentored and openness to new ideas, resilience when faced with difficulties, and a good capacity for self-regulation (2020).

There are also a series of organisational and contextual factors which can impact on the relationship. These can include some of the following factors (Knight, 2009):

- The organisation has an ethos of continuous improvement and is open to change and, therefore, learning is supported and risk-taking and experimenting with practice are encouraged. There needs to be strong relational trust between leaders and staff and time and resources for mentors and mentees to participate in mentoring provided by them (Chidiac, 2018). Leaders also need to support mentees in applying learning from their engagement in mentoring and provide recognition and reward for mentors.
- The issue of inadequate timetable allowance for mentoring activities was a key finding from Stevenson *et al.*'s (2023) survey of current mentoring practice in schools. To give mentoring programmes targeting mentees a chance to succeed, mentors need to be given sufficient time off the timetable to prepare for and meet with their mentees (2023).

Mentoring and cultural factors

Kochan and Pascarelli (2012) conceptualised the Cultural Framework for mentoring. The framework suggests that there are three cultural purposes for mentoring, traditional, transitional, and transformative, and that the cultural purpose determines the roles that mentors and mentees assume. For example, in the traditional mode, the purpose of the mentoring relationship is to transmit organisational and institutional values and practices, in the transitional mode it is to foster collaborative growth but still to maintain individual cultural identity, and in the transformative mode it is mutual growth and holistic development (2012).

The mentor/mentee relationship will also be impacted by a number of other variables. These include individual cultural dimensions such as gender and social class, life experiences, and personal attributes such as congruence and openness. In addition, the culture of the organisation can also impact the relationship in terms of the ways it defines the purposes of mentoring. For example, whether the approach is traditional, transitional, and transformative, which can also impact the power dynamics between mentor and mentee (Kochan *et al.*, 2015).

Some cultural barriers to an effective relationship

According to research by Kochan *et al.* (2015), there are four main cultural barriers: Matching mentors and mentees; mentee attitude towards matching; lack of organisational support; and static or closed organisational culture and cultural values.

- Matching processes

    Pairing mentors and mentees is at face value a relatively simple process using fairly transparent criteria such as subject specialism, teaching experience, availability, and willingness to mentor. These can be problematised by a variety of factors, however.

    For example, one of the main obstacles is the mismatch of personalities and teaching styles between mentors and mentees. A harmonious relationship between them is vital for effective communication, support, and collaboration. If there is a lack of compatibility in personalities or teaching approaches, it can hinder the mentoring process and lead to a strained relationship (2015).

    Different teaching styles can also impede a mentor/mentee teaching relationship (Straw, Walker and Binfield, 2020). This can manifest itself in several different ways:

Communication

Mentors using an authoritative style can come across as directive and may limit open communication with their mentees, leading to a more hierarchical relationship.

Feedback and Support

Mentors with authoritarian tendencies may provide feedback in a critical or commanding manner, which can create tension or discourage mentees from seeking guidance.

Learning Environment

Mentors following traditional teaching practices may rely on lecture-style instruction, which can limit mentees' active engagement and involvement in the learning process.

If you have a mentee who has a different teaching style from your own, how will you manage the potential issues raised in these three areas?

Mentoring areas	Your approaches
Communication	
Feedback and support	
Learning environment	

Another obstacle can be perceptions of power dynamics between mentors and mentees. In some cases, mentors may struggle to find a balance between providing guidance and support while allowing the mentee to take ownership of their learning and growth. This imbalance can lead to a lack of autonomy and independence for the mentee, impacting their development and confidence in their teaching practice (Kram, 1985).

Additionally, logistical challenges such as conflicting schedules, geographical distance, or workload pressures can obstruct the pairing of mentors and mentees. Finding time for regular meetings, observations, and feedback sessions can be challenging, especially in busy educational environments where teachers have multiple responsibilities and commitments (Cullimore and Simmons, 2010).

Moreover, the lack of training and support for mentors in effectively mentoring their trainees can be a significant obstacle. Mentoring requires specific skills such as active listening, constructive feedback, and goal setting, which mentors may not possess without proper training. Inadequate support for mentors can hinder their ability to guide and nurture their mentees effectively (Bachkirova and Cox, 2007).

- Mentee attitudes to matching

Some mentees may have preferences towards particular characteristics of their mentors, such as gender, age, or ethnic background. Some research also stresses the value of having mentor/mentee pairs with similar backgrounds (O'Broin and Palmer, 2010; van Ginkel, van Drie and Verloop, 2018), but this can be difficult, especially when there is a lack of either of them from a global majority group (Clutterbuck, 2012). It has also been argued that mentoring relationships across gender and racial lines yields benefits on both sides as it can produce a cross fertilisation of different and diverse opinions and perspectives and can enhance understanding on both sides (O'Broin and Palmer, 2010).

- Lack of organisational support
  This can manifest itself in different ways. For example, a lack of integration of programmes into the institution's operations, or a lack of financial or administrative support. There can also be an issue when there is no reward or recognition within the institution for those who volunteered to be mentors which can make it challenging for the mentor coordinator to find and keep good mentors. Lack of specific training for mentors can also be a feature of a disinterested institution (Tedder and Lawy, 2009).
- A closed organisational culture and cultural values
  This kind of set of cultural values can result in the focus of the mentoring endeavour being on having the mentee accept all the ways, mores, and ideas of the institution and then being judged on how they implement these in practice. It can also impact the way mentees are seen by other staff and mentors. For example, they could be seen to be as individuals capable of introducing new ideas and energies to the institution or a necessary incumbrance that needs to either be whipped into shape or babysat until they finish their qualification (Hargreaves, 2010).

Self-reflection task

How will you negotiate the following barriers to developing an effective relationship with your mentee?

Potential barriers	Your ideas
Mentee attitudes to matching?	
Lack of organisational support?	
A closed organisational culture and cultural values?	

References

Bachkirova, T. and Cox, E. (2007) 'Coaching with emotion in organisations: investigation of personal theories', *Leadership & Organization Development Journal*, 28, pp. 600–612. doi:10.1108/01437730710823860.

Blau, P.M. (1964) *Exchange and power in social life*. John Wiley & Sons.

Bourdieu, P. (1977) *Reproduction in education, culture and society*. SAGE Publications.

Bronfenbrenner, U. (1993) 'Ecological models of human development', in Gauvain M., Cole M. (eds) *Readings on the development of children*. 2nd edn. Freeman, pp. 37–43.

Byars-Winston, A., Estrada, Y., Howard, C., Davis, D. and Zalapa, J. (2010) 'Influence of social cognitive and ethnic variables on academic goals of underrepresented students in science and engineering: a multiple-groups analysis', *Journal of Counseling Psychology*, 57(2), pp. 205–218.

Chidiac, M.-A. (2018) *Relational organisational gestalt: an emergent approach to organisational development*. 1st edn. Routledge. doi:10.4324/9780429452833.

Clutterbuck, D. (2008). *Mentoring and Employee Well-being in Employee Well-being Support: A Workplace Resource*. in Kinder, A., Hughes, R. and Cooper, C. (eds) John Wiley, pp. 260–297.

Clutterbuck, D. (2012), 'Understanding diversity mentoring', in Clutterbuck, D., Poulsen, K.M. and Kochan, F. (eds.) *Developing successful diversity mentoring programmes: an international casebook*. Open University Press, pp. 1–17.

Colley, H. (2003) *Mentoring for social inclusion, a critical approach to nurturing mentor relationships*. Routledge.

Cox, E. and Bachkirova, T. (2007). 'Coaching with emotion: How coaches deal with difficult emotional situations', *International Coaching Psychology Review*, 2, pp. 165–178.

Cullimore, S. and Simmons, J. (2010) 'The emerging dilemmas and challenges for mentors and mentees in the new context for training in-service teachers for the Learning and Skills sector,' *Research in Post-Compulsory Education*, 15, pp. 223–239.

Duckworth, V. and Maxwell, B. (2015) 'Extending the mentor role in initial teacher education: embracing social justice', *International Journal of Mentoring and Coaching in Education*, 4, pp. 4–20. doi:10.1108/IJMCE-08-2014-0032.

Feldman, D.C. and Lankau, M. (2005) 'Executive coaching: a review and agenda for future research', *Journal of Management*, 31(6), pp. 829–848.

Guedes, B.A.M. (2021) What effect does the coaching model of professional development have on the building of teacher capacity? Unpublished Thesis. https://core.ac.uk/download/420293653.pdf.

Hardman, F. and Jan, A.K., (2010) 'Classroom discourse: towards a dialogic pedagogy', *The Routledge international handbook of English, language and literacy teaching*. Routledge, pp. 254–263.

Hargreaves, E. (2010) 'Knowledge construction and personal relationship: insights about a UK university mentoring and coaching service', *Mentoring & Tutoring: Partnership in Learning*, 18(2), pp. 107–120.

Hudson, P. (2013) 'Developing and sustaining successful mentoring relationships', *Journal of Relationships Research*, 4, p. 1–10.

Ingleby, E. (2010) 'Robbing Peter to pay Paul: the price of standards-driven education', *Research in Post-Compulsory Education*, 15(4), pp. 427–440.

Knight, J. (2009) *Instructional coaching: a partnership approach to improving instruction*. Corwin Press.

Kochan, F. and Pascarelli, J.T. (2012) 'Culture and mentoring in the global age', in Fletcher, S.J. and Mullen, C.A. (eds.) *Handbook of mentoring and coaching in education*. Sage Publications, pp. 184–194.

Kochan, F., Searby, L., Manju, P.G. and Edge, J.M. (2015) 'Cultural influences in mentoring endeavors: applying the cultural framework analysis process', *International Journal of Mentoring and Coaching in Education*, 4(2), pp. 86–106.

Kram, K. (1985) 'Mentoring at work: developmental relationships in organisational life', *Administrative Science Quarterly*, 30. doi:10.2307/2392687.

Lai, Y.-L. and McDowall, A. (2014) 'A systematic review of (SR) coaching psychology: focusing on the attributes of effective coaching psychologists', *International Coaching Psychology Review*, 9(2), pp. 118–134.

Lent, R.W., Brown, S.D. and Hackett, G. (1994) 'Toward a unifying social cognitive theory of career and academic interest, choice, and performance', *Journal of Vocational Behavior*, 45(1), pp. 79–122.

McHenry, L.K. (2018) A qualitative exploration of unconditional positive regard and its opposite constructs in coach-athlete relationships. Master's Thesis, University of Tennessee. https://trace.tennessee.edu/utk_gradthes/504.

O'Broin, A. and Palmer, S. (2010) 'Building on an interpersonal perspective on the coaching relationship', in Palmer, S. and McDowall, A. (eds.) *The coaching relationship: putting people first*. Routledge/Taylor & Francis Group, pp. 34–54.

Office of Standards in Education (Ofsted) (2007) The annual report of Her Majesty's Chief Inspector of Education, Children's Services and Skills 2006/07. (HMI 2677). London.

Office of Standards in Education (Ofsted) (2008) *The initial training of further education teachers (070194)*. Ofsted.

Stevenson, J., Kiss, Z., Jørgensen, C., Maxwell, B. and Hobson, A. (2023) Mentoring and coaching for trainee and early career teachers: a rapid evidence review. https://niot.s3.amazonaws.com/documents/3._Rapid_evidence_review_-_NIOT.pdf.

Straw, S., Walker, M. and Binfield, P. (2020) *Mentoring for early career chemistry teachers (MECCT): pilot report*. Education Endowment Foundation (EEF).

Tedder, M. and Lawy, R. (2009) 'The pursuit of "excellence": mentoring in further education initial teacher training in England', *Journal of Vocational Education & Training*, 61, pp. 413–429. doi:10.1080/13636820903363634.

van Ginkel, G., van Drie, J. and Verloop, N. (2018) 'Mentor teachers' views of their mentees', *Mentoring & Tutoring: Partnership in Learning*, 26(2), pp. 122–147. doi: 10.1080/13611267.2018.1472542.

van Nieuwerburgh, C. (2017) *An introduction to coaching skills: a practical guide*. Sage Publications.

Wenger, E., McDermott, R.A. and Snyder, W. (2002) *Cultivating communities of practice: a guide to managing knowledge*. Harvard Business Press.

Whitmore, J. (2009) *Coaching for performance: GROWing human potential and purpose: the principles and practice of coaching and leadership. People skills for professionals*. 4th edn. Nicholas Brealey.

Chapter 7

Supporting planning and observing classroom practice

The importance of reciprocity

Many researchers have evidenced how the ways that mentors collaborate with mentees by observing, reflecting, and enacting the teaching process and the resulting relationships often influence the quality of learning to teach and the overall mentoring experience (John, 2006; Powell, 2023; Pylman, 2016).

According to Alnajjar (2022), reciprocity between them is key to the prime roles of a mentor as educational trainer, sentimental underpinning, and social facilitator. The processes of sharing academic knowledge, resources, and experiences can lead to the building of trust and respect, to normalise, build rapport, and educate, and to bridge the gap between their expectations of teaching and reality.

Reciprocity provides preservice teachers with practical knowledge, strategies, advice, and live examples. Arguably, field experiences can enrich the lived curriculum of teacher education, and the role of the mentor should be to assist, not prescribe, practice. Other research suggested that involving preservice teachers in conversation and fostering thinking allowed them to address bigger teaching and learning challenges and broaden their perspectives (O'Leary, 2020).

Mentor and mentee reciprocity also enables mentees to feel safe disclosing failure experiences and motivates supervisors to self-disclose similar difficult experiences. As a result, the confidence of mentees improved. During these situations, mentors are aware of their mentees' feelings of incompetence when they make mistakes. Thus, the mentors reflect on their own experiences to encourage their mentees to accept challenges and missteps and thus support them in their early stage of career development (Pylman, 2016).

The gradual release of responsibility model of instruction, which is based on Vygotskian notion of the Most Knowledgeable Other (MKO) concept, suggests that learning should shift slowly and purposefully from teacher-as-model to joint responsibility, to independent practice and application by the learner (Vygotsky, 1962). Through gradual release, the student becomes a competent and independent learner.

According to Wexler (2020), 'Educative Mentors' in this role focus on growth-producing experiences looking towards long-term goals whilst also attending to immediate purposes. The educative mentor helps the novice learn to be a reflective and inquiry-based practitioner by jointly inquiring into teaching with the novice. This can be done by engaging novices in conversations through co-planning, observing and debriefing, and analysing the reflective practices of their mentors and students' work.

Central to this process is the role that the mentor must take to allow the student to experiment and learn by making mistakes within growth producing learning experiences in an environment where the mentee teacher feels safe to experiment (2020).

Self-reflection exercise

Ways in which you could prompt your mentee to experiment with new teaching strategies.

Mentor actions to take

- Ask questions that encourage the mentee to consider that they are using a specific strategy, the challenges they think they will confront, and how they imagine the strategy to look.
- Reflect with them to examine the success of the new strategy and how it can be improved.

The questions the mentor could use include the following:

- What did you try today that was new/different? How did it go? How do you know?
- Would you like to try a different approach to that?
- Is there a different/better way you think we could do _____?
- What have you learnt in your teaching classes that you would like to try out?
- Why are you interested in trying this new strategy? What do you envision it will look/sound like?
- What challenges do you anticipate might occur as you try this?

Now list some changes you think they could make in their practice.

For example,

- Different kinds of starters? or
- Introducing a new digital application?

Schwille (2008) suggested there are both 'inside' (i.e. mentoring that takes place during teaching while students are present) and 'outside' mentoring practices (i.e. mentoring that takes place before or after a teaching episode).

Lesson planning

Lesson planning is one of the main 'outside' mentoring practices. According to Mutton, Hagger and Burn (2011), there are six key characteristics of lesson planning:

- It occurs at different levels. This can be short term, medium term, or long term. It can be weekly, termly, or yearly. Mentors should encourage their mentees to plan ahead but also to prepare to change their planning in order to follow the learners' paths of learning.
- It is mostly informal for experienced teachers but formal for trainees. Mentors may need to supply them with exemplars of lesson plans, Schemes of Work, etc. to work from at the very beginning of their placement.
- It is creative. Mentors can play a prominent role in developing this in their trainees by allowing them to express their own ideas freely and to experiment in their sessions.
- It is knowledge based. Mentors should be mindful that trainees may depend too heavily in their planning on subject-content and not enough on the overall structuring of learning which lies at the heart of lesson planning (Mutton, Hagger and Burn, 2011).
- It must allow flexibility. Mentees must be encouraged to learn that a lesson plan is not a straitjacket and that they should be prepared to deviate from it when occasion calls.
- It occurs within a practical and ideological context and therefore mentors should be mindful not to impose their own ideologies of teaching on their mentees, even inadvertently, and to help them navigate some of the contextual planning issues such as class sizes and access to resources.

Why learning to plan lessons is important for a trainee teacher

Learning how to write a lesson plan is a crucial skill for trainee teachers as it serves as a roadmap for effective teaching and learning in the classroom. An average trainee teacher can expect to design between 150 and 200 lesson plans whilst they are in their placement. Institutions tend to have slightly different lesson plan formats, but in general, well-designed lesson plans outline the objectives, instructional strategies, assessment methods, and resources needed to deliver a successful lesson.

A lesson plan provides structure and organisation to the teaching process, ensuring that the trainee teacher has a clear direction and purpose for each lesson. It helps them stay focused on the learning objectives and key concepts they want students to understand (Redfern, 2020).

Lesson plans help trainee teachers align their instructional goals with the curriculum standards and learning outcomes set by educational authorities. By clearly articulating the objectives and assessments in the lesson plan, they ensure that their teaching addresses the required content and skills.

Effective lesson planning involves considering the diverse learning needs of students and incorporating strategies to engage and support all learners. Trainee teachers can use lesson plans to design activities that cater to various learning styles, abilities, and interests, promoting inclusive and engaging classroom environments (2020).

By incorporating formative and summative assessments into their lesson plans, they can monitor student progress, provide feedback, and reflect on the effectiveness of their instructional practices.

Barriers to lesson planning for mentees (John, 2006)

Teaching beginning teachers how to plan is not solely down to one party or the other; the provider can deliver the theory, explain the rationale, and present alternatives while the placement is able to demonstrate how context influences a teacher's lesson design decisions. Essentially, student-teachers are expected to improve their ability to plan their lessons by learning from their mistakes (Powell, 2023).

Mentees, especially early in their training, have to confront a series of barriers to effective lesson planning. These include:

- Finding their way around the linearity of lesson plan structures.
- Mentees describe their planning as time-consuming as they struggle to make sense out of the multitude of decisions they have to make regarding content, management, time, pacing, and resources.
- Trainees, particularly early on in their training, have difficulty making predictions about student responses and have problems adjusting their practice according to the exigencies they encounter (John, 2006).
- They tend to define learning and teaching more literally because they lack a range of teaching skills.
- Many student teachers, particularly early in their training, have difficulty matching goals, objectives, and forms of evaluation; many also fail to understand the conceptual (and sometimes semantic) distinctions between aims, objectives, and goals (2006).
- Many trainee teachers have difficulty integrating subject topics, understanding the concepts or tasks embedded in curriculum materials, and juggling conflicting goals when there is uncertainty about how to achieve multiple desired outcomes.
- Dealing with a lack of knowledge of their learners.

- Using the lesson plan as a script and the difficulty in seeing planning as a form of visualisation and anticipation of what might happen rather than their determination of what would happen and planning as a template (Mutton et al., 2011).
- An inability to embrace flexibility in the lesson prevented them from thinking 'on their feet' at times (Mullen, 2000).
- A lack of confidence which impacted their willingness to try different teaching strategies.
- Adapting the lesson plans of other teachers in order to teach other teachers' classes.
- Personality factors and preferences related to teaching style can also impact the multitude of decisions to be made during the planning stages of a lesson (Pylman, 2016).

Trainee teachers are taught the discipline of writing lesson plans from a variety of sources. These can include their tutor, line manager at their placement or their mentor and all three.

Lesson planning with the mentor

Mentors who assist the mentee's performance and learning through educative co-planning get to know them as learners. They mentor responsively, scaffold learning about and through planning, and gradually release mentees to independent planning (Pylman, 2016). Pylman identified a general pattern in the structure of co-planning sessions. She found that effective mentor teachers and/or interns explored content, designed learning activities, coached for teaching, and clarified roles (2016).

Some writers argue that co-planning is a powerful form of mentoring because mentors and mentees can develop shared understandings about the meaning and purpose of activities, and the trainee can gradually internalise certain ways of thinking, problem-solving, and decision-making (Brondyk and Searby, 2013; Manning and Hobson, 2017; Redfern, 2020).

The benefits of co-planning a lesson

Benefits for the mentor

These can include the following.

Enhanced professional growth

Collaborating with a mentee on lesson planning provides the mentor with opportunities to reflect on their teaching practices, try new strategies, and stay current with innovative approaches.

Skill development

Co-planning allows mentors to refine their communication, collaboration, and leadership skills. It also provides a chance to model effective instructional planning techniques for the mentee (Brondyk and Searby, 2013).

Increased job satisfaction

Mentors often find joy and fulfilment in supporting the growth and development of their mentee, contributing to greater job satisfaction and a sense of accomplishment (Chan and Luo, 2022).

Benefits for the mentee

These can include the following.

Enhanced learning experience

Co-planning lessons with a mentor provides the mentee with valuable insights, guidance, and expertise that can help improve their teaching skills and effectiveness in the classroom.

Professional development

Working collaboratively with a mentor on lesson planning exposes the mentee to different pedagogical approaches, instructional strategies, and classroom management techniques.

Develop self-reflection

It can also help to support their self-evaluations of planning and understanding of the needs of the learners (Manzey, 2010).

Increased confidence

The support and guidance provided by the mentor during the co-planning process can help boost the mentee's confidence in their teaching abilities, reduce imposter syndrome, and enhance their overall self-efficacy (Mullen, 2000).

WAYS IN WHICH LESSON PLANNING CAN BE SUPPORTED BY MENTORS

There are many different ways in which a mentor can support a mentee's planning, teaching, and assessing (Pylman and Bell, 2021). These include the following:

- Modelling
  The mentor can start by providing the mentee with example lesson plans that demonstrate key components such as learning objectives, instructional

activities, assessment methods, and resources. By analysing and deconstructing these models, the mentee can gain a better understanding of how to structure and organise their own lesson plans.
- Reflection and Feedback

    After the mentee has written a lesson plan, the mentor can facilitate a reflective discussion to help the mentee analyse the strengths and weaknesses of their plan. By providing constructive feedback and guidance, the mentor can help them identify areas for improvement and adjustments to enhance the quality of their lesson plans (Powell, 2023).
- Peer Review

    Encouraging the mentee to engage in peer review activities can also be beneficial to their lesson planning skills. By sharing their lesson plans with peers or other educators for feedback and critique, the mentee can gain valuable insights and perspectives that can inform their practice and help them refine their lesson plans (2023).
- Tutor Collaboration

    The mentor can work in partnership with the trainee's tutor to develop a common template for lesson planning that can be used by the mentee in their assignments and in their teaching practice. This will provide the mentee with a structure to work from and ensure a uniformity of practice and a clarity of standards (Pylman and Bell, 2021).

The stages of co-planning a lesson

- First stage

    During this stage, student teachers need to know what a lesson plan actually is, as well as understanding the crucial nexus that exists between planning and teaching. Mentors will need to help them to the crucial connection between classroom management, subject content, and the curriculum and will tend to rely on concrete, even prosaic models of planning to guide their thinking. Model lesson plans and exemplars can help support their progress in this area (Mullen, 2000).

    The key to co-planning is that it involves discussion between the mentor and the student-teacher about the lesson before it is taught by the mentor. During a co-planning meeting, the mentor and the student-teacher work together to plan the lesson, and therefore the student-teacher can participate in the lesson planning alongside an experienced practitioner who explains the rationale behind their thinking.

    The goal during this phase is not for the mentee to learn to imitate the mentor but to develop their own adaptive expertise as they learn to pay attention to student needs and knowledge, standards and objectives, time management, and other pedagogical choices (Chan and Luo, 2022).

    The role of the mentor during this stage is also to share knowledge of common misconceptions students often bring with them to the lesson or to draw attention to concepts which they tend to find particularly

difficult to grasp during the lesson. Mentors will be sharing their Pedagogical Content Knowledge (PCK) with their mentee (Tedder and Lawy, 2009).

According to research by Powell (2023), co-planning has several benefits. These include:

- It enables student-teachers to think differently about lesson planning as their focus shifted away from the content, they were going to deliver, to learning they wanted the pupils to achieve.
- It becomes a means for mentors to share their tacit knowledge of teaching and thus enables student-teachers to anticipate what may happen in a lesson and thus plan for responsiveness and greater flexibility.
- It can also give student-teachers confidence to try new approaches and afford mentors an opportunity to reflect on their own practice.

These plans can then become the basis of structured observations focussing on particular, more complex aspects of the lesson plan such as differentiation. Mentees should be encouraged to develop a stronger understanding of the learning needs of their groups and how to develop their planning to accommodate them differently in every session (2003).

- Final stage

    During this stage, the mentee should be given the opportunity to fly solo and develop their own lesson plans. Mentors need only to preview the lesson plans before they are used in class. During this stage, the mentor needs to step back and allow the mentee to make their own mistakes in the planning and to support them during feedback afterwards (Edwards and Protheroe, 2004).
- Second stage

    As soon as student teachers begin the practical phase of their courses, the role of the mentor becomes more prominent as the novices move through a form of 'Legitimate Peripheral Participation' (LPP) (Lave and Wenger, 1991). LPP is a process in which newcomers become experienced members and eventually old timers of a community of practice or collaborative project (1991). LPP identifies learning as a contextual social phenomenon, achieved through participation in a community practice. During this phase, mentees should be scaffolded through a dialogue with real teaching situations. This process can be partly mimetic in that various routines and representations are internalised and layered onto their evolving practical theories.
- Third stage

    As mentee confidence develops, the process of lesson planning needs to become more co-operative as both parties will benefit from discussing options and jointly informing one another of the process as it evolves.

Aguirre-Garzón *et al.* (2022) suggest that, because of the fundamental thought process involved, the process of planning a lesson can be regarded as a significant analytical tool for beginning teachers to unpack their own thinking about teaching and learning. Co-planning can lead to long-term and transferable learning on behalf of the student-teacher.

Co-planning can also be used as an ongoing developmental process and not just one used at the beginning of training. Mentees should be encouraged to seek the advice of their mentors for planning when they feel short of inspiration, stuck in a rut as regards new approaches, or just needing a different way to approach their teaching (2022). This can also help mentees become more creative and confident teachers who are willing to experiment with new techniques and to take risks.

From their research Mutton, Hagger and Burn (2011) suggest that co-planning can help long term and suggest that teachers learn most about how to plan once they gain much greater knowledge of what it can and cannot achieve and that ongoing learning about planning can be a powerful vehicle for ongoing learning about teaching as a whole. They suggest that as trainee teachers progress in their placement, it can be that through planning they learn about teaching and through teaching that they are able to learn about planning. In doing so, mentors should be developing their understanding of the role and process of planning itself, and how to plan for flexibility (2011).

There are several techniques that mentors can develop in order to support their mentees in their planning. One of these is the Think Aloud.

Think Alouds

One technique that has been used to evaluate comprehension monitoring abilities is the oral Think Aloud procedure. Think Alouds involve the overt, verbal expression of the normally covert mental processes readers engage in when constructing meaning from a text.

Bereiter and Bird (1985) analysed protocols of adults' Think Alouds during reading and identified four strategies:

a restatement (paraphrasing and summarising),
b backtracking (looking back and rereading),
c demanding relationships (self-questioning and inferring unstated information), and
d problem formulation (hypothesising and predicting).

The Think Aloud was developed to help enhance students' abilities in the thinking process and understand what they comprehend, and it allows the reader to connect meaning and understanding with the text (1985).

Teachers could show their thinking process and how their thoughts are occurring during the reading for students who are struggling with comprehension. Through using a Think Aloud, teachers vocalise how they think as they read (Ortlieb and Norris, 2012).

The Think Aloud strategy can be used as a scaffolding model by mentors to develop higher thinking and learning in their mentees and can allow for the clarification of difficult concepts or tasks. In a Think Aloud, mentors can model their own thinking strategies for their mentees as they need. The goal of the Think Aloud strategy is that eventually mentees will develop a similar thinking process when they are planning independently, thereby improving their comprehension (Ortlieb and Norris, 2012).

There are two types of Think Alouds, concurrent and retrospective Think Aloud (Kuusela and Paul, 2000).

Concurrent

The former is elicited while a learning task is being performed. The participant typically either voices aloud thoughts, feelings, and reasoning as the primary learning activity is going on or stops the primary task every now and then, usually at the prompt of a visual, acoustic, or semantic reminder, so that they can tell the other participant what has been going on in their mind.

Retrospective or reflective Think Aloud

Retrospective Think Aloud happens at the end of a learning task and is meant to collect the participants' thinking and reasoning processes while they are still in the short-term memory of the learner.

Benefits of using Think Alouds

These include the following:

- Modelling Thought Processes
  Think Alouds provide mentors with a structured way to model their expert thinking processes as they plan lessons. By vocalising their decision-making, considerations, and reflections, mentors can demonstrate effective lesson planning strategies to their mentees (2000).
- Cognitive Apprenticeship
  Using Think Alouds in lesson planning allows mentees to observe and understand the cognitive processes involved in effective planning. Through this apprenticeship model, mentees can internalise the reasoning behind decision-making and adapt these strategies in their own lesson planning endeavours.

- Enhancing Metacognitive Skills
  Think Alouds can encourage metacognitive awareness by prompting both mentors and mentees to reflect on their own thinking processes. This metacognition can lead to a deeper understanding of lesson planning principles, strategies, and potential areas for improvement.
- Facilitating Dialogue and Collaboration
  They can create opportunities for rich dialogue and collaboration between mentors and mentees during the lesson planning process. By articulating their thoughts, mentors and mentees can engage in discussions, ask questions, and receive feedback, fostering a supportive and collaborative learning environment (Ortlieb and Norris, 2012).
- Promoting Reflective Practice
  Think Alouds encourage mentors and mentees to engage in reflective practice by actively considering and articulating the rationale behind their decisions. This reflective approach can lead to continuous improvement, refinement of planning skills, and enhanced critical thinking abilities (2012).

Case study

According to Dimitrios (Mentor for Construction Students)

First, I sit down with a mentee with a blank lesson plan. Then I bring up the course spec or the Scheme of work, and then I verbalise what I want to do and why I am going to do it. I break the lesson down stage by stage and keep saying what I am going to do and why I am doing it this way. It's also a two-way thing as I normally respond to questions as we go along. I try to break things down in my head and explain different options to the trainee so that they can see there are always alternatives to the way you plan things and that there is never just one right way in teaching anything.

The importance of co-planning

Some mentees approach planning on a short-term basis, being concerned about tomorrow rather than seeing the whole, long-range picture. They can therefore benefit from mentors' experience, because they would tend to have a broader perspective because they know what students learnt before their mentees started teaching and they know the direction the curriculum is going throughout the rest of the semester (Manzey, 2010).

During this process, mentee will need to be encouraged to move beyond technical reflections based on the immediate effectiveness of their approaches to comparative reflections, characterised by asking questions about their practice, such as 'would another approach better suit my students' needs?' and 'is my assessment of students realistic or equitable?' (2010).

Pylman (2016) suggested that using video-recorded co-planning sessions was an effective way to reflect on and improve mentoring practice. Her research explored the ways in which a mentor used talk in co-planning sessions to model their thinking process, to teach the mentee how to plan, and to gradually release planning responsibility to engage the mentee in learning to plan for instruction.

She showed how the mentor used the filmed sessions to 'notice' elements of their teaching practice and to stimulate reflection on how they used talk during a co-planning session to explain, to inform, to model, to clarify, to question, and to Think Aloud.

Her results suggest the importance of co-planning and the potential for supporting mentor teacher development through the use of video to aid in reflecting on mentoring practice (2016).

Using rubrics

Mentors can also provide their mentees with a set of prompts within a rubric for co-planning and co-reflections. These can be encapsulated in the form of phrases or questions, key considerations that mentees should consider in their planning decisions. This can have several benefits for both parties including the following.

Clarity and consistency

Prompts within a rubric can provide clear guidelines and criteria for planning and reflection, ensuring that both mentors and mentees focus on key aspects of lesson design. This promotes consistency and helps align expectations between the mentor and the mentee and also serves as a structured framework for reflection, guiding mentors and mentees through a comprehensive review of their lesson planning process. This helps to deepen understanding, identify strengths and areas for improvement, and promote meaningful dialogue between them (Shanks, 2017).

Skill development

By using them, mentors can help mentees develop specific skills and competencies related to effective lesson planning. The guided reflection facilitated by the prompts allows mentees to critically evaluate their planning decisions and consider alternative approaches, thus promoting professional growth.

Formative assessment

Prompts within a rubric can aid in formative assessment, allowing mentors to provide targeted feedback to mentees on their lesson plans. This feedback is valuable for supporting mentees' learning and development, fostering a continuous improvement mindset, and enhancing the quality of future lesson plans (2017).

Collaboration and communication

The use of prompts within a rubric encourages collaboration and open communication between mentors and mentees. By engaging in structured co-planning and co-reflection activities guided by the prompts, both parties can work together to set goals, address challenges, and celebrate successes in a supportive and constructive manner (Sachs, Fisher and Cannon, 2011).

> **Rubric prompt checklist for a co-planning production meeting**
>
> Here are some of the most important questions to be discussed by mentor and mentee before planning:
>
> 1. What is the topic of this class?
> 2. Where does it fit in with the current Scheme of Work?
> 3. What are the learning objectives for this lesson?
> 4. What are the specific needs of the students in this group?
> 5. How will I engage them at the beginning of the lesson?
> 6. What teaching strategies and activities will I use to teach the content?
> 7. How will I differentiate my approaches to meet their diverse needs?
> 8. How will I promote Inclusion and Diversity in the lesson?
> 9. How will I embed English, Maths, and digital literacy in this class?
> 10. What resources and materials will I need for it?
> 11. Which formative assessment methods will I use?
> 12. How will I address any potential challenges or disruptions during the lesson?
> 13. How will I promote student participation and engagement?
> 14. How will I provide feedback and support during the lesson?
> 15. How will I evaluate the effectiveness of the lesson and reflect on my teaching practice afterwards?

According to Pylman's (2016) research, there are six most effective types of talk used in co-planning lessons:

- Mentor telling
  This is where a mentor explains how to teach a particular topic.
- Transparent thinking
  This happens when a mentor is thinking out aloud and explaining how and why they made particular decisions.
- Mentor questioning and feedback
  Here, the mentor poses questions to the mentee which prompt them to think about their own assumptions and form a type of feedback.

- Mentee questioning

  Here, the mentee would be encouraged to ask the mentor to provide more examples of situations or techniques.
- Mentee telling

  In this situation, the mentee is prompted to describe their plans and recap on what they did previously or what they intended to do in a future session.
- Transparent thinking

  In this situation, the mentee is prompted to problem solve, make decisions, and plan for instruction in a process of metacognition.

> Video or audio record one of your own mentoring sessions and analyse the way in which you use the different types of talk to shift the responsibility for leading the co-planning sessions from you to your mentee and develop their autonomy as a teacher.

> **Self-reflection scenario exercise**
>
> Imagine that you have a new mentee who says they prefer to work on their lesson planning on their own. You have allowed them to plan this way for the past two lessons, but there are issues with the areas of her planning.
>
> What would you do?
>
> Allow her to continue experimenting and hope that she finally gets the hang of it?
>
> Provide her with a model lesson plan that she can base her own on?
>
> Insist that she plans a lesson with you?
>
> Convince her of the benefits of co-planning and see if she comes around to the idea voluntarily?

The importance of questioning during co-lesson planning

In co-planning sessions, mentors have the opportunity to scaffold mentees' learning and prepare them for independent decision-making. One way they can scaffold learning is through questioning. Mentors can help mentees grow as thoughtful and reflective practitioners by not only encouraging them to analyse what they will teach but also probing them to explain when, where, how, and why they are using particular teaching approaches. This will enable them to develop metacognition and build connections between what they choose to teach, how they teach the material, and what their students learn (Oti, 2012).

Research by Pylman and Bell (2021) suggests that mentors need to think carefully about the importance of questioning their mentee during lesson planning. They argued that mentors should be doing the following during this stage:

- To check in to see if mentees knew what they need to know,
- To see if mentees were able to apply that knowledge to make good plans,
- To allow them to make decisions and encourage them to envision possibilities, and
- To probe to see if they knew why they were making these decisions.

It has been suggested that there are three main types of cognitive questions:

- Input questions
  The first type of questions causes mentees to input data, encouraging them to name, describe, or recall data.
- Process questions
  Mentors ask and encourage mentees to process the data they have acquired. They are asked to make sense or meaning out of the data by explaining, organising, comparing, or sequencing.
- Output questions
  These require students to go beyond the concepts and principles they have developed and use their knowledge in new or hypothetical situations. In this manner, they are asking students to develop output as they are applying, hypothesising, evaluating, designing, or defending.

> Write three questions that you might use in a mentoring session for each category.

Supporting a mentee's scheme of work design

Learning how to design a scheme of work from a mentor is crucial for a trainee teacher because it will form the backbone of their teaching and assessment over the next academic year and will prepare them for employment after finishing the course (Redfern, 2020). In particular, it is essential for them to learn:

- Curriculum Alignment: A scheme of work outlines the sequence and structure of topics to be covered throughout a school year or term. By learning how to design a scheme of work from a mentor, the mentee can ensure that their teaching is aligned with the curriculum requirements and learning objectives.
- Effective Planning: Designing a scheme of work involves breaking down the curriculum into manageable units and planning the sequence of lessons and

activities. This skill is essential for effective lesson planning and ensuring that the content is covered in a coherent and logical manner (John, 2006).
- Differentiation: A well-designed scheme of work reflects the abilities of students. By learning how to design a scheme of work from the mentor, a trainee teacher can develop strategies for differentiation and catering to the individual needs of all students in the classroom (Martin and Johnson, 2013).
- Time Management: Designing a scheme of work involves allocating time for each topic, lesson, and assessment. This skill is crucial for effective time management in the classroom and ensuring that all curriculum content is covered within the allocated time.
- Assessment and Evaluation: A scheme of work typically includes assessments and evaluation strategies to measure student progress and learning outcomes. By learning how to design a scheme of work, the mentee can develop effective assessment practices and tools to monitor student learning (Manning and Hobson, 2017).
- Collaboration: Designing a scheme of work often involves collaboration with colleagues, university tutors, subject coordinators, and other stakeholders. By working with a mentor to design a Scheme of Work, the mentee can develop skills in collaborating with others to plan and deliver effective teaching and learning experiences.

There are many different ways in which a mentee can be supported in designing a Scheme of Work. They include the following ideas:

Understanding Curriculum Requirements: By providing a copy of the curriculum specification. This can help the mentee understand the curriculum guidelines, standards, and requirements that need to be addressed in the Scheme of Work.
Modelling Best Practice: The mentor can show them copies of their own Schemes of Work to draw inspiration from and to help them develop an understanding of teaching and learning as a whole (Holland, 2018).
Setting Measurable Learning Objectives: The mentor can assist their mentees in their defining and the writing of clear and measurable learning objectives that align with the curriculum and student needs of the teaching group (Chan and Luo, 2022).
Sequencing Content: Mentors can guide mentees in structuring and sequencing content in a logical and coherent manner to facilitate effective learning progression.
Incorporating Differentiation: Mentors can support mentees in designing activities and assessments that cater to the diverse needs and learning styles of students.
Assessments: The mentor can help their mentees align assessments with learning objectives and suggest strategies for designing formative and summative

assessments that gauge student progress (Aderibigbe, Gray and Colucci-Gray, 2018).

Integrating Technology: Mentees can be introduced to different types of technology and to help them to integrate technology effectively to enhance teaching and learning in the scheme of work (2018).

Cultivating Critical Thinking: Mentors can encourage mentees to incorporate activities and tasks that promote critical thinking, problem-solving, and higher-order thinking skills.

Providing Resources: Mentors can share resources, materials, and teaching strategies that can enrich the scheme of work and support student learning (Martin and Johnston, 2013).

Offering Feedback. Mentors can provide constructive feedback on the draft scheme of work, highlighting areas for improvement and offering suggestions for enhancement.

Reflecting and Revising: Mentees can be guided in reflecting on the effectiveness of the scheme of work through formative evaluation and revision based on feedback, student performance, and teaching experiences (John, 2006).

> **Coaching exercise – scheme of Work design**
>
> Provide the mentee with the curriculum guidelines or standards for the chosen subject and grade level and encourage the mentee to choose a specific topic or unit to focus on for the exercise.
>
> Ask them to create a short scheme of work outlining the sequence of lessons, learning objectives, teaching strategies, and assessment methods for the chosen topic. The scheme of work should cover a period of 2–4 weeks, depending on the complexity of the topic. Allow them time to work on designing the scheme of work, providing guidance and feedback as needed.
>
> Once the mentee has completed the scheme of work, review it together and discuss areas for improvement or refinement. Encourage the mentee to reflect on the process of designing the scheme of work and discuss how they can apply these skills in their future lesson planning and teaching practice.
>
> Ask the mentee to expand the SoW to cover an entire term and then review the results with them.

Developing teaching resources

Teaching resources are the tools of a teacher's trade and having the right ones in the toolbox can make a difference to the success of a teaching session. Teaching resources are essential tools that enable teachers to effectively deliver instruction, engage students, and enhance the learning experience. These resources come in various forms, including textbooks, worksheets, multimedia materials, manipulatives, and online resources, and play a crucial role in supporting teachers in their instructional practices (Martin and Johnston, 2013).

Firstly, teaching resources help teachers plan and organise their lessons effectively. By providing a framework for instruction, resources such as lesson plans and schemes of work enable teachers to structure their teaching in a coherent and logical manner. This helps ensure that all necessary content is covered, learning objectives are met, and assessments are aligned with student learning outcomes (2017).

Secondly, teaching resources facilitate differentiation and personalised learning. By using a variety of resources that cater to different learning styles, abilities, and interests, teachers can create inclusive and engaging learning experiences for all students. For example, visual aids can help visual learners understand complex concepts, while hands-on activities can support kinaesthetic learners in mastering practical skills (Lofthouse and Thomas, 2017).

Moreover, teaching resources can save teachers time and effort by providing ready-made materials that can be easily adapted to suit the needs of their students. Preparing high-quality resources in advance allows teachers to focus on facilitating learning, providing feedback, and addressing individual student needs during the teaching session. Additionally, using diverse and interactive resources can make lessons more interesting and engaging, capturing students' attention and motivating them to participate actively in the learning process (Mutton, Hagger and Burn, 2011).

Some of the challenges that a mentee faces when undertaking the design of teaching resources for the first time include the following (Aguirre-Garzón *et al.*, 2022).

Lack of experience

Trainee teachers may have limited experience in designing teaching resources, which can make the process challenging and overwhelming.

Uncertainty about student needs

They may struggle to anticipate the learning preferences and needs of their students when creating teaching resources for the first time and have limited access to a variety of teaching materials, such as textbooks, technology, or manipulatives, which can constrain their ability to design effective resources (2022).

Time constraints

Designing teaching resources can be time-consuming, and they may find it difficult to balance this task with other responsibilities, such as lesson planning, assessment, and classroom management.

Lack of knowledge of learning levels

Mentees may not have had many opportunities to observe the ability of their class and hence may find it difficult to teach at the right level and may not receive sufficient guidance or support from their mentors or experienced colleagues when designing their own teaching resources, leading to uncertainty, frustration, and inappropriateness (Holland, 2018).

However, there are many different ways in which a mentee can be supported in designing their teaching resources. They include the following ideas (Brondyk and Searby, 2018).

Identifying resource needs

They can be helped to identify the specific resources needed for a lesson or unit, considering factors such as student learning preferences, learning needs, curriculum requirements, and available materials.

Sourcing materials

They can be introduced to quality teaching resources, such as textbooks, online tools, manipulatives, or multimedia resources, or shown how to modify or adapt existing teaching resources to better meet the needs of their students or align with the learning objectives of a lesson. In addition, mentors can support mentees in developing original teaching resources, such as lesson plans, worksheets, assessments, or multimedia presentations (Manning and Hobson, 2017).

Ensuring accessibility

Mentors can help mentees ensure that teaching resources are accessible to all students, including those with diverse learning needs or language backgrounds (Brondyk and Searby, 2018).

Providing feedback

They can review and provide constructive feedback on the teaching resources created by mentees, offering suggestions for improvement or enhancement.

Integrating technology

They can be guided into integrating technology tools and resources effectively into their teaching, enhancing student engagement and learning outcomes.

Differentiating instruction

Mentors can help mentees design teaching resources that support differentiated instruction, catering to the unique needs and abilities of individual students, and help your mentees to align teaching resources with curriculum standards, learning objectives, and assessment criteria to ensure coherence and consistency (Willy, 2023).

Promoting sustainability

Mentors can encourage mentees to develop teaching resources that can be reused, adapted, and shared with other educators, promoting collaboration and sustainability in resource development (2023).

> **Coaching exercise – designing teaching resources**
>
> Provide your mentee with a specific teaching topic or concept to focus on for the resource design challenge. Ask the mentee to review the curriculum guidelines or standards related to the chosen topic to ensure alignment.
>
> Encourage the mentee to research different types of teaching resources that could be used to teach the topic effectively and have them select one specific type of teaching resource to design (e.g., a worksheet, a hands-on activity, a multimedia presentation).
>
> Set a time limit for them to design the resource and provide them with a set of criteria ensuring they consider factors such as clarity, engagement, and relevance to student learning.
>
> When they have completed it, have the mentee present their teaching resource to you explaining the rationale behind their design choices. Provide feedback on the resource design, highlighting the strengths and areas for improvement.
>
> Encourage the mentee to revise and refine the teaching resource based on the feedback received and then reflect on the activity together, discussing the challenges faced and the skills developed in the process of designing teaching resources.
>
> Ask your mentee to trial the resource with their learners and ask them to provide feedback on it. Then have another meeting to discuss its strengths and any possible areas of improvement.

Co-teaching

Co-teaching includes features where mentors share teaching episodes with their mentees and where mentors directly assist while their trainees are teaching (Schwille, 2008). One of the unique features of this co-teaching model is the use of three strategies: follow-me episodes, reverse-follow-me episodes, and team-teaching episodes.

Follow-me

The follow-me episodes are designed so mentors model expert inquiry-based science teaching behaviours during one period and then have trainees try their hand at teaching the same lesson during the next period. This strategy has its roots in Schon's (1987) work on developing practitioners in professions that are considered ill-structured, professions where practitioners do not have one set course of action. Schon's work suggests that learning how to reflect-in-action is facilitated when mentees see their mentors model such reflection and then have opportunities to try it themselves.

Some of the benefits for mentors and mentees of using follow-me episodes include the following.

Real-time observation

The mentee can observe the mentor's teaching strategies, methods, and instructional approaches first-hand during the teaching session. This allows for immediate feedback and clarification on demonstrated practices (Sachs, Fisher and Cannon, 2011).

Active learning

By actively following and participating in the mentor's teaching actions, the mentee engages in experiential learning, which can deepen their understanding and retention of effective teaching practices (Alnajjar, 2022).

Immediate feedback

Through the follow-me modelling method, mentors can provide instant feedback to mentees on their teaching approaches, helping them to adjust and improve their techniques in real-time, and mentees can tailor their learning experience based on their personalised needs and preferences by observing and mirroring the mentor's actions and instructional strategies (2022).

Demonstrating best practices

The mentor's modelling of effective teaching practices serves as a practical demonstration of best practices in action, offering mentees valuable insights and strategies to incorporate into their own teaching repertoire (Willy, 2023).

Building trust and rapport

The collaborative nature of the 'follow-me' modelling method fosters a strong mentor-mentee relationship, promoting trust, open communication, and mutual respect in the teaching partnership.

Reverse-follow-me

Reverse-follow-me episodes are also based on Schon's work and his suggestion that during apprenticeships practitioners should rotate their lead, especially when confronted by novel situations. In reverse-follow-me episodes, mentees teach part of a lesson, such as a starter, an activity, or a plenary, then their mentors enact the same part of the lesson but modify it with their own expertise (Robson and Mtika, 2017).

By rotating the lead, Schon suggested pairs have a common context which ideally should trigger rich conversations and reflections. These reflections ought to prompt candidates to think beyond just the technical aspects of teaching as they see the effect a different style of teaching has on student learning (1987).

Some of the benefits for mentors and mentees of using reverse-follow-me episodes include the following.

Active participation

The reverse 'follow-me' approach encourages active engagement from the mentee, as they are responsible for leading the teaching session and demonstrating their understanding and application of teaching techniques. This active participation can enhance the mentee's confidence and ownership of their teaching practice (Robson and Mtika, 2017).

Reflection and feedback

By taking on the role of the teacher and leading the session, the mentee gains the opportunity to reflect on their instructional decisions and receive constructive feedback and an opportunity to observe experienced practice from the mentor. This feedback and demonstration can help the mentee improve their teaching skills and refine their instructional approach (Jones and Smith, 2022).

Peer learning

The reverse 'follow-me' modelling method promotes a collaborative learning environment where both can learn from each other. The mentor can gain insights into the mentee's teaching style and approaches, while the mentee can benefit from the mentor's practical teaching expertise and feedback (Schon, 1987).

Skill development

Through using the method, the mentee can practice and refine their teaching skills in a real-time, practical environment that is also constructive and supportive. This hands-on experience can help the mentee build confidence, develop effective teaching strategies, and enhance their overall teaching proficiency (Robinson and Hobson, 2017).

Team-teaching

Team-teaching episodes are inspired by Roth and Kleiner's research (1998) and suggest that mentees and mentees team-teaching of any length of time can add layers of awareness that are not possible during solo teaching episodes. He found that both members of the pair had to share authority and be sensitive to what was happening in the classroom from both teacher's and student's perspectives. This mode of teaching appears to be especially promising during inquiry instruction because mentors are immediately available to aid and advise their trainees.

Some of the benefits for mentors and mentees of using the team-teaching strategy include the following (1998).

Shared expertise

The team-teaching approach allows both the mentor and the mentee to bring their unique strengths, experiences, and perspectives to the teaching process. This collaboration can lead to a more comprehensive and holistic approach to instruction (Robson and Mtika, 2017).

Professional growth

It can provide mentees with opportunities to learn from the mentor's expertise while also contributing their own ideas and innovations. Mentors, in turn, can benefit from fresh perspectives and insights shared by mentees.

Immediate feedback

They can provide each other with real-time feedback and support. This collaborative approach fosters a culture of continuous improvement and mutual learning which can enhance student engagement by incorporating diverse teaching styles and strategies. The presence of both in the classroom can provide students with varied instructional approaches and personalised attention (Sachs, Fisher and Cannon, 2011).

Building trust and rapport

Collaborating can strengthen the mentor-mentee relationship by fostering trust, open communication, and shared goals. This collaborative experience can deepen the professional bond between them.

Mentor and mentee joint reflection exercise

With your mentee, schedule the three different episodes of mentor and mentee co-teaching, and with your mentee, complete the table below.

Co-teaching approaches	Mentor reflections	Mentee reflections
Follow-me		
Reverse-follow-me		
Team-teaching		

References

Aderibigbe, S., Gray, D.S. and Colucci-Gray, L. (2018) 'Understanding the nature of mentoring experiences between teachers and student teachers', *International Journal of Mentoring and Coaching in Education*, 7(1), pp. 54–71.

Aguirre-Garzón, E.A., Ubaque-Casallas, D., Salazar-Sierra, A. and López-Hurtado, M.E. (2022) 'Learnings on conflicts and reconciliations in EFL preservice teachers' pedagogical practicum', *Íkala, Revista De Lenguaje Y Cultura*, 27(3), pp. 646–662. doi:10.17533/udea.ikala.v27n3a04.

Alnajjar, K. (2022) 'Can new teachers learn teaching by reciprocating?', *International Journal of Health Sciences*, 6(S6), pp. 6294–6311. doi:10.53730/ijhs.v6nS6.10987.

Bereiter, C. and Bird, M. (1985) 'Use of thinking aloud in identification and teaching of reading comprehension strategies', *Cognition and Instruction*, 2(2), pp. 131–156. http://www.jstor.org/stable/3233543.

Brondyk, S. and Searby, L. (2013) 'Best practices in mentoring: complexities and possibilities', *International Journal of Mentoring and Coaching in Education*, 2(3), pp.189–203.

Chan, C.K. and Luo, J. (2022) 'Towards an inclusive student partnership: rethinking mentors' disposition and holistic competency development in near-peer mentoring.' *Teaching in Higher Education*, 27(7), pp. 874–891.

Edwards, A. and Protheroe, L. (2004) 'Teaching by proxy: understanding how mentors are positioned in partnerships', *Oxford Review of Education*, 30(2), pp. 183–197.

Holland, E. (2018) 'Mentoring communities of practice: what's in it for the mentor?' *International Journal of Mentoring and Coaching in Education*, 7(2), pp. 110–126.

John, P.D. (2006) 'Lesson planning and the student teacher: re-thinking the dominant model', *Journal of Curriculum Studies*, 38(4), pp. 483–498.

Jones, J. and Smith, H.A. (2022) 'A comparative study of formal coaching and mentoring programmes in higher education', *International Journal of Mentoring and Coaching in Education*, 11(2), pp. 213–231.

Kuusela, H. and Paul, P. (2000) 'A comparison of concurrent and retrospective verbal protocol analysis', *American Journal of Psychology*, 113, pp. 387–404.

Lave, J. and Wenger, E. (1991) *Situated learning: legitimate peripheral participation*. Cambridge University Press.

Lofthouse, R. and Thomas, U. (2017) 'Concerning collaboration: teachers' perspectives on working in partnerships to develop teaching practices', *Professional Development in Education*, 43(1), pp. 36–56.

Manning, C. and Hobson, A.J. (2017) 'Judgemental and developmental mentoring in further education initial teacher education in England: mentor and mentee perspectives', *Research in Post-Compulsory Education*, 22(4), pp. 574–595.

Manzey, C. (2010) Exploring the role of a coteaching model of student teaching in supporting candidates learning to teach inquiry science. Unpublished Doctoral thesis. https://api.semanticscholar.org/CorpusID:61088621.

Martin, E.M. and Johnson, C. (2013) 'The where of Teaching May Matter as much as the how: Teaching Perspectives From Three Different Institutions', *High impact teaching for sport and exercise psychology educators*. Routledge. pp. 238–250.

Mullen, C.A. (2000) 'Constructing co-mentoring partnerships: walkways we must travel', *Theory into Practice*, 39(1), pp. 4–11.

Mutton, T., Hagger, H. and Burn, K. (2011) 'Learning to plan, planning to learn: the developing expertise of beginning teachers', *Teachers and Teaching*, 17(4), pp. 399–416. doi:10.1080/13540602.2011.580516.

Mutton, T., Hagger, H. and Burn, K. (2011) 'Learning to plan, planning to learn: the developing expertise of beginning teachers', *Teachers and Teaching, Theory and Practice*, 17(4), pp. 399–416.

O'Leary, M. (2020) *Classroom observation*. Routledge.

Ortlieb, E. and Norris, M. (2012) 'Using the Think Aloud strategy to bolster reading comprehension of science concepts', *Current Issues in Education*, 15, pp. 1–10.

Oti, J. (2012) *Mentoring and coaching in further education. The Sage handbook of mentoring and coaching in education*. Sage Publications, pp. 354–367.

Powell, C. (2023) 'Co-planning lessons: experiences of mentors and beginning teachers', *LINK*, 7(1).

Pylman, S. (2016) 'Reflecting on talk: a mentor teacher's gradual release in co-planning', *The New Educator*, 12(1), pp. 48–66.

Pylman, S. and Bell, J. (2021) 'Levels of mentor questioning in assisted performance: what mentors should ask student teachers while co-planning,' *Mentoring and Tutoring: Partnership in Learning*. doi: 10.1080/13611267.2021.1986796.

Redfern, A. (2020) *The essential guide to classroom practice*. Routledge.

Robinson, C. and Hobson, A. (2017) Mentor education and development in the Further Education sector in England. Available from https://www.brighton.ac.uk/education-research-centre/research-projects/mentor-education-and-development-in-the-further-education-sector-in-england.aspx.

Robson, D. and Mtika, P. (2017) 'Newly qualified teachers' professional learning through practitioner enquiry: investigating partnership-based mentoring', *International Journal of Mentoring and Coaching in Education*, 6(3), pp. 242–260.

Roth, G. and Kleiner, A. (1998) 'Developing organizational memory through learning histories', *Organizational Dynamics*, 2, pp. 43–60.

Sachs, G., Fisher, T. and Cannon, J. (2011) 'Collaboration, mentoring and co-teaching in teacher education', *Journal of Teacher Education for Sustainability*, 13(2), p. 70.

Schön, D.A. (1987) *Educating the reflective practitioner: toward a new design for teaching and learning in the professions*. Jossey-Bass.

Schwille, S.A. (2008) 'The professional practice of mentoring', *American Journal of Education*, 115, pp. 139–167. doi:10.1086/590678.

Shanks, R. (2017) 'Mentoring beginning teachers: professional learning for mentees and mentors', *International Journal of Mentoring and Coaching in Education*, 6(3), pp. 158–163.

Tedder, M. and Lawy, R. (2009) 'The pursuit of "excellence": mentoring in further education initial teacher training in England', *Journal of Vocational Education and Training*, 61(4), pp. 413–429.

Vygotsky, L.S. (1962) *Thought and language*. MIT Press.

Wexler, L.J. (2020) '"Empowering" instead of "crushing an idea": one student teacher/mentor teacher pair's story of learning and growing', *The New Educator*. doi:10.1080/1547688X.2020.1727594.

Willy, T. (2023) Lived experiences of teacher mentors; the importance of context and partnership in mentoring arrangements in the English school system. Doctoral dissertation. UCL (University College London).

Chapter 8

Lesson observations and feedback

Observations

Lesson observations are an important part of monitoring standards in institutions. Given that student experience of teaching and learning is a key issue in institutions, lesson observation can be an opportunity for trainees to receive advice and guidance, to provide material for professional reflection, and to identify areas for professional development and further training. It is normally part of the developmental processes of a training course and should be objective and transparent to those being observed (Hairon *et al.*, 2020).

Why it is important for a mentor to observe teaching practice

Observing a mentee's teaching practice is a fundamental aspect of effective mentoring in education. Through direct observation, mentors can gain valuable insights into their teaching techniques, classroom management skills, and overall delivery of instruction. By actively observing them in action, they can provide targeted feedback, tailored guidance, and constructive criticism to enhance the mentee's teaching abilities (Lindorff *et al.*, 2020).

Observation allows mentors to assess the mentee's strengths and areas for development, providing a comprehensive understanding of their teaching style and classroom dynamics. Observing teaching practice also enables them to identify effective teaching strategies that can be shared with the mentee to improve their effectiveness in class (Hairon *et al.*, 2020).

In addition, observation can help to foster a collaborative and supportive mentoring relationship, creating a platform for open communication, reflective discussions, and mutual learning opportunities. It can also allow a mentor to model best practices and demonstrate pedagogical techniques, inspiring mentees to enhance their teaching skills and professional growth. In essence, observing a mentee's teaching practice is essential for promoting continuous improvement, professional development, and effective mentorship in the educational setting (O'Leary, 2012).

DOI: 10.4324/9781003527374-8

In the initial observations, mentors should take into account the stage of development of the mentees they are observing. For example, trainees in the early stages of their development may be focussing their efforts on the 'basics' such as planning, communication, etc., particularly if they have no previous experience of teaching.

Preparing the mentee for the teaching observation

Mentally preparing a mentee for a teaching observation is crucial for several reasons, including:

- Anxiety reduction

    Teaching observations can be a stressful and anxiety-provoking experience for mentees, especially if they feel under pressure to perform well. Mentally preparing them can help alleviate anxiety, boost confidence, and create a more positive mindset leading up to the observation (Lofthouse and Wright, 2012).
- Confidence building

    It can enhance their confidence in their teaching abilities, lesson plans, and classroom management strategies. By discussing expectations, providing support, and offering reassurance, mentors can help mentees feel more self-assured and capable on the day of the observation (Page, 2016).
- Focus and preparedness

    It can also help them to maintain focus, stay organised, and be mentally prepared for the observation. Mentees who are mentally prepared are more likely to exhibit effective teaching practices, engage students successfully, and handle unexpected challenges with composure (2016).
- Professional development

    Teaching observations can be valuable opportunities for professional growth and development. Mentally preparing the mentee can help them approach the observation as a learning experience, reflect on their teaching practices, and identify areas for improvement. This proactive mindset can lead to a more meaningful and impactful observation process (Sullivan, 2024).

Some practical steps to prepare them for the observation process are as follows (Wragg, 1990):

- Establish clear expectations

    Clearly communicate the purpose, goals, and expectations of the teaching observation to the mentee. Explain what will be observed, evaluated, and discussed during the observation process.

    Provide guidance and support: Offer guidance and support to help them prepare for the observation. Share any relevant criteria, rubrics, or evaluation frameworks that will be used during the observation (Peake, 2006).

- Collaboratively set goals
  Work with the mentee to collaboratively set specific, achievable goals for the teaching observation. These should align with the mentee's professional development needs and focus on areas for growth and improvement.
- Conduct pre-observation meeting
  Hold a pre-observation meeting to discuss the upcoming observation, review the lesson plan or teaching materials, and address any questions or concerns the mentee may have. This meeting can help the mentee feel more prepared and confident (2006).
- Practice and rehearse
  Encourage them to practice and rehearse the lesson or teaching activities before the observation. Offer feedback, suggestions, and support to help the mentee refine their teaching strategies and delivery (O'Leary, 2016).
- Provide resources and tools
  Ensure that they have access to any necessary resources, materials, or technology needed for the observation. Provide guidance on how to effectively utilise these resources during the lesson.
- Create a supportive environment
  Foster a supportive and encouraging atmosphere for them during the observation. Reassure them that the observation is a learning opportunity and encourage them to approach it with a growth mindset (2016).
- Encourage reflection
  Encourage the mentee to reflect on their teaching practice before, during, and after the observation. Reflection can help them gain insights, identify areas for improvement, and make meaningful connections between theory and practice.

Self-reflection exercise

Preparing your mentee for an observation

Arrange two chairs. One for the mentor and one for the mentee.
Imagine that you are a mentee and are about to be observed for the first time.
Verbalise and write down all the feelings and thoughts that you are experiencing.
Note down all the key questions that you would like your mentor to answer about the observation.
Switch chairs and imagine you are now the mentor.
Note down your responses to the mentee's questions.
When you hold your next pre-observation meeting with your mentor, compare your notes with the actual responses of the mentee.

Summative and formative approaches to teaching observations

A summative observation

When conducting a summative teaching observation, a mentor typically approaches the process with the goal of evaluating the mentee's teaching performance against established criteria, standards, or expectations (OFSTED, 2018). Here are some steps a mentor may take when conducting a summative teaching observation:

- Pre-observation preparation
  They may ensure that the mentee is aware of the purpose and criteria for the summative observation. They may also review any specific standards, rubrics, or evaluation frameworks that will be used to assess the mentee's teaching performance.
- Observation
  During the observation, the mentor carefully assesses various aspects of the mentee's teaching practice, including instructional strategies, student engagement, classroom management, assessment techniques, and overall effectiveness. They may use a structured observation tool or checklist to document observations.
- Data collection
  They may gather data, evidence, and specific examples to support the evaluation of the mentee's teaching performance, taking note of strengths, areas for improvement, and any noteworthy observations during the lesson.
- Evaluation and feedback
  Following the observation, the mentor conducts a feedback session with the mentee to discuss observations, provide a comprehensive evaluation of their teaching performance, and offer constructive feedback. They will highlight areas of strength, identify areas for improvement, and suggest strategies for continued professional growth.
- Written feedback
  The mentor will probably provide a written summative evaluation report or feedback document summarising the observations, feedback, strengths, areas for improvement, and recommendations for the mentee's professional development. This written feedback can serve as a formal record of the observation and evaluation process. If the observation is done as part of a formal training programme, a grade may be generated which may form part of the wider course assessment programme (Cohen and Goldhaber, 2016).
- Goal setting and follow-up
  The mentor may go on to collaboratively set goals with the mentee based on the feedback provided during the summative observation and to discuss strategies for improvement, professional development opportunities, and

next steps for continued growth as a teacher. Follow up with the mentee to provide ongoing support and guidance in achieving their goals.

A formative observation

When transitioning from a summative to a formative approach in teaching observation, a mentor may adjust their methods, focus, and feedback strategies to map against the goals of formative assessment and ongoing professional development. Here are some ways a mentor may change their approach (Gitomer *et al.*, 2014):

- A shift in observation focus
  In a formative observation, the focus is on providing feedback for growth and improvement rather than evaluating performance against predetermined standards or criteria. The mentor may emphasise strengths, areas for growth, and support mechanisms to help the mentee develop as a classroom practitioner.
- Collaborative planning
  They may prioritise collaborative planning and goal-setting with the mentee to establish areas of focus, learning goals, and strategies for improvement. They may both co-create a plan for professional development based on identified needs and goals.
- Feedback delivery
  In formative observations, feedback is often more descriptive, specific, and supportive, focusing on actionable recommendations and resources to enhance teaching practices. The mentor may provide ongoing, timely feedback to address immediate needs and promote continuous improvement (2014).
- Reflective practice
  The mentor may encourage reflective practice by engaging the mentee in self-assessment, dialogue, and critical reflection on their teaching practice. They may also facilitate discussions on teaching strategies, student outcomes, classroom dynamics, and ways to refine instructional approaches.
- Professional growth
  The mentor may provide opportunities for the mentee to engage in additional professional development activities, workshops, readings, or peer observations to support their growth as an educator. The ultimate goal of a formative observation is to support the mentee's continuous improvement and professional development (Hudson, 2016).

A tip from a mentor

'When the observation has finished, ask your mentee whether they want you to write it up as a summative or a formative. If it went well, they may ask for the former; if it went badly, the latter'.

Quantitative and qualitative approaches to observation

A quantitative approach to a teaching observation

If a mentor adopts a quantitative approach to lesson observation, they will typically focus on quantifiable, measurable data and indicators to assess the quality of the lesson and provide feedback to the mentee. By focusing on quantitative data and observable behaviours, a mentor can provide specific, objective feedback to the mentee and identify areas for growth and development in their teaching practice (Wright, 2016). Some key aspects that a mentor may look for when using a quantitative approach to lesson observation include the following.

Time management

Observing how effectively the trainee manages time during the lesson, including pacing, transitions between activities, and adherence to the lesson plan schedule.

Student engagement

Quantifying student engagement levels, such as active participation, attentiveness, and responsiveness to questions and tasks throughout the lesson. This may involve using observation rubrics or checklists to track engagement indicators (2016).

Classroom management

Assessing the trainee's ability to maintain a positive and orderly classroom environment, including behaviour management strategies, student interactions, and response to disruptions.

Instructional strategies

Evaluating the variety and effectiveness of teaching strategies used during the lesson, such as differentiation, scaffolding, questioning techniques, and the use of technology. This may involve counting the number of times specific strategies are employed (van der Lans *et al.*, 2016).

Learning outcomes

Measuring student learning outcomes and achievement as a result of the lesson, such as completion of tasks, mastery of content, and demonstration of understanding. This could involve quantitative assessment data, quizzes, or performance measures (2016).

Use of resources

Monitoring how effectively the teacher utilises instructional resources, materials, and technology to support learning objectives and enhance student engagement in the lesson.

Feedback and reflection

Quantifying the quality and frequency of feedback provided by the teacher to students, as well as the teacher's own reflection on the lesson and opportunities for improvement.

A qualitative approach to teaching observation

If a mentor adopts a qualitative approach to lesson observation, they will focus on in-depth analysis, descriptive feedback, and qualitative data to assess the quality of the lesson and provide feedback to the mentee (Hudson, 2016). This qualitative approach will emphasise self-reflection, open-ended discussions, and dialogue aimed at enhancing teaching effectiveness and supporting continuous improvement. Some key aspects that a mentor may look for when using a qualitative approach to lesson observation include the following.

Teaching strategies and approaches

Observing and analysing the effectiveness of teaching strategies, instructional approaches, and pedagogical techniques employed during the lesson. This may involve reflecting on the rationale behind the strategies used and their impact on student learning.

Student engagement and interaction

Evaluating the level of student engagement, participation, and interaction during the lesson. This includes observing how well the teacher fosters a supportive learning environment, encourages student voice, and promotes active student involvement (O'Leary and Gewessler, 2014).

Differentiation and personalisation

Assessing the teacher's ability to differentiate instruction, address diverse student needs, and provide personalised learning opportunities tailored to individual students. This involves observing how the teacher adapts instruction to cater to varying learning styles, abilities, and interests.

Classroom environment and atmosphere

Analysing the overall classroom environment, atmosphere, and dynamics, including rapport between students and teacher, respect for diverse perspectives, and a sense of inclusivity and belonging (Ivanova, 2023).

Reflection and professional growth

Encouraging the teacher to reflect on their teaching practice, analyse the lesson's strengths and areas for improvement, and set goals for professional growth.

Examples of quantitative observation tools

These are often dubbed systematic observation approaches and have been developed for use in schools. They include the following:

- Flanders Interaction Analysis Categories (FIAC). It focusses on three domains of communication, Teacher Talk, Pupil Talk, and Silence (Sharma and Tiwari, 2021).
- Classroom Assessment Scoring System (CLASS) (Paro, Pianta and Stuhlman, 2004). The CLASS model links teacher behaviours with student achievement as part of an observational teacher-assessment tool. The model is about enhancing the overall relationship between teachers and students and their learning. It uses three broad domains of interactions among teachers and children: Emotional support, classroom organisation, and instructional support. Each domain includes several dimensions that relate to what is directly observed and indicators for each of the dimensions.
- International Comparison Analysis of Learning and Teaching (ICALT). ICALT can be described as an event-sampling observation instrument. There are six domains of behaviour which include: Safe learning climate, classroom management, clear instruction, activating teaching methods, learning strategies, and differentiation. Observers rate the items within these domains on a four-point scale (1 = mostly weak; 2 = more often weak than strong; 3 = more often strong than weak; 4 = mostly strong) (Chun, Lee and Kim, 2023).
- Mathematical Quality of Instruction framework (MQI) (2018). This is a content-specific observational rubric. It focusses predominantly on the nature and quality of Mathematical content and instruction through the observation of teacher–student, teacher–content and student–content interactions (Charalambous and Litke, 2018).

The strengths of using a quantitative observation tool

Using a quantitative observation tool in lesson observation offers several strengths that can provide valuable insights into teaching practices and student engagement. Some of the key strengths include:

- Objectivity

    Quantitative observation tools provide a structured framework for assessing specific behaviours, actions, and outcomes, which can help minimise

subjective biases in the observation process. The use of quantifiable data and indicators allows for a more objective evaluation of teaching performance (Cohen and Goldhaber, 2016).
- Measurable Data

    Quantitative tools allow for the collection of measurable data and statistics, such as frequency counts, timings, and ratings, which can be used to track trends, patterns, and progress over time. This data can help mentors and teachers identify areas of strength and improvement (Gibson, 2006).
- Standardisation

    Quantitative observation tools typically have standardised criteria, rubrics, and rating scales, which promote consistency and reliability in the evaluation process. This standardisation ensures that all observers are assessing teaching practices and student engagement using a common set of criteria (OFSTED, 2019).
- Comparative Analysis

    Quantitative data collected through observation tools can facilitate comparative analysis between different lessons, teachers, or classrooms. This comparative analysis can help mentors identify effective teaching practices, pinpoint areas for improvement, and make data-informed decisions.
- Efficiency

    Quantitative observation tools can streamline the observation process by focusing on specific behaviours, actions, and outcomes. By using a structured tool with clear indicators, mentors can efficiently assess teaching performance, provide targeted feedback, and track progress over time (Mikeska *et al.*, 2019).
- Accountability

    The use of quantitative observation tools promotes accountability by establishing clear expectations, goals, and criteria for effective teaching practices. Teachers and mentors can use the data collected through observation tools to reflect on performance, set goals for improvement, and demonstrate progress.

The weaknesses of using a quantitative observation tool

While quantitative observation tools offer several benefits, they also have some weaknesses that should be considered when using them in lesson observation. Some of the weaknesses include:

- Limited Context

    Quantitative observation tools may focus on measurable aspects of teaching practice, such as behaviours, actions, or outcomes, but they may not capture the rich context, nuances, or complexity of the teaching and learning process. This limited context may overlook important qualitative aspects of teaching effectiveness (Ivanova, 2023).
- Lack of Depth

    Quantitative tools are often focused on collecting numerical data or ratings, which may not provide a comprehensive understanding of the

underlying reasons, motivations, or strategies behind observed behaviours. They may lack the depth needed to uncover underlying issues or opportunities for improvement (Cohen and Goldhaber, 2016).
- Narrow Focus

  Quantitative observation tools are typically designed to assess specific teaching practices or student behaviours, which may result in a narrow focus that overlooks other important factors contributing to effective teaching and learning, such as student engagement, motivation, or socio-emotional dynamics (2023).
- Reliance on Observation Skills

  The effectiveness of quantitative observation tools depends on the observer's ability to accurately collect and interpret data. If observers lack training, experience, or reliability in conducting observations, the quality of the data collected may be compromised (Mikeska et al., 2019).
- Potential for Misinterpretation

  Quantitative data collected through observation tools can be misinterpreted or misused if not analysed and interpreted correctly. Misinterpretation of data may lead to inaccurate judgements, biased assessments, or ineffective feedback.

Examples of qualitative approaches

There are three types of qualitative approaches to observation: Structured, Semi-structured, and Unstructured (narrative).

- Structured teaching observations

A structured teaching observation is a systematic and intentional process in which an observer observes a teacher's instructional practices and interactions with students using a predetermined framework or set of criteria. The structured observation typically involves the use of a standardised observation tool, checklist, rubric, or protocol to guide the observation process and assess specific aspects of teaching performance (O'Leary, 2012).

In a structured teaching observation, the observer focuses on observing and documenting specific behaviours, practices, strategies, and outcomes during a classroom lesson or instructional session. The structured observation tool outlines the criteria for effective teaching, student engagement, classroom management, assessment practices, and other relevant factors that contribute to successful teaching and learning.

Strengths and weaknesses of using a structured approach to teaching observations

Using a structured approach to teaching observations by a mentor offers several strengths and weaknesses that can influence the effectiveness of the observation process. Here are some key points for each.

Strengths

Consistency

A structured approach ensures that all teaching observations are conducted using a common framework, criteria, and set of guidelines, promoting consistency in the evaluation process. This is also vital if the observations need to be mapped across to meet the assessment criteria of a teaching qualification

Clear criteria

The use of a structured observation tool provides clear criteria and benchmarks for assessing teaching performance, making it easier for mentors to evaluate and provide feedback to the mentee (Lindorff *et al.*, 2020).

Objective assessment

They allow for a more objective assessment of teaching practices, as observations are based on observable behaviours and evidence rather than subjective opinions.

Data collection

Structured observations enable mentors to collect data on teaching practices, student engagement, and learning outcomes, which can be used to track progress, identify trends, and make data-informed decisions (Adelman, Adelman and Walker, 2003).

Professional development

By following a structured approach, mentors can identify specific areas for improvement, offer targeted feedback, and support the professional development of the mentee.

Weaknesses

Limited flexibility

It may limit the flexibility of the observation process, as mentors may be required to follow a predetermined framework that may not capture all aspects of effective teaching.

Overemphasis on compliance

A rigid adherence to a structured observation tool can shift the focus towards compliance with criteria rather than fostering a reflective and growth-oriented approach to teaching improvement (Charalambous and Litke, 2018).

Time-consuming

Implementing a structured approach to teaching observations may require more time and effort from both mentors and mentees, particularly in terms of preparing observation tools, conducting observations, and providing feedback.

One-size-fits-all

Structured observation tools may not always be adaptable to the unique needs, contexts, and teaching styles of individual mentees, potentially limiting their effectiveness in supporting diverse educators.

Lack of nuance

A structured approach may lack the nuance and depth required to capture the full complexity of teaching practices, student interactions, and classroom dynamics, potentially leading to oversimplified or superficial observations (Cameron, 2014).

This is an example of a structured observation feedback form based on one used in an FE college in the UK for assessing new teachers. It is mainly quantitative and based on four domains. It breaks down each domain into seven specific subcategories for a more detailed assessment of teaching performance. The quantitative rating in percentage terms allows for a numerical evaluation, while the qualitative feedback offers additional context and suggestions for improvement.

Observer: *Teacher:* *Date:* *Group:* *Duration:*	*Percentages*
Domain 1: Planning Lesson Objectives: Alignment with Curriculum Standards: Differentiation for Diverse Learners: Materials and Resources: Timeliness and Organisation: Assessment Alignment: Adaptation to Student Needs:	25%
Domain 2: Teaching Engaging Instructional Strategies: Clear Communication: Classroom Management: Student Engagement: Questioning Techniques: Technology Integration: Time Management:	25%

(Continued)

Observer: Teacher: Date: Group: Duration:	Percentages
Domain 3: Learning Opportunities for Active Learning: Feedback and Support: Group Work/Collaboration: Differentiated Instruction: Student Participation: Critical Thinking Skills: Feedback to Teachers:	25%
Domain 4: Assessment Variety of Assessment Methods: Alignment with Objectives: Timely Feedback to Students: Authentic Assessment: Assessment for Learning: Assessment of Learning: Assessment Data Analysis:	25%
Overall grade:	
Overall Comments: Strengths: Areas for Growth:	
Observer's Signature: Date:	

Mentee		**Date:**	
College		**Subject:**	Health and Social Care
Group/Level:	BTEC Level Two	**Number in Class:**	7
Topic:	Liaising with carers	**Lesson Time:**	9.30–10.30
Observer:		**Joint Observer:**	

Focus for observation
Classroom management (PS13). Building relationships with students (PS14)

Strengths and what went well?
Clear logical structure to the class – developing narrative structure. Supported by a clearly designed PowerPoint. PS15
Good use of differentiated questions and answers with clear verbal praise and verbal feedback. PS16
Good use of encouraging and motivating language used at times. PS4
Clear awareness of different learners' needs, applying knowledge of SEN at times to scaffold individual learning. PS3 and PS11
Clear promotion and support of positive behaviour and confident demeanour. PS13 and PS14
Clear promoting and supporting positive learners.

(Continued)

Areas to develop?
The teacher might have used visual examples such as mind maps and graphics to support learning more frequently. PS16
Might also have used a range of examples when explaining aspects support drawn from own knowledge and experience working in the industry. PS8
Tasks might have been broken down into smaller ones and then peer reviewed. PS19
Challenge could have been raised in places by asking students to provide their own examples from placements and develop them in discussions. PS3
Sometimes answers given to questions before the group had time to struggle with them. PS19
Might have used digital technology in places to enhance learners' engagement and to provide a greater range of examples.

- Semi-structured observations

A semi-structured teaching observation is a type of observation where the observer follows a flexible framework or guide while observing a teacher's instructional practices and interactions with students. Unlike a fully structured observation, which typically involves a predetermined set of criteria or a checklist, a semi-structured observation allows for some level of adaptability and customisation based on the specific context, goals, and focus of the observation.

In a semi-structured observation, the observer may have a general framework or outline to guide the observation process, but there is room for flexibility to explore additional aspects of teaching and learning that may emerge during the observation (Granström, Kikas and Eisenschmidt, 2023). The observer may focus on specific areas of interest or priority while also remaining open to unexpected observations or interactions that could provide valuable insights into the teacher's instructional effectiveness.

During a semi-structured teaching observation, the observer may use a combination of predetermined criteria or guidelines along with open-ended questions, reflective prompts, or follow-up probes to gather more in-depth information, clarify observations, and engage in meaningful dialogue with the teacher (Montgomery, 2002).

Strengths and weaknesses of using a semi-structured approach to teaching observations
Using a semi-structured approach to teaching observations by a mentor offers several strengths and weaknesses that can impact the effectiveness of the observation process. Here are some key points for each.

Strengths

Flexibility

A semi-structured approach allows the mentor to adapt the focus and direction of the observation based on the specific needs, goals, and priorities of the mentee. This flexibility enables a more personalised and tailored observation experience.

Holistic view

By incorporating both structured elements and flexibility, a semi-structured approach allows the mentor to capture a broader and more holistic view of the teacher's instructional practices, teaching style, and interactions with students (Montgomery, 2002).

Responsive feedback

It enables the mentor to provide timely and relevant feedback that is responsive to the specific context and observations made during the observation and to comment on the unpredictable. This can lead to more meaningful, relevant, and actionable feedback for the teacher.

Professional growth

The flexibility of a semi-structured approach can support the professional growth and development of the teacher by encouraging reflection, dialogue, and exploration of various aspects of teaching practice.

Weaknesses

Lack of standardisation

A semi-structured approach may lack the consistency and standardisation of a fully structured observation, leading to variability in the focus, criteria, and feedback provided by different mentors. This could potentially result in inconsistent evaluations. If the data is to be used as part of a teacher training assessment, it may be difficult to make it fit the assessment criteria (Puttick and Wynn, 2021).

Subjectivity

The flexibility in a semi-structured approach opens the door to subjective interpretations and biases in observation and feedback, as the mentor may emphasise certain aspects of teaching over others based on personal preferences or perspectives (Wragg, 1990).

Time and preparation

It may require more time and preparation on the part of the mentor to design, customise, and implement the observation process, leading to increased demands on resources and planning.

Focus and clarity

The flexible nature of a semi-structured approach may sometimes result in a lack of clear focus or direction in the observation, making it challenging to provide targeted feedback or address specific areas for improvement (Cameron, 2014).

> Here is an example of a semi-structured summative assessment feedback form. In this example, all comments have been mapped to Education and Training Foundation Professional Standards (et-foundation.co.uk). It is typical of a summative feedback form used in teaching qualifications at Further Education level in the UK.
>
> **Mentee**
> **Date:**
> **College**
> **Subject**: Health and Social Care
> **Group/Level**: BTEC Level Two
> **Number in Class**: 7
> **Topic**: Liaising with carers
> **Lesson Time**: 9.30–10.30
> **Observer: Joint Observer**
>
> **Focus for observation**
>
> Classroom management (PS13). Building relationships with students (PS14),
>
> **Strengths and what went well**
>
> Clear logical structure to the class – developing narrative structure. Supported by a clearly designed PowerPoint. PS15
> Good use of differentiated questions and answers with clear verbal praise and verbal feedback. PS16
> Good use of encouraging and motivating language used at times. PS4

Clear awareness of different learners' needs, applying knowledge of SEN at times to scaffold individual learning. PS3 and PS11

Clear promoting and supporting of positive behaviour and confident demeanour. PS13 and PS14

Clear promoting and supporting positive learner (PS11).

Areas to develop

The teacher might have used visual examples such as mind maps and graphics to support learning more frequently. PS16

Might also have used a range of examples when explaining aspects of support drawn from own knowledge and experience working in the industry. PS8

Tasks might have been broken down into smaller ones and then peer reviewed. PS19

Challenge could have been raised in places by asking students to provide their own examples from placements and develop them in discussions. PS3

Sometimes answers given to questions before the group had time to struggle with them. PS19

Might have used digital technology in places to enhance learners' engagement and to provide a greater range of examples.

Targets for improvement

Targets should be SMART, fit for purpose, trainee and student progress driven, and written using the language of the Professional Standards and grade descriptors and used to inform the targets set in the weekly progress meeting.

Suggested training activities/actions to be taken to support progress towards targets

1. Use more visual examples which will enable you to select and use digital technologies safely and more effectively to promote learning. This will be more effective than using handwritten diagrams on the whiteboard (PS16).
2. Observe mentor and experiment with different applications (PS2).
3. Develop and update knowledge of your subject specialism and use this to embed your lessons with more examples drawn from a wider range of literature and from your own professional practice (PS8).
4. Consult BTEC reading lists for suggestions and discuss with your mentor how you can use your own working experience more effectively (PS3).

5 Break down the longer tasks into short ones by asking students to work on sections of a narrative and then peer review them. This would enable you to apply appropriate and fair methods of assessment and provide constructive and timely feedback to support learning and achievement (PS19).
6 Review your previous research on Assessment and Feedback and research on chunking (Dylan Wiliam, for example).

- Unstructured teaching observations

An unstructured teaching observation is a type of classroom observation that involves the observer watching a teacher's instructional practices and interactions with students without a specific framework, checklist, or predetermined criteria. In an unstructured observation, the observer does not follow a set agenda or guidelines but instead observes the teaching and learning process in a more open-ended and flexible manner.

The goal of an unstructured teaching observation is to gain a comprehensive and naturalistic view of the teacher's classroom practices, teaching style, student engagement, and overall dynamics without imposing a specific evaluation framework (Cockburn, 2005).

During an unstructured observation, the observer may focus on capturing the overall teaching environment, verbal and nonverbal communication between the teacher and students, instructional strategies used, student responses, classroom management, and other relevant aspects of teaching and learning. The observer may take detailed notes, make observations, and reflect on the interactions and dynamics happening in the classroom without predetermined expectations or biases.

Strengths and weaknesses of using an unstructured approach to lesson observations

Using an unstructured approach to teaching observations by a mentor offers several strengths and weaknesses that can impact the effectiveness of the observation process. Here are some key points for each.

Strengths

Flexibility

An unstructured approach allows the mentor to have the freedom and flexibility to observe various aspects of teaching practice and classroom dynamics without being constrained by predetermined criteria or checklists. This flexibility can lead to a more authentic and naturalistic observation experience.

Naturalistic insights

Observing teaching practices in an unstructured manner can provide the mentor with naturalistic insights into the teacher's instructional strategies, interactions with students, classroom management, and overall teaching style. This can lead to a more comprehensive understanding of the teacher's strengths and areas for growth (Sullivan, 2024).

Personalised feedback

The open-ended nature of unstructured observations allows the mentor to provide personalised and context-specific feedback to the teacher based on their unique observations and insights. This personalised feedback can be tailored to address specific strengths and areas for improvement (Archer *et al.*, 2016).

Relationship building

An unstructured approach to teaching observations can foster a more collaborative and trusting relationship between the mentor and the teacher as it allows for open communication, reflection, and dialogue about teaching practices (Gibson, 2006).

Weaknesses

Lack of consistency

The lack of a structured framework or checklist in unstructured observations may result in variability in the observations conducted by different mentors, leading to inconsistencies in evaluation and feedback. As in the case of semi-structured observations, if the data is to be used as part of a teacher training assessment, it may be difficult to make it fit the assessment criteria (Cockburn, 2005).

Subjectivity

Without clear criteria or guidelines, there is a risk of subjectivity in the observations and feedback provided by the mentor, which may limit the objectivity and reliability of the evaluation process.

Missed opportunities

An unstructured approach might overlook specific aspects of teaching practice or key areas of improvement that could have been identified with a more structured observation framework. This could limit the effectiveness of the observation process in supporting teacher growth (2006).

Limited actionability

The open-ended nature of unstructured observations may result in feedback that is less actionable or specific compared to structured observations, which could hinder the teacher's ability to make targeted improvements in their teaching practices.

> Here is an example of a completed unstructured observation feedback form.
> Where relevant, please offer feedback on some or all of these:
>
> a Assessing learners needs
> b Planning & preparing teaching
> c Developing & using range of methods
> d Managing the learning process
> e Providing learners with support
> f Assessing learning
> g Subject knowledge
>
> Observer's feedback
>
> 1 Supportive Presence: The teacher demonstrated an excellent supportive presence throughout the class, going round to each learner to aid and guide as needed. This approach ensured that every student felt valued and supported in their learning journey.
> 2 Interactive Questioning: The distribution of questions to elicit responses was an effective strategy employed by the teacher. By actively engaging students through questioning, the teacher encouraged participation to enrich the learning experience.
> 3 Motivational Techniques: The teacher employed motivational techniques to inspire students' interest and engagement in the lesson. Through enthusiastic delivery and relevant examples, students were encouraged to actively participate and invest in their learning.
> 4 Live Feedback: The teacher provided live feedback to students. This immediate feedback not only reinforces positive behaviours but also helps students correct mistakes promptly.
>
> Observer's suggestions/targets for improvement
>
> 1 Effective Pacing: While the lesson was well-structured, there were moments where pacing could have been improved. Some segments felt rushed.

> Adjusting the pace to allow for deeper exploration and understanding would have enhanced learning outcomes.
> 2 Scaffolding for Engagement: While the teacher effectively supported students individually, there's room to enhance scaffolding techniques to foster greater engagement across the class. Implementing varied instructional strategies, such as group activities or peer-to-peer learning, could further enhance student involvement and interaction.
>
> Signature of observer:

OFSTED criteria for teaching observations (2019)

Some mentors modify their formative approaches by using elements of OFSTED's approach to lesson observation to prepare their mentees for an OFSTED inspection. The OFSTED approach is specific and related to the purpose of inspection. The data gathered from individual observations is part of an overall judgement of the quality of teaching and learning across the school. Observations focus on teaching, which can be observed and measured, rather than learning, which cannot (OFSTED, 2019). Learners' attitudes towards learning and motivation are also avoided by them.

These criteria include the following:

- To set high expectations which inspire, motivate, and challenge pupils and manage behaviour effectively.
- To demonstrate good, detailed subject and curriculum knowledge which is communicated well at the appropriate age level.
- To plan and teach well-structured lessons which make accurate and productive use of assessment.
- To use assessment information which is gathered from looking at pupils' prior knowledge and understanding well as a result of useful feedback, written or oral, from teachers.
- To use relevant and appropriate resources during presentation to clarify meaning to pupils.
- To demonstrate good questioning skills.

Here's an analysis of some of the strengths and weaknesses of using them in mentor observations.

Strengths

- OFSTED criteria can provide a structured and standardised framework for observing and evaluating teaching which can help to ensure that

observations are guided by clear, evidence-based principles, which can help mentors focus on key aspects of effective teaching and learning.
- By using them mentors can ensure that their feedback aligns with national expectations and standards which can help trainees or early career teachers understand what is required to meet or exceed professional expectations (Adelman, Adelman and Walker, 2003).
- Because OFSTED places a strong emphasis on the impact of teaching on student progress and learning outcomes, this can encourage mentors to focus not just on teaching techniques but also on how these techniques translate into meaningful learning for students.
- The criteria can prompt detailed discussions between mentors and mentees about areas of strength and areas for improvement. This can facilitate reflective practice and targeted professional development (Peake, 2006).
- It can promote consistency in how observations are conducted and evaluated across different mentors or institutions, which can help standardise expectations and reduce subjectivity.
- Familiarity with OFSTED criteria can prepare mentees for future inspections or performance evaluations and help them to understand what inspectors are likely to focus on and how to meet those expectations.

Weaknesses

- Applying formal OFSTED criteria in mentoring situations can create unnecessary pressure for mentees, especially if they are still in the early stages of their development. This may discourage experimentation and risk-taking in their teaching.
- The criteria are designed for inspection purposes, not developmental mentoring. Their use in mentor observations risks shifting the focus away from professional growth and onto meeting external standards, which may hinder genuine learning (O'Leary, 2016).
- They may not always be appropriate for the developmental needs of mentees. For example, they may not account for the specific challenges faced by trainee teachers or allow for incremental progress over time (2016).
- While student outcomes are important, focusing too heavily on them during mentoring may overlook the process of learning to teach and stifle experimentation and creativity. Mentees need space to develop foundational skills before they can consistently achieve strong student outcomes.
- Arguably, mentoring is most effective when it is tailored to the unique needs of the mentee. Rigid adherence to OFSTED criteria may reduce the mentor's ability to provide personalised, context-specific guidance (Page, 2016).
- They tend to emphasise formal evaluation, which can create a one-way, judgemental process. This may undermine the collaborative, developmental nature of mentoring, where dialogue and trust are key to promote gradual, sustainable growth over time (2016).

Validity and reliability of teaching observations

Teaching observations play a crucial role in assessing and improving the quality of instruction in educational settings. However, there are several contentious issues related to the validity and reliability of teaching observations that impact their effectiveness and credibility.

One major contentious issue is subjectivity in the observation process. The subjective nature of observations can lead to biases, personal interpretations, and differences in judgement among observers, raising concerns about the validity of the feedback provided. Observers may have varying perspectives on what constitutes effective teaching practices, leading to inconsistencies in evaluations (van der Lans *et al.*, 2016).

Another contentious issue is the reliability of teaching observations. Reliability refers to the consistency and stability of observation results when conducted multiple times or by different observers. Factors such as observer training, observation instruments, and contextual factors can influence the reliability of observations. Lack of standardised observation protocols, unclear criteria for evaluation, and differences in observer expertise can all contribute to inconsistencies in feedback and ratings, undermining the reliability of the observation process (2016).

Additionally, there are challenges related to the limited scope and duration of observations, such as the focus on visible behaviours rather than underlying pedagogical principles, and the lack of opportunities for teacher reflection and dialogue following observations. All these can impede the validity and reliability of teaching observations.Addressing these contentious issues requires clear criteria for evaluation, comprehensive training for observers, ongoing feedback and calibration processes, and a focus on collaborative and formative approaches to observation and feedback (O'Leary, 2012).

Impact of the Hawthorne effect on validity and reliability of an observation

The Hawthorne effect is a phenomenon in which individuals modify their behaviour or performance in response to being observed, leading to an artificial improvement or change in their actions. In the context of teaching observations, the Hawthorne effect can have a significant impact on the reliability of the observation process.

When teachers are aware that they are being observed, they may alter their teaching practices, behaviour, or interactions with students in an attempt to present themselves in a favourable light or meet perceived expectations. This behaviour change can be subconscious or intentional, but it can distort the observer's perception of the teacher's usual instructional practices and effectiveness (O'Leary, 2020).

The Hawthorne effect can create a false impression of the teacher's performance during the observation period, leading to inflated ratings or feedback that do not accurately reflect their everyday teaching practices. Observers may observe improved engagement, more effective lesson delivery, or better classroom management during the observation due to the teachers' heightened awareness and effort, masking any underlying issues or areas for improvement (Page, 2016).

As a result, the reliability of the teaching observation may be compromised, as the observed behaviour may not be representative of the teacher's typical performance or instructional practices. The artificial changes in behaviour induced by the Hawthorne effect can distort the observer's assessment and lead to inaccuracies in the evaluation process (Lofthouse and Wright, 2012). To mitigate the impact of the Hawthorne effect on the reliability of teaching observations, observers should be mindful of the phenomenon and try to minimise its influence.

Minimising the impact of the Hawthorne effect

This is crucial to ensuring the accuracy and reliability of the feedback provided to educators. Several strategies can be employed to reduce the impact of this phenomenon and mitigate its influence on the observation process.

One approach is to establish a culture of trust and transparency between observers and teachers. By fostering open communication and emphasising the purpose of observations as a tool for professional growth rather than evaluation or judgement, teachers may feel less pressured to modify their behaviour during observations (Wragg, 1990).

Providing clear guidelines and expectations for the observation process can also help mitigate the Hawthorne effect. By communicating specific criteria, objectives, and focus areas for the observation in advance, teachers can align their efforts with the intended goals of the observation, reducing the likelihood of artificial changes in their behaviour.

> **A tip from a mentor**
>
> Try asking your mentee which areas you should focus on during the observations; this will help you build SMARTer targets after the session
>
> Conducting unannounced or surprise observations can help minimise the Hawthorne effect. By catching teachers off guard, observers are more likely to capture a true and authentic snapshot of the teacher's typical instructional practices and classroom dynamics. Unannounced observations encourage teachers to maintain consistency in their teaching approaches and provide a more accurate reflection of their day-to-day performance.

Finally, ensuring that observers are trained and experienced in conducting objective and unbiased observations is essential for minimising the Hawthorne effect. Observers should be knowledgeable about effective teaching practices, familiar with the observation tool or rubric being used, and equipped to provide constructive feedback that is focused on professional development and growth (Farrell, 2011).

There are also other ways to maintain objectivity and manage the observer effect. These can include using multiple sources of data, conducting unannounced or frequent observations, and focusing on the consistency of performance over time rather than isolated observations. Additionally, establishing trust and rapport with teachers can help create a more authentic observation experience and reduce the likelihood of artificial changes in behaviour.

Minimising the Hawthorne effect

Self-reflection activity

Here are some strategies to minimise its effects on the teaching observation.

- Develop a rapport with your mentee.
- Discuss aims and objectives of the observation in depth with your mentee before the observations.
- Use small ad hoc observations to build up the mentee's confidence.
- Brief students in advance to put them at ease and also to encourage them to be their usual selves when your mentee is being observed.
- Conduct some of the observations online via Zoom or MS Teams (Ceven, 2012).
- Film the session without your presence and assess it afterwards (Cooper, 2015).

The representativeness of a teaching observation

The representativeness of a teaching observation refers to the extent to which the observed teaching practices and interactions accurately reflect the teacher's typical performance and instructional approaches. Several factors can impact the representativeness of a teaching observation, raising concerns about the validity and reliability of the feedback provided (Archer *et al.*, 2016).

One issue related to representativeness is the timing and frequency of observations. A single observation conducted at a specific time may not capture the full range of a teacher's instructional practices or the variability in student learning experiences. To address this issue, multiple observations over different days, times, and class periods can provide a more comprehensive and representative view of the teacher's teaching effectiveness.

Another challenge to representativeness is the selection of observation criteria and focus areas. If the observation instrument or rubric used does not encompass all relevant dimensions of effective teaching or fails to align with the teacher's instructional goals and strategies, the observation may not accurately capture the teacher's strengths and areas for growth. Ensuring that the observation criteria are comprehensive, relevant, and tailored to the specific context can enhance the representativeness of the observation (2016).

Additionally, the observer's expertise, familiarity with the teacher's instructional practices, and potential biases can impact the representativeness of the observation. An observer who lacks subject-specific knowledge or experience in the observed teacher's grade level or content area may not fully appreciate the nuances of the instructional strategies employed (Gibson, 2006).

Mentor subjectivity and bias

This is a significant variable in the observation of teaching. It raises the question, 'Do we only see what we are looking for and only look for what we know about?' There is also the question about whether it is easier to observe using a qualitative or a quantitative approach? All our interpretations can be impacted upon by our individual learning preferences, the observation instrument being used, the purpose of the observation, and whether we are observing high inference factors, such as independent thinking, or low, such as pace of less and projection of voice (Hudson, 2016).

Mentor subjectivity and bias can have a significant impact on the reliability and validity of observation results in various contexts, including research, education, and professional practice. Mentor subjectivity refers to the unique perspective, experiences, and attitudes that mentors bring to their observations, shaping how they perceive, interpret, and evaluate observed behaviours, interactions, or outcomes. When they bring their personal beliefs, assumptions, and preferences into the observation process, their subjective interpretations and judgements can influence the data collected and the conclusions drawn (Lofthouse and Wright, 2012).

Bias, on the other hand, refers to systematic errors or distortions in the observation process, resulting from preconceptions, prejudices, or unconscious assumptions that affect the objectivity and accuracy of the data. Mentor bias can manifest in various forms, such as confirmation bias, halo effect, and or cultural bias:

- Confirmation bias
    Confirmation bias, a cognitive bias where individuals selectively focus on information that aligns with their pre-existing beliefs or expectations, can

significantly impact the reliability of observation results when exhibited by a mentor. In the context of mentoring and observation, confirmation bias can lead mentors to unconsciously seek out, interpret, or remember information that confirms their prior assumptions or biases, while disregarding or downplaying evidence that contradicts them. This biased approach to observation can distort their perception of the mentee's performance, behaviour, or progress, potentially leading to inaccurate assessments and unreliable feedback (Montgomery, 2002).

When a mentor succumbs to confirmation bias, they may selectively notice and emphasise instances that support their existing beliefs about the mentee's abilities or qualities, while dismissing or ignoring evidence that challenges these beliefs. This can result in an incomplete and skewed representation of the mentee's performance, as well as a lack of objectivity in their observations and evaluations (O'Leary, 2020). It can also reinforce stereotypes, assumptions, or prejudices held by the mentor, influencing their interpretations of the mentee's behaviour and potentially leading to unfair or biased assessments.

Ultimately, it undermines the trustworthiness and credibility of observation results, compromising the validity and reliability of the feedback provided to the mentee. To mitigate its impact on observation results, mentors must strive to remain open-minded, self-aware, and reflexive in their approach to observation, actively challenging their own assumptions and seeking diverse perspectives to ensure the objectivity and accuracy of their assessments (Peake, 2006).

- Halo and the Horn effects

  The Halo and Horn effects are cognitive biases that can significantly impact the reliability of observation results when exhibited by a mentor in a mentoring relationship. The Halo effect occurs when a mentor forms a favourable overall impression of a mentee based on a single positive trait, behaviour, or characteristic. This can lead them to overlook or downplay the mentee's flaws, mistakes, or areas for improvement, resulting in an inflated and biased assessment of the mentee's performance. It can distort the mentor's perception of the mentee's abilities and potential, leading to exaggerated praise, lenient feedback, and inaccurate evaluations. As a result, the reliability of observation results may be compromised, as the mentor's positive bias may overshadow objective observations and critical feedback (Hudson, 2016).

  Conversely, the Horn effect, also known as the Devil effect, occurs when a mentor forms a negative overall impression of a mentee based on a single negative trait, behaviour, or characteristic. This bias can lead them to focus excessively on the mentee's shortcomings, mistakes, or perceived weaknesses, while ignoring or discounting their strengths, achievements, or positive qualities. The Horn effect can skew the mentor's perception of the mentee's performance, leading to overly critical feedback, unjustified judgements, and inaccurate assessments. This bias can undermine the reliability of observation results, as the mentor's negative bias may overshadow genuine progress or potential displayed by the mentee. In both cases, the Halo and Horn effects can introduce subjectivity, inconsistency, and inaccuracies into the observation process, affecting the validity and trustworthiness of the mentor's evaluations and feedback (2016).

- Cultural bias

Cultural bias in a mentor can have a significant impact on the reliability of observation results in a mentoring relationship. Cultural bias refers to the tendency to interpret behaviours, interactions, or outcomes based on one's own cultural norms, values, beliefs, or stereotypes, often leading to subjective judgements and distorted perceptions. When a mentor exhibits cultural bias in their observations, they may unintentionally apply their own cultural lens to evaluate the mentee's performance, behaviour, or progress, potentially leading to misinterpretations, misjudgements, and unreliable feedback (Apter, Sulla and Swinson, 2020).

Cultural bias can manifest in various forms, such as ethnocentrism (viewing one's own culture as superior), stereotyping (generalising assumptions about individuals based on cultural identities), or cultural incompetence (lack of understanding or sensitivity towards cultural differences). When a mentor's cultural bias influences their observations, it can impact the accuracy, fairness, and objectivity of their assessments, as well as the quality of feedback provided to the mentee (Adelman, Adelman and Walker, 2003).

Cultural bias may result in them overlooking or misinterpreting culturally specific behaviours, misattributing motivations, or misjudging the mentee's competencies, potentially leading to biased evaluations and assessments. Moreover, cultural bias may hinder effective communication, trust, and rapport between the mentor and mentee, affecting the overall mentoring relationship and the mentee's development (O'Leary, 2016). Addressing cultural bias in mentoring requires self-awareness, cultural sensitivity, and openness to diverse perspectives in order to promote fair, equitable, and culturally responsive observations and feedback.

Self-reflection exercise

Exploring unconscious biases
  Objective
  The objective of this self-reflection activity is to help mentors examine and identify their unconscious biases towards their mentees, raise

awareness of potential biases, and develop strategies to mitigate their impact on the mentoring relationship.

1 Set aside dedicated time and a quiet, reflective space for this activity.
2 Use a journal, notebook, or digital note-taking tool to record your reflections.
3 Reflect on the following prompts and questions:

- What are some assumptions or stereotypes I hold about my mentee based on their background, identity, or experiences?
- Have I ever made snap judgements about my mentee without fully understanding their perspective or context?
- How do my personal beliefs, values, or cultural norms influence my interactions with my mentee?
- Have I ever experienced discomfort or resistance when my mentee challenges my perspectives or approaches?
- In what ways might my unconscious biases impact my feedback, assessments, or decision-making processes regarding my mentee?

4 Analyse any patterns, recurring thoughts, or emotional reactions that arise during this reflection process.
5 Consider how your unconscious biases may affect your mentoring relationship and the mentee's growth and development.
6 Identify specific strategies or actions you can take to mitigate the impact of your biases:

- Seek diverse perspectives and feedback from colleagues or mentors.
- Attend workshops or training on unconscious bias awareness and cultural competence.
- Engage in reflective practices and self-awareness exercises regularly.
- Foster open communication and trust with your mentee to address biases openly.

7 Set goals for ongoing self-reflection and improvement in addressing unconscious biases in your mentoring practice.
8 Reflect on the insights gained from this activity and consider how you can apply them in your mentoring interactions with your mentee.

References

Adelman, C., Adelman, C. and Walker, R. (2003) *A guide to classroom observation.* Routledge.
Apter, B., Sulla, F. and Swinson, J. (2020) 'A review of recent large-scale systematic UK classroom observations, method and findings, utility and impact', *Educational Psychology in Practice*, 36(4), pp. 367–385.

Archer, J., Cantrell, S., Holtzman, S.L., Joe, J.N., Tocci, C.M. and Woo, S. (2016) *Better feedback for better teaching: a practical guide to improving classroom observations*. John Wiley & Sons.

Cameron, D.L. (2014) 'An examination of teacher–student interactions in inclusive classrooms: teacher interviews and classroom observations', *Journal of Research in Special Educational Needs*, 14(4), pp. 264–273.

Ceven, J.A. (2012) 'Learning from one's own teaching: New teachers analyzing their practice through video recorded classroom observation cycles in an e-mentoring program', *Journal of Research in Science Teaching*, 53(3) pp. 473–501.

Charalambous, C.E. and Litke, E. (2018) 'Studying instructional quality by using a content-specific lens: the case of the Mathematical Quality of Instruction framework', *ZDM Mathematics Education*. https://link.springer.com/article/10.1007/s11858-018-0913-9.

Chun, S., Lee, O. and Kim, D.-J. (2023) An explanation of the ICALT instrument's measurement of teaching quality in relation to teacher education and policy in South Korea. doi:10.1007/978-3-031-31678-4_14.

Cockburn, J. (2005) 'Perspectives and politics of classroom observation', *Research in Post-Compulsory Education*, 10(3), pp. 373–388.

Cohen, J. and Goldhaber, D. (2016) 'Building a more complete understanding of teacher evaluation using classroom observations', *Educational Researcher*, 45(6), pp. 378–387.

Cooper, D.G. (2015) 'The lesson observation on-line (evidence portfolio) platform', *Australian Journal of Teacher Education (Online)*, 40(1), pp. 83–93.

Farrell, T.S. (2011) '"Keeping SCORE": reflective practice through classroom observations', *RELC Journal*, 42(3), pp. 265–272.

Gibson, S.A. (2006) 'Lesson observation and feedback: the practice of an expert reading coach', *Literacy Research and Instruction*, 45(4), pp. 295–318.

Gitomer, D., Bell, C., Qi, Y., McCaffrey, D., Hamre, B.K. and Pianta, R.C. (2014) 'The instructional challenge in improving teaching quality: lessons from a classroom observation protocol', *Teachers College Record*, 116(6), pp. 1–32.

Granström, M., Kikas, E. and Eisenschmidt, E. (2023) 'Classroom observations: how do teachers teach learning strategies?' in *Frontiers in education*, Vol. 8. Frontiers Media SA, p. 1119519.

Hairon, S., Loh, S.H., Lim, S.P., Govindani, S.N., Tan, J.K.T. and Tay, E.C. (2020) 'Structured mentoring: principles for effective mentoring', *Educational Research for Policy and Practice*, 19(2), pp. 105–123.

Hudson, P. (2016) 'Identifying mentors' observations for providing feedback', *Teachers and Teaching*, 22(2), pp. 219–234.

Ivanova, I.N. (2023) 'Lesson observation: the challenge of seeing beyond observable behaviours', *Studies in Linguistics, Culture, and FLT*, 11(3), pp. 9–26.

Lindorff, A., Jentsch, A., Walkington, C., Kaiser, G. and Sammons, P. (2020) 'Hybrid content-specific and generic approaches to lesson observation: possibilities and practicalities', *Studies in Educational Evaluation*, 67, p. 100919.

Lofthouse, R. and Wright, D. (2012) 'Teacher education lesson observation as boundary crossing', *International Journal of Mentoring and Coaching in Education*, 1(2), pp. 89–103.

Mikeska, J.N., Holtzman, S., McCaffrey, D.F., Liu, S. and Shattuck, T. (2019) Using classroom observations to evaluate science teaching: implications of lesson sampling for measuring science teaching effectiveness across lesson types. *Science Education*, 103(1), pp. 123–144.

Montgomery, D. (2002) *Helping teachers develop through classroom observation second edition*. David Fulton Publishers.

O'Leary, M. (2012) 'Exploring the role of lesson observation in the English education system: a review of methods, models and meanings', *Professional Development in Education*, 38(5), pp. 791–810.

O'Leary, M. (2016) *Reclaiming lesson observation*. Routledge.

O'Leary, M. (2020) *Classroom observation. a guide to the effective observation of teaching and learning*. Routledge.

O'Leary, M. and Gewessler, A. (2014) 'Changing the culture: beyond graded lesson observations', *Adults Learning*, 25(3), pp. 38–41.

OFSTED (2018) Six models of lesson observation: an international perspective. https://assets.publishing.service.gov.uk/government/uploads/system/uploads/attachment_data/file/708815/Six_models_of_lesson_observation.pdf.

OFSTED (2019) How valid and reliable is the use of lesson observation in supporting judgements on the quality of education? June 2019, No. 190029. https://assets.publishing.service.gov.uk/government/uploads/system/uploads/attachment_data/file/936246/Inspecting_education_quality_Lesson_observation_report.pdf.

Page, L. (2016) 'The impact of lesson observation on practice, professionalism and teacher identity', in *Reclaiming lesson observation*. Routledge, pp. 62–74.

Paro, K., Pianta, R. and Stuhlman, M. (2004) 'The classroom assessment scoring system: findings from the prekindergarten year', *Elementary School Journal*, 104, pp. 409–426. doi:10.1086/499760.

Peake, G. (2006) Observation of the practice of teaching. Research findings from the University of Huddersfield Consortium for PCET. https://s3.eu-west-2.amazonaws.com/assets.creode.advancehe-document-manager/documents/hea/private/3060_1568036830.pdf.

Puttick, S. and Wynn, J. (2021) 'Constructing "good teaching" through written lesson observation feedback', *Oxford Review of Education*, 47(2), pp. 152–169.

Sharma, M. and Tiwari, N. (2021) 'A study of class interaction analysis using Flanders's FIAC', *International Journal of Scientific Research in Science, Engineering and Technology*, pp. 171–179. doi:10.32628/IJSRSET218432.

Sullivan, S., (2024). 'Observing a lesson', in *Mentoring mathematics teachers in the secondary school*. Routledge, pp. 81–92.

van der Lans, R.M., van de Grift, W.J., van Veen, K. and Fokkens-Bruinsma, M. (2016) Once is not enough: establishing reliability criteria for feedback and evaluation decisions based on classroom observations. *Studies in Educational Evaluation*, 50, pp. 88–95.

Wragg, E.C. (1990) *An introduction to classroom observation second edition*. Routledge.

Wright, V. (2016) 'Giving lesson observation feedback', *Teacher Education Advancement Network Journal (TEAN)*, 8(1), p. 1.

Chapter 9

Approaches to mentor feedback and maintaining ethical boundaries

Four levels of feedback

Hattie and Timperley (2007) distinguish four levels at which the feedback can be aimed, which is an expansion of a previously developed model by Kluger and DeNisi (1996). They distinguish between the self, task, process, and regulation levels.

- Feedback at the self level is not related to the task performed but is aimed at learner characteristics such as attitudes and classroom behaviours.
- Feedback at the task level is aimed at correcting errors in the work.
- Process-level feedback relates to the process that was followed to perform a particular task and gives suggestions regarding how the process can be improved.
- Feedback at the regulation level relates to affective processes in the mind of the learner, such as self-assessment, willingness to receive feedback, and self-regulation in learning.

> Think about a feedback session in which you have been involved either as an observer or an observer and answer the following questions:
>
> To what extent was the feedback aimed at?
> The self-level and why?
> The task level and why?
> The process level and why?
> The regulation level and why?
> Was the balance of feedback right? If not, how could it have been improved?

Why mentor feedback is important for a trainee teacher

Mentor feedback is crucial for a trainee teacher's professional growth and development for several reasons.

Improvement and reflection

Mentor feedback provides trainee teachers with valuable insights into their strengths, areas of improvement, and areas for growth(Cunningham and Austin, 2007). Constructive feedback helps them identify specific areas where they can enhance their teaching practices, lesson planning, classroom management, and instructional strategies. This feedback encourages trainee teachers to reflect on their performance, adjust, and continuously improve their teaching skills (Ellis and Loughland, 2017).

Professional development

It plays a key role in the professional development of trainee teachers by offering guidance, advice, and support. Mentors can share their expertise, knowledge, and experiences to help trainee teachers navigate challenges, overcome obstacles, and build confidence in their teaching abilities (O'Leary, 2022). Effective feedback from mentors can equip trainee teachers with the necessary tools and strategies to excel in their teaching careers.

Validation and encouragement

Mentor feedback serves as a form of validation and encouragement for trainee teachers by recognising their achievements, efforts, and progress. Positive and affirming feedback from mentors can boost trainee teachers' confidence, motivation, and morale. It reinforces their strengths, fosters a sense of accomplishment, and encourages them to continue pursuing excellence in their teaching practice (2022).

Accountability and growth

It holds trainee teachers accountable for their performance, professionalism, and commitment to their teaching roles. Feedback can help trainee teachers set goals, monitor progress, and take ownership of their learning and development. Mentors provide guidance and support to help trainee teachers grow professionally, adapt to challenges, and strive for continuous improvement in their teaching practice (Jordan, 2023).

> **Self-evaluation prompts for the mentee**
>
> Here is a checklist of prompt questions that you might give to your mentee to help them reflect on their session before receiving feedback from their mentor:
>
> What do I think I achieved overall in this session?
> Which parts of the lesson do I regard as most effective? and which is the least effective?
> To what extent did all my students achieve all their LOs?
> How did they react to my teaching?
> To what extent am I satisfied with my planning and resources?
> How effective were my teaching and assessment strategies?
> What worked? What did not? Why?
> If I could teach this again, what would I change? and why?
> Did I achieve my previous targets? Why?
> What are the three key targets I need to work on for my next observation? How will I achieve them?

Hattie and Timperley (2007) model of feedback

Hattie and Timperley's (2007) model identifies three key questions related to effective feedback: (1) Where am I going? addresses the clarification and discussion of aims and criteria and the characteristics of good performance. This shared understanding of aims and criteria supports the answers to the questions that follow: (2) How am I going there? and (3) Where do I go next? The answers to these questions should yield high-quality information about current performance and how to improve achievement (Hattie and Timperley, 2007; Nicol and Macfarlane, 2006; Ruiz-Primo, 2011). In addition to these three questions, Hattie and Timperley (2007) relate powerful feedback to different levels of learning: Task, process, self-regulation, and self.

Some preconditions for successful mentor feedback

Hattie and Timperley argue that feedback on the process level and self-regulation is found to be most powerful when it focuses on deep processing and the mastery of tasks. Consequently, feedback is powerful when information about tasks can help the students to improve their strategy processing and self-regulation (Andrade, 2010; Zimmerman, 2002).

Students' interpretations and use of feedback (Boud and Molloy, 2012; Gamlem and Smith, 2013), as well as teachers' responses to students' interpretations of feedback (Black and Wiliam, 2009; Hattie and Timperley, 2007), also suggest that students are aware of their own learning processes and their perceptions of learning and can thus find feedback to be useful (Boud and Molloy, 2012; Wiliam, 2011). The effect of feedback is mediated by students' ability and their skill at monitoring, directing, and regulating their actions (Hattie and Timperley, 2007).

Main phases of feedback

Three main phases of feedback are Feed up, Feedback, and Feedforward (Hattie and Timperley, 2007).

- Feed up

During this phase, the aims and the criteria for learning are clarified with the mentee. This phase in the assessment is crucial as it sets the foundation for the entire learning and evaluation process. During this phase, clear and precise learning objectives are established, which help guide trainees on what they are expected to achieve. It provides students with a sense of direction and purpose, ensuring that they understand the goals and the criteria against which their performance will be measured.

It is also important for motivating trainees, as it helps them to see the relevance and value of their learning activities. By knowing what is expected, mentees can better focus their efforts on the desired outcomes, thus enhancing their engagement and commitment to the learning process. In addition, it allows educators to communicate expectations effectively, reducing ambiguity and fostering a more focused and organised learning environment. It also provides for initial feedback. Mentors can use this phase to assess students' prior knowledge and skills, identifying any gaps that need to be addressed (2007).

- Feedback

The feedback phase is the most comprehensive and diverse category and is normally presented as the mentor's perceptions of content and performance. The feedback phase in assessment is crucial for several reasons. First and foremost, it allows trainees to understand their strengths and areas for improvement. Additionally, it helps to bridge the gap between current performance and desired learning outcomes. It offers them clear, actionable steps to improve their work, which can lead to better results.

- Feedforward

Feedforward in assessment refers to the process of providing constructive feedback to students that focuses on future learning and improvement rather than solely reflecting on past performance. This approach aims to guide students on how to enhance their skills and understanding, thereby promoting continuous development. It is proactive and, unlike traditional feedback, which often looks back at completed tasks, feedforward emphasises upcoming assignments and projects. This helps mentees to anticipate challenges and equips them with strategies to tackle them effectively (2007).

It is also specific as effective feedforward provides clear, actionable suggestions rather than vague comments. It pinpoints particular areas where trainees can improve and offers concrete advice on how to achieve these improvements. This makes it easier for students to understand what is expected of them and how they can progress.

Feedforward also tends to be more positive and encouraging. Whilst acknowledging areas that need improvement, it focuses on potential and growth, motivating trainees to strive for better outcomes. This positive reinforcement helps to build confidence and fosters a more constructive learning environment (Burgess *et al.*, 2020).

It is typically forward-looking and goal oriented. It aligns with the learning objectives and helps students to see the path ahead, identifying the steps they need to take to reach their goals. It can ensure that trainees are not just working on tasks but are also moving towards their broader training aims.

Some obstacles to effective feedback

- The power relationship is asymmetric with high stakes for the student teachers, who are heavily dependent on the mentor's feedback and assessment as the mentor who provides feedback in the development process (formative feedback) may also be responsible for part of the final evaluation of the teaching placement (summative feedback), which may be considered to be particularly challenging for both the student teachers and mentors.
- Overly critical feedback may create negative emotional reactions, threatening the student teachers' self-image (and contribute to tensions or conflicts in their relationship). Some research shows that student teachers may respond to the feedback in ways that may impact the quality of the mentoring. They may become less verbally active, withhold information, and, in particular, refrain from sharing problems with their mentor to avoid negative evaluations (Brandt, 2008).
- Trainees might also hide any disagreement with their mentors and feel obliged to conform to the feedback without actually agreeing with it (Beck and Kosnik, 2002; Bonilla-Medina *et al.*, 2008). They may also deflect or ignore their mentor's feedback.
- It may also become a bone of contention between the mentor, the mentee, and the college tutor who may be asked to intercede on the mentee's behalf if they feel that the grade or feedback is not justified (Beck and Kosnik, 2002).

- Relational factors can influence willingness to provide honest and constructive feedback. de Lange and Wittek (2018) found that observers in their studies avoided critique and constructive feedback, fearing the risk of damaging collegiality by making their observers feel threatened or defensive. Instead, they opted to provide positive feedback and focus on the mechanics of teaching rather than more complex or problematic aspects. This decision compromised the goal of fostering professional growth in teaching, leading de Lange and Wittek to recommend explicitly shifting from polite to exploratory talk (2018).

How to use critical feedback effectively using face work theory

Face work derives from Erving Goffman's concept of face (1963), which, he argued, was the positive self-image a person tries to establish in social interactions, or the positive social value a person effectively claims for himself.

Goffman's claims were:

1 that people normally value their own and others' faces;
2 that a person normally attempts to save their own and the other party's face;
3 that when a person loses it, they try to restore or repair it; and
4 that when one party loses face, the other party often tries to help them restore or repair it.

Lim and Bowers (1991) reconstructed a previously established conceptual framework from Brown and Levinson (1978), arguing that face reflects three wants:

- Fellowship face (want to be included),
- Autonomy face (want not to be imposed on), and
- Competence face (want to have one's abilities respected).

Face threatening situations can occur when people are challenged by others, such as through criticism, which can cause emotional reactions as shame, humiliation, confusion, or frustration. Several factors determine how severely face threats are experienced in a context: Power differentials, degrees of dependence, and the perceived importance of maintaining a particular face (Redmond, 2015).

All these factors suggest that the placement context and the professional scrutiny they routinely undergo in it must be viewed as especially challenging for mentees' competence faces, and this is particularly the case with regard to feedback. Thus, the mentor's communication becomes key to providing clear and constructive feedback but also ensuring that the mentee's face is saved (Lim and Bowers, 1991).

Self-reflection activity

Complete the table with your own examples drawn from mentoring practice

Different wants	How do you satisfy this want in your mentee?
Fellowship face (want to be included) Autonomy face (want not to be imposed on) Competence face (want to have abilities recognised and respected)	

According to the research of Bjørndal and Gjesdal (2020), four strategies used by mentees when receiving post-observational feedback were common. These were:

- withdrawing,
- contradicting,
- repairing (balancing, normalising, or extenuating), and
- emphasising a competent, self-reflective, and progressive face.

Self-reflection activity

Mentees' strategies.
How would you respond to these reactions from your mentee?
Withdrawing
Contradicting
Repairing and justifying
Emphasising a competent self-reflective face

Phases of mentor feedback

The phases of mentor's feedback tend to fall into the following three approaches:

Firstly, the mentor encourages the student teachers to evaluate his or her own teaching. In these cases, the mentor will sometimes tend to confirm the student teachers' critical self-evaluation, or, in contrast, initiate feedback by adding critical nuances to the trainees' self-evaluation or contradicting it (Copland and Donaghue, 2021).

Secondly, the mentor's contribution starts as a neutral exploration or positive evaluation of aspects of the mentee's practice, only for it to become clear later in the conversation that they have a critical agenda related to the topic (2021).

Thirdly, the mentor interweaves critical feedback with positive and supportive feedback as well as familiar communication patterns involving politeness.

> **Self-reflective questions**
>
> What are the strengths and weaknesses of each mentoring approach?
> Which of the three do you tend to use more often when you give feedback?
>   Why is this the case?
>
> Developing approaches to post-observation feedback

Develop approaches to facework, e.g. using strategies such as preambles, hesitation, laughter, and modifiers, to soften potentially face threatening moves while being careful not to mitigate an important message to the extent that it is obscured (Copland, 2008; Copland and Donaghue, 2021).

- Studies suggest that mentor power moves, such as initiating topics, controlling the floor, and taking longer turns (Copland, 2008; Hyland and Lo, 2006), leave the observed teacher with little space to talk.
- Mentee feedback literacy

  Feedback literacy is an important set of capacities to develop. Firstly, students with more developed feedback literacy are likely to understand the benefit of using feedback to improve their learning and performance (Carless and Boud, 2018). Secondly, being able to make and refine evaluative judgements means that students can understand the quality of their own and others' work (Molloy, Boud and Henderson 2019).

  Thirdly, working with emotions productively means that mentees can manage the potentially negative affective reactions to receiving critical feedback and are also able to seek out further feedback in ways that portray sensitivity towards the feedback giver. Finally, understanding how to use feedback information to act is a key self-regulatory capacity (Carless and Boud, 2018).
- Teacher feedback literacy

  This involves the movement away from the provider to the designer of learning environments that support students to develop feedback literacy (Hyland and Lo, 2006).

When mentor feedback could be given

Ad hoc feedback can be provided by the mentor as much as possible to develop a strong working relationship between mentor and mentee and to support their professional development. There are also several occasions where more formal and more in-depth feedback is advisable. These include:

Feedback during observation planning
Feedback post-observation
Feedback during professional development target setting

- Feedback during observation planning

    Offering feedback during the lesson planning stage allows the mentor and the mentee to establish a supportive and collaborative relationship. By providing constructive feedback and guidance, the mentor demonstrates their commitment to the mentee's professional growth, fostering trust, respect, and open communication in the mentoring process (McCarthy, 2017).

    Providing feedback during the lesson planning stage is also crucial for several reasons such as the following.

Enhancing learning outcomes

It allows the mentor to assess the effectiveness of the planned activities, objectives, and assessments. By providing feedback, the mentor can help the mentee make necessary adjustments to ensure that the lesson plan is in alignment with the learning objectives and promotes student engagement and understanding.

Promoting reflection and growth

It can encourage them to reflect on their teaching strategies, instructional methods, and learning goals. It can also prompt them to consider different perspectives, approaches, and techniques, leading to professional growth and development (Ferguson, 2011).

Increasing preparedness and confidence

The feedback can help the mentee feel more prepared and confident in delivering the lesson. The mentee can address potential challenges, gaps, or areas of improvement in the lesson plan beforehand and therefore approach the teaching experience with greater confidence and competence.

Aligning teaching practices

Feedback during the lesson planning stage can help to ensure that their teaching practices are in alignment with best practices, pedagogical principles, and curriculum requirements.

- Feedback post-observation

    It is important for a mentor to provide feedback to their mentee after a teaching observation for several reasons.

Reflection and learning

Feedback allows the mentee to reflect on their teaching practice, classroom management, and student interactions. By receiving it, they can identify strengths, areas for improvement, and strategies to enhance their teaching skills and also to help them identify professional development goals and areas for growth (Puttick and Wynn, 2021).

Validation and encouragement

Positive feedback from a mentor can validate the mentee's efforts, achievements, and successes. Encouraging feedback boosts their confidence, motivation, and morale, developing a positive and supportive relationship.

Accountability and progress monitoring

Feedback serves as a form of accountability for the mentee to implement suggested changes and strategies. Regular feedback sessions allow the mentor and mentee to monitor progress, track improvements, and adjust goals as needed (Tyrer, 2023).

Mentorship and support

Feedback from a mentor demonstrates their commitment to the mentee's professional development and growth. It shows that the mentor is invested in the mentee's success, providing guidance, advice, and support to help the mentee succeed in their teaching practice.

- Feedback during professional development target setting
  This is essential for several reasons (Cunningham and Austin, 2007).

Clarity and focus

Feedback provides the trainee teacher with clear guidance on setting specific, measurable, achievable, relevant, and time-bound (SMART) professional development targets. Feedback helps align the targets with the trainee's goals, needs, and areas for growth.

Motivation and accountability

Feedback serves as a source of motivation for the trainee teacher, encouraging them to set challenging yet attainable professional development targets. Regular feedback also holds the trainee accountable for working towards their targets and maintaining progress.

Reflection and self-awareness

Feedback during target setting encourages the trainee teacher to reflect on their strengths, weaknesses, and areas for improvement. Constructive feedback helps build self-awareness and enables the trainee to identify specific actions to enhance their teaching practice.

Customisation and personalisation

Feedback supports the customisation and personalisation of professional development targets based on the trainee teacher's unique needs and aspirations. Mentors can help the trainee set realistic and relevant targets that align with their professional growth (2007).

Approaches to mentor feedback

Directive feedback approach (White, 2007)

Main Features:

The directive feedback approach involves providing specific instructions, suggestions, or recommendations to guide the trainee teacher's actions or behaviours. The mentor takes a more authoritative stance, offering clear direction on what needs to be done or improved.

- Focus: The mentor places the emphasis on correcting errors, addressing deficiencies, and providing step-by-step guidance to help the trainee teacher achieve desired outcomes.
- Example: 'I noticed that your classroom management could be more effective. Here are some strategies you can implement to create a more structured and engaging learning environment'.

Evaluative feedback approach (Brown and Glover, 2006)

Main Features:

The evaluative feedback approach involves providing an assessment or judgement of the trainee teacher's performance based on set criteria or standards. The mentor evaluates the strengths and weaknesses of the trainee teacher's work.

- Focus: The focus is on measuring performance against predetermined benchmarks, highlighting areas of success and areas in need of improvement.
- Example: 'Your lesson planning demonstrates creativity and engagement with students, but there is room for improvement in your assessment strategies to ensure student learning outcomes are met'.

Appreciative feedback approach (Cogan, 1995)

Main Features

The appreciative feedback approach involves recognising and acknowledging the trainee teacher's strengths, achievements, and positive attributes. The mentor values their efforts and contributions.

- Focus: There is an emphasis placed on building confidence, reinforcing good practices, and fostering a positive learning environment by celebrating successes and encouraging progress.

Example: 'I appreciate your enthusiasm and dedication to creating inclusive lessons that cater to diverse student needs. Your commitment to student success is commendable'.

Transformative feedback approach

Main Features:

The transformative feedback approach involves empowering and challenging the trainee teacher to reflect critically on their beliefs, assumptions, and practices. The mentor aims to stimulate deep learning, growth, and self-awareness.

Focus: The focus is on promoting transformative change, encouraging self-reflection, and inspiring the trainee teacher to question their perspectives, experiment with new approaches, and continuously evolve as an educator.

Example: 'Your teaching style shows potential for growth and innovation. Let's explore different pedagogical approaches together and experiment with strategies that can elevate your teaching practice to the next level'.

> **Strengths and weaknesses of the main feedback approaches**
>
> *Directive feedback approach*
>
> Strengths:
>
> Provides clear guidance and specific instructions for improvement
> Helps trainee teachers understand what needs to be done to enhance performance
> Offers immediate actionable steps for growth
>
> Weaknesses:
>
> May come across as authoritarian or controlling
> Could limit the trainee teacher's autonomy and creativity
> May not promote deeper reflection or critical thinking
>
> *Evaluative feedback approach*
>
> Strengths:
>
> Provides a clear assessment of performance against set criteria
> Identifies areas of strength and areas for improvement
> Helps trainee teachers understand where they stand in terms of progress

Weaknesses:

Can be perceived as judgemental or overly critical
May focus more on outcomes rather than the learning process
Could create a performance-driven culture that discourages risk-taking

Appreciative feedback approach

Strengths:

Recognises and celebrates the trainee teacher's achievements
Builds confidence and motivation
Fosters a positive and supportive mentor-trainee relationship

Weaknesses:

May overlook areas for improvement or constructive feedback
Could be perceived as insincere or superficial if not balanced with constructive criticism
May not provide specific guidance for further growth and development

Transformative feedback approach

Strengths:

Encourages self-reflection, critical thinking, and a growth mindset
Inspires trainee teachers to explore new perspectives and innovative approaches. Focuses on personal and professional development beyond performance evaluation

Weaknesses:

Requires a high level of trust, openness, and vulnerability from both the mentor and trainee teacher
Can be time-consuming and challenging to implement in practice
May be less prescriptive and structured, potentially leading to ambiguity

Self-reflective activity

According to Bunton, Stimpson and Lopez-Real (2002), there are four types of written/verbal post observation feedback. Complete the following table with examples from your own practice

Types of feedback	How do you implement this approach in your feedback?
Descriptive: Narrativising to the trainee what happened in a non-evaluative way, for example, you asked a general question to the class and then waited for volunteers to answer...	
Questioning/reflective: Asking the trainee genuine questions and inviting the trainee to speculate; for example: Why not introduce structures at this point? This is NOT a criticism, just a question.	
Evaluative: Assessing strengths and weaknesses; for example, this is a very carefully planned lesson. But you might have differentiated it more carefully with a range of activities.	
Advisory: Giving advice or making suggestions of what the trainee could or should do; for example: Don't rush through your plan if you are running out of time and haven't met your learning outcomes.	

Self-reflection task

Self-reflection activity

Complete the table below with examples drawn from your own practice.

Impacts of discussing feelings	Examples of how you implement this
Creating a supportive environment	
Building trust	
Developing self-awareness and reflection	
Managing emotional responses	
Enhancing communication	

Self-reflection task

Complete the following table with examples of your own practice.

Roles of discussion in feedback	Examples of how you undertake these
Promotes reflective practice Enhances understanding Encourages active participation Supports critical thinking skills Encourages Dialogue and Feedback Loops	

Face to face feedback

Goal, reality, options, and will (GROW)

In this approach, the mentor helps the mentee identify their goals, assess the current reality of their teaching practice, explore different options for improvement, and commit to specific actions or strategies moving forward. This structured model provides a framework for focused and goal-oriented feedback sessions that guide the mentee towards professional growth (Grant, 2022).

Strengths

Goal-Oriented
It is highly goal-oriented, focusing on the mentee's specific objectives, aspirations, and desired outcomes. This approach can help the mentee clarify their teaching goals and align feedback with their professional development needs (Dowden *et al.*, 2013).
Structured and Systematic
It provides a clear and structured framework for feedback sessions, guiding mentors and mentees through a systematic process of setting goals, evaluating current reality, exploring options, and committing to actions, and this can help to ensure that feedback is focused, productive, and action-oriented (Grant, 2022).

Empowering and Reflective
By encouraging the mentee to reflect on their teaching practice, identify areas for improvement, and generate options for growth, the GROW model empowers the mentee to take ownership of their professional development. This reflective process fosters self-awareness, accountability, and proactive learning.

Weaknesses

Rigidity
One potential weakness of the GROW method is its rigidity and linearity, as it follows a sequential process of setting goals, assessing reality, exploring

options, and determining actions. This rigid structure may limit flexibility and adaptability in feedback sessions, potentially overlooking important nuances or complexities in the mentee's teaching practice (Leach, 2020).

Lack of Emphasis on Relationship

It primarily focuses on the mentee's goals, actions, and outcomes, sometimes at the expense of building a strong mentor-mentee relationship. Feedback sessions may become transactional rather than fostering trust, rapport, and open communication between the mentor and the mentee (2020).

Overemphasis on Goals

While goal setting is a central component of the GROW model, an overemphasis on achieving specific goals may overshadow the importance of process-oriented learning, continuous improvement, and holistic development in teaching practice. This narrow focus on outcomes could undermine the mentee's exploration, experimentation, and creativity in their professional growth journey (Rubtcova, Pavenkov and Pavenkov, 2016).

Situation, behaviour, impact (SBI)

In this model, the mentor begins by describing a specific situation or teaching scenario, then observes and provides feedback on the mentee's teaching behaviour during that situation, and finally discusses the impact of the behaviour on student learning or engagement. This structured feedback session helps the mentee understand the specific behaviours that are effective or need improvement, fostering targeted and actionable feedback (Sorensen, 2024).

Strengths

Specific and Focused

The SBI method provides a structured framework for delivering feedback that is specific and focused on observable behaviours in a given situation. By pinpointing concrete behaviours, mentors can offer targeted feedback that is actionable and relevant to the mentee's development (2024).

Clarity and Objectivity

The approach encourages mentors to describe the situation, behaviour observed, and its impact, promoting clarity and objectivity in feedback delivery. This structured format can help to eliminate ambiguity and ensure that feedback is grounded in observable evidence rather than subjective interpretations.

Promotes Accountability

By linking behaviours to their impact on student learning or engagement, the SBI method fosters a sense of accountability in the mentee. This accountability can encourage them to reflect on the consequences of their actions and take responsibility for addressing areas of improvement (Watson and Williams, 2004).

Weaknesses

Limited Contextual Understanding: While the SBI method focuses on specific behaviours and their impact, it may lack the depth needed to address broader contextual factors influencing performance. This limitation could hinder a comprehensive understanding of the mentee's challenges and hinder the mentor's ability to provide holistic feedback (Seiler, 2021).

Potential for defensiveness

Incomplete Feedback Loop

The SBI method primarily emphasises delivering feedback on observed behaviours and their impact, potentially neglecting opportunities for exploring underlying motivations, emotions, or beliefs that may be driving the behaviour. This can result in a partial feedback loop that fails to address deeper root causes of performance issues (Sorenson, 2024). This may sometimes come across as overly critical or confrontational to the mentee, leading to defensiveness or resistance to feedback. Therefore, mentors should exercise sensitivity and skill in delivering SBI feedback to ensure it is received constructively.

Pendleton rules aka Pendleton's 'Feedback Sandwich'

This involves the mentee's self-assessment before the mentor provides feedback. The mentor asks the mentee about their strengths, areas for improvement, and action steps they can take to address those areas. The mentor then shares their observations and suggestions for further improvement, leading to a collaborative and reflective feedback dialogue (Esmaeeli *et al.*, 2023).

The Pendleton rules method of feedback, also known as the approach, has both strengths and weaknesses that should be considered when using this structured feedback model in mentoring sessions.

Strengths

Emphasises Self-Assessment

It places a strong emphasis on the mentee's self-assessment before receiving feedback from the mentor. This encourages them to reflect on their own performance, identify strengths and areas for improvement, and take ownership of their professional development.

Collaborative approach

By involving the mentee in the feedback process and allowing them to share their self-assessment first, it promotes a collaborative and participatory dynamic between the mentor and mentee which can enhance the mentee's engagement, motivation, and commitment to implementing feedback, boosting their confidence, self-esteem, and receptivity to critical feedback (2023).

Weaknesses

Potential for Bias

The method relies heavily on the mentee's self-assessment as the initial step in the feedback process. This self-assessment may be influenced by their subjective perspectives, biases, or blind spots, potentially leading to inaccurate or incomplete self-reflection. Therefore, if the mentor provides feedback based solely on this without offering an objective evaluation, there is a risk of losing objectivity and overlooking critical areas for improvement, which could hinder the mentee's professional growth and development (Donaghy *et al.*, 2021).

Lack of Structure

The method may lack a structured framework for guiding feedback sessions, as it primarily focuses on the sequence of self-assessment, positive feedback, and constructive feedback. This lack of structure could result in less focused, comprehensive, or actionable feedback discussions (2021).

How would you use these three approaches in your mentoring?
Which one better supports your practice?

Feedback models	How would you apply them?
GROW	
SBI	
Pendleton rules model	

Barriers to effective feedback

According to Burgess *et al.* (2020), there are four main obstacles. These include the following.

Lack of direct observation of tasks

Feedback has the greatest impact on trainees' behaviour when it is provided based on direct observation of a specific task. In the busy classroom setting, direct observation is often lacking.

Feedback can be more difficult to provide when the mentee's performance is below par and may be disappointing to them. The provision of such feedback requires an understanding of the process and skill. Although there may be a desire to avoid upsetting a trainee, this can result in 'vanishing feedback' where meaningful feedback is avoided (Cogan, 1995).

Lack of trust

A lack of trust between the mentor and mentee can impede the effectiveness of feedback. If the mentee does not trust the mentor's intentions or expertise, they may be less receptive to feedback and less likely to implement suggested changes. In addition, power dynamics in the mentoring relationship can create barriers to effective feedback. If the mentee perceives the mentor as having significantly more authority or control, they may feel reluctant to challenge or question the feedback provided (Irons, 2008).

Communication style

Differences in communication styles between the mentor and mentee can lead to misunderstandings or misinterpretations of feedback. If the mentor's feedback is unclear, ambiguous, or overly critical, it may be challenging for the mentee to understand and act upon.

Cultural and diversity factors

Cultural differences between the mentor and mentee, such as language barriers, values, or beliefs, can impact the effectiveness of feedback. Misunderstandings related to cultural norms or expectations may hinder the mentee's ability to receive and act upon feedback (Jordan, 2023).

Emotional reactions

Emotional reactions from either the mentor or mentee, such as defensiveness, resistance, or sensitivity to criticism, can impede the feedback process. Emotional barriers may prevent open and honest communication, making it difficult to address feedback constructively.

Lack of specificity

Vague, general, or non-specific feedback can hinder the effectiveness of the mentoring relationship. If feedback is not tailored to the mentee's needs and specific areas for improvement, it may be less actionable and impactful.

Time constraints

Limited time for feedback discussions or coaching sessions can also be a significant barrier. If the mentor and mentee do not have sufficient time to discuss feedback in depth, address concerns, or develop action plans, the feedback may lack depth and effectiveness (Le and Vásquez, 2011).

Organising a successful feedback session

An effective format for a feedback session between a teaching mentor and mentee typically follows a structured approach that promotes meaningful dialogue, reflection, and actionable outcomes. Here is an outline of the key components of an effective feedback session. According to Burgess *et al.* (2020), there are six key areas:

- Structure
  Schedule the feedback session at a convenient time for both mentor and mentee.
1 Setting the Stage
    - Establish a positive and supportive environment that encourages open communication and trust in which you clarify the purpose and goals of the feedback session, agree on confidentiality and respect for each other's perspectives, and make the purpose of the meeting clear (2020).

      The seating arrangement in the room should show the mentor and the mentee as equals, and the feedback should focus on what was observed in the session, such as knowledge, attitudes to students, and teaching and learning strategies.
    - Format
        - The aim of the feedback session is to improve the mentee's performance, and the session structure should be made clear to include student self-assessment, teacher assessment, and joint development of an action plan and should be based upon an appropriate feedback model, e.g. Pendleton's. It is important to both give positive feedback and areas requiring improvement and to provide concrete examples (Pendleton *et al.*, 1984).
    - Content
        - Mentor and mentees need time to prepare their respective content for the session. The mentee should assess their own learning objectives for the teaching placement, including formal objectives and personal objectives. The mentor should prepare for the session by making direct observations of the student's performance and gaining feedback from others on the team. They should review notes and only select a few points to cover (1984).
2 Feedback Process
    a Self-Assessment
      Allow the mentee to reflect on their teaching practice and identify strengths, areas for improvement, and goals.
    b Mentor Observation
      The mentor shares observations, either oral or written, of the mentee's teaching behaviours, strategies, and interactions with students

and provides specific, behaviour-based feedback using a structured framework balancing positive feedback with constructive feedback and offering suggestions for improvement (Puttick and Wynn, 2021).

3 Reflection and Discussion
- Engage in a two-way dialogue where the mentee can ask questions, seek clarification, and share their perspective and reflect on the impact of feedback on teaching practice and student learning.

4 Action Planning
- Collaboratively develop an action plan that outlines specific goals, strategies, and timelines for implementing feedback based on SMART (Specific, Measurable, Achievable, Relevant, Time-bound) goals to track progress (Tyrer, 2023).

5 Follow-Up and Support
- Schedule follow-up meetings to review progress, address challenges, and provide ongoing support and encourage ongoing reflection, self-assessment, and growth in teaching practice.

6 Closure
- Summarise key points discussed during the feedback session and express appreciation for the mentee's receptiveness and commitment to professional growth and reiterate the mentor's support and availability for further guidance.

Some practical tips for effective verbal observation feedback (O'Leary, 2020)

Mentors should:

- Say what they see
  Feedback should be clearly stated and not interpretative, evaluative, or judgemental. It should be supported by mentor questions.
- Be sensitive
  Mentors should avoid offering solutions and saying what the mentee should have done unless it is requested by them. This can come across as patronising and demeaning (White, 2007).
- Avoid generalised statements
  For example, 'I think you should work on your formative assessment strategies'. These should be supported by detailed examples and specific advice aimed to progress mentee's development in particular areas.
- Use Socratic questioning
  This will encourage deeper thinking, prompting the mentee to examine the reasoning behind their choices and to link their responses

to wider theory and to reflect upon their own philosophy of learning (O'Leary, 2011).
- Use a range of questions

    Switch from generalised questions to more specific ones based on particular occurrences, such as 'You chose to use gapped handouts twice in this class. Why did you use this approach a second time?' This will encourage the mentee to reflect in more depth and take greater ownership of their strategies.
- Balance the feedback

    Highlight strengths as well as areas for improvement and always provide examples of both and encourage the mentee to see that they are making progress.
- Ensure that feedback is dialogic

    Effective feedback comes out of a process of discussion. It should not be dominated by a mentor telling a mentor what they need to 'put right' in their teaching. Mentees should be prompted to discuss their decision-making and to reflect upon the consequences of this and the options they considered before making these decisions (O'Leary, 2022).
- Collaborate with the mentee on areas of development

    These should be jointly arrived at to make them more relevant to the mentee and to help develop their ownership of their own learning and development. These will also allow the mentee to reflect on achievable targets and record them for timely review.
- Prioritise areas of development

    Keeping the list short will make them more achievable in the short term rather than developing a long list, which is demotivating and unlikely to be achieved.
- Provide timely feedback

    There are debates about the most effective time to provide feedback. According to O'Leary (2020), it should be provided ideally within a day of the observation or at least within a week. He argues that this will ensure that the observation will still be 'fresh' in the minds of both mentor and mentee. The downside of this could be that their responses could be clouded by emotion and fatigue and lacking in dispassionate judgement (Watson and Williams, 2004).

    Alternatively, they suggest (2004) that it is better to feedback at least a few days after the observation to allow both mentor and mentee to reflect on the observation and to be able to take a more objective and less emotional interpretation of it.

    It can be useful to provide immediate post-observation feedback if the mentee requests it as it may help to calm their nerves and to help them reflect on it in more depth before they receive the more formal feedback.
- Ensure enough time is available for detailed feedback

    According to research by O'Leary (2011), the average time spent by school observers was between 10 and 20 minutes and he suggests a minimum of 30 minutes (O'Leary, 2020). This will allow a more in-depth mutual discussion of the observation rather than a top down direction from the mentor.

> **Self-reflective activity**
>
> Think about a recent observation that you have been involved in either as an observer or as an observee. Reflect on the feedback you gave or were given and answer the following questions:
> Was the discussion useful? If not? Why not?
> How did you feel about giving or receiving the feedback?
> Did you feel that you or your mentee played an active role in it? If not, why not?
> What was most challenging about the context of the feedback?
> Did you feel that the areas of self-development that you agreed were SMART?
> What will you take from the experience? How would you improve it if you have to repeat the experience?

Written observation feedback

Written teaching observation feedback should be comprehensive, constructive, and actionable, highlighting both strengths and areas for improvement. Research suggests that it is the most popular feedback form amongst students (Brown and Glover, 2006). Some key features of effective written teaching observation feedback include:

- Clear and specific
  Feedback should be clear, specific, and focused on observable behaviours, actions, and outcomes. It should provide detailed examples to support feedback and make it easier for the trainee to understand and act upon. Therefore, it should be based on clearly stated evidence from the teaching observation focussing on factual incidences and data. It can also be useful to write in bullet points (Glover and Brown, 2006).
- Provide balanced comments
  It is important to recognise the mentee's strengths, effective practices, and accomplishments as acknowledging strengths can boost teacher motivation, self-esteem, and confidence, and the specific areas where the teacher can enhance their teaching practice, such as classroom management, instructional strategies, and student engagement.
- Provide constructive criticism
  The feedback should be evaluative and written in a constructive and professional style using language that is supportive, respectful, and encouraging, emphasising growth and development rather than fault-finding or criticism (2006).
- Provide opportunities for the mentee's feedback
  Feedback should be dialogic, allowing mentees to comment or reply or ask questions either through a comment box on the feedback form or a follow-up feedback session.

- Actionable recommendations
  It should make direct reference to criteria/rubrics and offer practical, realistic, and achievable recommendations for implementing future short-term changes and enhancements in teaching practice (Cunningham and Austin, 2007).
- Followed up and supported
  The mentor should ensure that the written feedback is followed up with verbal feedback if required to clarify and elaborate on what was written and also to discuss the outcomes with the trainee. This will then open the door to further ongoing support, coaching, extra resources, and mentoring to help the mentee implement changes and monitor progress.

Oral feedback and written observation feedback

Written and verbal teaching observation feedback have distinct strengths and weaknesses that can impact their effectiveness in providing valuable insight and support for teachers.

Strengths of written teaching observation feedback

- Clarity and Detail
  Written feedback allows for the inclusion of detailed observations, examples, and recommendations. Mentees can refer back to written feedback for reference and clarification (Dowden *et al.*, 2013).
- Reflection Tool
  They can review it at their own pace, enabling deeper reflection and analysis of their teaching practice.
- Documentation
  Written feedback provides a documented record of observations and recommendations that can be easily referenced and reviewed over time (Esmaeeli *et al.*, 2023).

Weaknesses of written teaching observation feedback

- Lack of Interaction
  Written feedback lacks the immediate dialogue and clarification that verbal feedback offers. Teachers may have questions or seek further explanation that is not readily available in written form. Without the opportunity for real-time discussion, they may misinterpret or misunderstand written feedback, leading to confusion or miscommunication (2023).
- Limited Context
  Written feedback may lack the context and nuance that verbal feedback can provide, making it challenging to address specific nuances or complexities in teaching practice (Dowden *et al.*, 2013).

Strengths of verbal teaching observation feedback

- Immediate Feedback
  Verbal feedback provides real-time interaction and discussion, allowing for immediate clarification and elaboration on observations and recommendations.
- Two-Way Dialogue
  Verbal feedback encourages an interactive exchange between the observer and teacher, fostering a deeper understanding and engagement.
- Personalised Approach
  Verbal feedback can be tailored to the individual teacher's communication style and preferences, enhancing its impact and receptivity (Ellis and Loughland, 2017).

Weaknesses of verbal teaching observation feedback

- Memory and Retention
  Verbal feedback may be less easily retained or remembered compared to written feedback, particularly if there is a large volume of information shared.
- Note-Taking Challenges
  Teachers may have difficulty capturing or recalling all aspects of verbal feedback, potentially missing key insights or recommendations.
- Documentation
  Verbal feedback may lack a documented record for future reference, making it harder to track progress or revisit specific recommendations (Ferguson, 2011).

> **Self-reflection task**
>
> Observe three teaching sessions
> Feedback to your mentee orally for one session
> Provide written for the second session
> Provide oral and written feedback for the third session
> Ask your mentee which one they preferred.

Using online feedback

Using online teaching feedback offers several advantages and disadvantages compared to traditional face-to-face or written feedback methods.
Strengths

- Accessibility
  Online teaching feedback can be accessed at any time and from any location, providing greater flexibility for both mentors and mentees (Tochon, 2001).

- Documentation
    Online feedback can be easily stored, organised, and revisited for future reference, allowing for ongoing reflection and improvement.
- Efficiency
    Online feedback can streamline the feedback process, enabling mentors to provide timely and targeted feedback to multiple mentees efficiently.
- Multimedia Integration
    Online platforms enable the integration of multimedia elements such as videos, images, or interactive resources to enhance the feedback experience (McCarthy, 2017).

Weaknesses

- Lack of Personal Interaction
    Online teaching feedback may lack the personal touch and direct interaction that can be established through face-to-face feedback, impacting rapport and relationship building.
- Misinterpretation
    Without the nuances of tone, body language, and facial expressions, online feedback may be more prone to misinterpretation or misunderstanding (Kerman *et al.*, 2024).
- Technical Issues
    Connectivity problems, platform glitches, or other technical issues can disrupt the online feedback process and hinder effective communication.
- Limited Depth
    Online feedback may have limitations in providing in-depth, nuanced feedback on certain aspects of teaching practice that require hands-on observation or detailed discussion (2024).

Self-reflection task

How would you manage to overcome some of the problems associated with online feedback?

Problems	Your solutions
Lack of personal interaction?	
Misinterpretation?	
Technical issues?	
Limited depth of response?	

References

Andrade, H. (2010) Students as the definitive source of formative assessment: academic self-assessment and the self-regulation of learning. NERA Conference Proceedings 2010. Available at: https://www.researchgate.net/publication/50236003 (Accessed 1 April 2025).

Beck, C. and Kosnik, C. (2002) 'Components of a good practicum placement: student teacher perceptions', *Teacher Education Quarterly*, 29, pp. 81–98.

Bjørndal, C. T. and Gjesdal, S. (2020). 'The role of sport school programmes in athlete development in Norwegian handball and football', *European Journal for Sport and Society*, 17(4), 374–396. doi:10.1080/16138171.2020.1792131.

Black, P. and Wiliam, D. (2009) 'Developing the theory of formative assessment', *Educational Assessment Evaluation and Accountability*, 21, pp. 5–31. doi:10.1007/s11092-008-9068-5.

Bonilla-Medina, S., Ximena, R. and Mendez, P. and Universidad Distrital Francisco José de Caldas-Colombia (2008) Mentoring in pre-service teaching: from reflection on practice to a didactic proposal. Actualidades Pedagógicas. https://repository.uel.ac.uk/item/864z0.

Boud, D. and Molloy, E. (2012) 'Rethinking models of feedback for learning: the challenge of design', *Assessment & Evaluation in Higher Education*, 38(6), pp. 698–712. doi:10.1080/02602938.2012.691462.

Brandt, C. (2008) 'Integrating feedback and reflection in teacher preparation,' *ELT Journal*, 62(1), pp. 37–46.

Brown, E. and Glover, C. (2006) 'Evaluating written feedback', in *Innovative assessment in higher education*. Routledge, pp. 101–111.

Brown, P. and Levinson, S. (1978) 'Universals in language usage: politeness phenomena', in Goody, E. (ed.) *Questions and politeness: strategies in social interaction*. Cambridge University Press, pp. 56–310.

Bunton, D., Stimpson, P. and Lopez-Real, F. (2002) 'University tutors' practicum observation notes: format and content', *Mentoring and Tutoring: Partnership in Learning*, 10(3), pp. 233–252. doi:10.1080/1361126022000037060.

Burgess, A., van Diggele, C., Roberts, C. and Mellis, C. (2020) 'Feedback in the clinical setting', *BMC Medical Education*, 20(Suppl 2), p. 460. doi:10.1186/s12909-020-02280-5.

Carless, D. and Boud, D. (2018) 'The development of student feedback literacy: enabling uptake of feedback', *Assessment & Evaluation in Higher Education*, 43(8), pp. 1315–1325. doi:10.1080/02602938.2018.1463354.

Cogan, D (1995) 'Using a counselling approach in teacher supervision', *The Teacher Trainer*, 9(3).

Copland, F. and Donaghue (2021) *Analyzing discourses in teacher observation feedback conferences 2021*. Routledge edition, Taylor & Francis Group.

Copland, F.M. (2008) *Professional encounters in TESOL: Deconstructing the discourse: Understanding the trainer's talk discourses of teachers in training*. Garton, S. and Richards, K. (eds.). Palgrave Macmillan, pp. 24–41.

Cunningham, T. and Austin, J. (2007) 'Using goal setting, task clarification, and feedback to increase the use of the hands-free technique by hospital operating room staff', *Journal of Applied Behavior Analysis*, 40, pp. 673–677. doi:10.1901/jaba.2007.673-677.

de Lange, T. and Wittek, L. (2018) 'Creating shared spaces: developing teaching through peer supervision groups', *Mind, Culture, and Activity*, 25(4), pp. 324–339. doi:10.1080/10749039.2018.1544645.

Donaghy, F., Mehay, R., Seigel, S. and Chahal, P. (2021) 'The skilful art of giving feedback', in *The essential handbook for GP training and education*. CRC Press, pp. 81–95.

Dowden, T., Pittaway, S., Yost, H. and McCarthy, R. (2013) 'Students' perceptions of written feedback in teacher education: ideally feedback is a continuing two-way communication that encourages progress', *Assessment & Evaluation in Higher Education*, 38(3), pp. 349–362.

Ellis, N.J. and Loughland, T. (2017) '"Where to next?": examining feedback received by teacher education students', *Issues in Educational Research*, 27(1), pp. 51–63.

Esmaeeli, B., Esmaeili Shandiz, E., Shojaei, H., Fazli, B. and Ahmadi, R. (2023) 'Feedback in higher education: an overview of reviews and systematic reviews', *Medical Education Bulletin*, 4(2), pp. 745–764.

Ferguson, P. (2011) 'Student perceptions of quality feedback in teacher education', *Assessment and Evaluation in Higher Education*, 36(1), pp. 51–62.

Gamlem, S. and Smith, K. (2013) 'Student perceptions of classroom feedback', *Assessment in Education: principles*, 20. doi:10.1080/0969594X.2012.749212.

Glover, C. and Brown, E. (2006) 'Written feedback for students: too much, too detailed or too incomprehensible to be effective?', *Bioscience Education*, 7(1), pp. 1–16. doi:10.3108/beej.2006.07000004.

Goffman, E. (1963) *Stigma*. Penguin.

Grant, A.M. (2022) Is it time to REGROW the GROW model? Issues related to teaching coaching session structures. In Tee, D. and Passmore, J. Wiley, *Coaching Practiced*, pp. 29–40.

Hattie, J. and Timperley, H. (2007) 'The power of feedback', *Review of Educational Research*, 77, pp. 81–112.

Hyland, F. and Lo, M.M. (2006) 'Examining interaction in the teaching practicum: issues of language, power and control', *Mentoring & Tutoring: Partnership in Learning*, 14(2), pp. 163–186.

Irons, A. (2008) *Enhancing learning through formative assessment and feedback*. Routledge.

Jordan, J.L. Sr. (2023) Understanding the experience of Black male collegiate students and exploring the factors that lead to their retention through mentorship programs. Unpublished Doctoral dissertation, Northern Kentucky University. Available from: https://www.proquest.com/openview/afa9b642e5cc6debb152ea539d9fba62/1?cbl=18750&diss=y&pq-origsite=gscholar.

Kerman, N.T., Banihashem, S.K., Karami, M., Er, E., Van Ginkel, S. and Noroozi, O. (2024) 'Online peer feedback in higher education: a synthesis of the literature', *Education and Information Technologies*, 29(1), pp. 763–813.

Kluger, A.N. and DeNisi, A. (1996) 'The effects of feedback interventions on performance: a historical review, a meta-analysis, and a preliminary feedback intervention theory', *Psychological Bulletin*, 119, pp. 254–284.

Le, P.T.A. and Vásquez, C. (2011) 'Discourse and intern perceptions', *Teacher Development*, 15(4), pp. 453–470.

Leach, S. (2020) 'Behavioural coaching: the GROW model', in *The coaches' handbook*. Routledge, pp. 176–186.

Lim, T.-S. and Bowers, J.W. (1991) 'Facework: solidarity, approbation, and tact', *Human Communication Research*, 17(3), pp. 415–450.

McCarthy, J. (2017) 'Enhancing feedback in higher education: students' attitudes towards online and in-class formative assessment feedback models', *Active Learning in Higher Education*, 18(2), pp. 127–141.

Molloy, E., Boud, D. and Henderson, M. (2019) 'Developing a learning-centred framework for feedback literacy', *Assessment & Evaluation in Higher Education*, 45(4), pp. 527–540. doi:10.1080/02602938.2019.1667955.

Nicol, D. and Macfarlane, D. (2006) 'Formative assessment and self-regulated learning: a model and seven principles of good feedback practice', *Studies in Higher Education*, 31, pp. 199–218. doi:10.1080/03075070600572090.

O'Leary, M. (2011) The role of lesson observation in shaping professional identity, learning and development in further education colleges in the West Midlands. Unpublished PhD thesis. Institute of Education, University of Warwick.

O'Leary, M. (2020) *Classroom observation: a guide to the effective observation of teaching and learning*. Routledge.

O'Leary, M. (2022) 'Rethinking teachers' professional learning through unseen observation', *Professional Development in Education*, 1–14. doi:10.1080/19415257.2022.2125551.

Pendleton, D., Schofield, T., Tate, P. and Havelock, P. (1984) *The consultation: an approach to learning and teaching*. Oxford University Press. https://www.tandfonline.com/action/showCitFormats?doi=10.1080/03054985.2020.1846289.

Puttick, S. and Wynn, J. (2021) 'Constructing "good teaching" through written lesson observation feedback', *Oxford Review of Education*, 47(2), pp. 152–169. doi:10.1080/03054985.2020.1846289.

Redmond, M. (2015) *Social exchange theory [White paper]*. Iowa State University. https://dr.lib.iastate.edu/entities/publication/3269a123-c890-4b0c-b114-fd12e43e7f4.

Rubtcova, M., Pavenkov, O. and Pavenkov, V. (2016) The grow-model in the coaching session. In 016 NSCA Coaches Conference in San Antonio, TX.

Rubtcova, M., Pavenkov, O. and Pavenkov, V. (2016) The grow-model in the coaching session. In NSCA Coaches Conference in San Antonio, TX. January 16th

Ruiz-Primo, M. (2011) 'Informal formative assessment: the role of instructional dialogues in assessing students' learning', *Studies in Educational Evaluation*, 37, pp. 15–24. doi:10.1016/j.stueduc.2011.04.003.

Seiler, H. (2021) *Using client feedback in executive coaching: improving reflective practicee*. McGraw-Hill Education.

Sorensen, B. (2024) Delivering negative feedback with empathy and effectiveness. https://www.amazon.co.uk/Delivering-Negative-Feedback-Effectiveness-Receiving-ebook/dp/B0DPWCQRZH.

Tochon, F.V. (2001) 'Education research: new avenues for video pedagogy and feedback in teacher education', *International Journal of Applied Semiotics*, 2, pp. 9–28.

Tyrer, C. (2023) 'Untangling the complexity of mentoring feedback practices in post-compulsory initial teacher education in the UK', *Journal of Further and Higher Education*, 47(1), pp. 31–44. doi:10.1080/0309877X.2022.2088271.

Watson, A. and Williams, M. (2004) 'Post-lesson debriefing: delayed or immediate? An investigation of student teacher talk', *Journal of Education for Teaching*, 30, pp. 85–96. doi:10.1080/0260747042000229726.

White, S. (2007) 'Investigating effective feedback practices for pre-service teacher education students on practicum', *Teaching Education*, 18(4), pp. 299–311.

Wiliam, D. (2011) 'What is assessment for learning?', *Studies in Educational Evaluation*, 37, pp. 3–14.

Zimmerman, B. (2002) 'Becoming a self-regulated learner: an overview', *Theory Into Practice*, 41, pp. 64–70. doi:10.1207/s15430421tip4102_2.

Chapter 10

Mentoring and inclusion

Mentoring, inclusion, and equity

Mentoring in education plays a pivotal role in fostering inclusivity and equity, especially in supporting underrepresented student populations. A mentorship relationship provides a supportive and guidance-based framework that can help underrepresented students navigate the complexities of the education system, overcome barriers to success, and thrive academically and personally.

Mentors can serve as role models, advocates, and allies for underrepresented students, offering them mentorship, advice, encouragement, and resources to help them succeed (Davies and Crozier, 2006). By providing personalised support and guidance, mentors can help underrepresented students build confidence, self-efficacy, and a sense of belonging within the educational environment. This support is crucial in addressing systemic inequalities, biases, and barriers that may hinder the academic achievement and well-being of underrepresented student populations.

They can also help underrepresented students develop essential skills, networks, and opportunities that can enhance their educational experiences and future prospects (Duckworth and Maxwell (2015). Mentoring relationships can provide access to resources, opportunities for growth, and exposure to diverse perspectives and pathways, empowering underrepresented students to reach their full potential and pursue their academic and career goals.

Inclusivity and equity in education are essential for creating a learning environment that is supportive, respectful, and accessible to all students, regardless of their backgrounds or identities. Mentoring plays a crucial role in promoting these values by fostering a sense of belonging, empowering underrepresented students, and addressing systemic inequalities. By investing in mentorship programmes that prioritise inclusivity and equity, educational institutions can create more supportive and equitable learning environments that benefit all students, particularly those who have been historically marginalised or disadvantaged (Duckworth and Maxwell, 2015).

Inclusive mentoring relationships

Mentor cultural awareness and sensitivity

Demonstrating cultural awareness and sensitivity towards their mentee is essential for mentors to build trust, rapport, and effective communication in the mentoring relationship. There are several ways in which they can exhibit this (Garner, 2003):

- Respect and value cultural differences

Mentors should demonstrate respect for their mentee's cultural background, traditions, values, and beliefs. Cultural backgrounds, traditions, values, and beliefs can significantly impact the dynamics of a mentor-mentee relationship in education. The intersection of diverse cultural identities between the mentor and mentee can influence communication, expectations, perceptions, and interactions within the mentoring partnership. Here are some ways in which cultural backgrounds can impact the mentor-mentee relationship (Hansman, 2002):

- Communication styles

Different cultural backgrounds may shape how individuals communicate, including verbal and nonverbal cues, language usage, tone, and expressions. Misinterpretations in communication styles can lead to misunderstandings or barriers to effective dialogue between the mentor and mentee. Different cultural backgrounds bring diverse communication norms, expectations, and preferences that can influence the effectiveness of mentorship interactions (Johnson-Bailey and Cervero, 2004).

- Verbal and nonverbal communication

Verbal and nonverbal cues play a critical role in shaping the dynamics of mentoring relationships in education, and these cues carry significant cultural implications that can impact communication, understanding, and rapport between mentors and mentees. Cultural differences in the interpretation of verbal and nonverbal cues can influence the effectiveness and success of mentoring interactions (Johnson-Bailey and Cervero, 2004).

Verbal communication

Language nuances

Cultural differences in language usage, expressions, and idiomatic expressions can affect the clarity and understanding of verbal communication between mentors and mentees. Mentors and mentees from diverse cultural backgrounds may interpret phrases or words differently, leading to potential miscommunication (Osipov, Ziyatdinova and Irismetova, 2020).

Nonverbal communication

Body language and gestures

Nonverbal cues such as gestures, facial expressions, and body language can convey emotions, attitudes, and intentions in communication. However, these cues can be culturally specific and may be interpreted differently based on a person's cultural background. Mentors and mentees need to be mindful of nonverbal signals to ensure mutual understanding and connection (Singh, 2022).

Personal space and proximity

Cultural norms around personal space, touch, and proximity can impact the nonverbal interactions between mentors and mentees. Some cultures may value close physical contact, while others prioritise maintaining distance (Singh, 2022). Respect for these cultural differences in nonverbal communication can promote comfort and trust in the mentorship relationship.

Direct vs. indirect communication

Some cultures value direct, explicit communication, while others tend to employ indirect, implicit communication styles. Mentors and mentees coming from different communication paradigms may find it challenging to align their expectations and preferences, affecting clarity, transparency, and the exchange of feedback within the mentoring relationship.

Hierarchical vs. egalitarian communication

Cultural norms around power distance and hierarchical structures can influence the dynamics of communication between mentors and mentees. In cultures where deference to authority is emphasised, mentees may be less likely to engage in open dialogue or express dissenting opinions, impacting the depth of the mentoring relationship and hindering mutual understanding (Young, Haffejee and Corsun, 2017).

Listening and feedback

The way individuals listen, process information, and provide feedback can vary across cultures. Mentors need to be attuned to their mentees' communication styles, active listening skills, and feedback preferences to ensure effective communication and meaningful engagement in the mentorship process (Tyrer, 2023).

> **Mentor training exercise**
>
> **Cultural iceberg exercise**
>
> Provide participants with a visual of an iceberg, with the tip above the water representing visible cultural aspects (e.g. food, clothing) and the submerged portion representing invisible aspects (e.g. values, beliefs). Discuss how these hidden cultural factors impact communication.

Navigating cultural differences in communication styles requires mentors to practice empathy, sensitivity, and adaptability, fostering a culture of openness, respect, and inclusivity in their mentoring relationships within the educational setting.

Expectations and goals

Cultural values and beliefs can influence the mentee's and mentor's expectations regarding the mentoring relationship, academic achievement, career aspirations, and personal development. Understanding and aligning these expectations can foster a more productive and supportive mentoring dynamic.

Academic expectations and goals are fundamental aspects of mentoring relationships in education, and they can be profoundly influenced by the cultural backgrounds of both mentors and mentees. The intersection of diverse cultural values, beliefs, and norms can shape how academic success is perceived, pursued, and supported within the mentoring dynamic (Davies and Crozier, 2006).

Cultural perceptions of success

Different cultures may have varying definitions of academic success and achievement. Some cultures prioritise grades, test scores, and external recognition as indicators of success, while others may value holistic development, creativity, and resilience. These divergent views can impact the academic expectations that mentors and mentees bring to the mentoring relationship.

Educational aspirations

Cultural backgrounds can influence the educational aspirations and career goals of mentees. Factors such as family expectations, societal norms, and economic constraints may shape a mentee's ambition to pursue higher education, specific fields of study, or certain career pathways. Mentors need to be attuned to these cultural factors when guiding and supporting their mentees in setting and achieving their academic goals (Blake-Beard, 2009).

Support systems and resources

Cultural backgrounds can also influence the availability of support systems and resources for academic success. Mentees from marginalised or underrepresented cultural groups may face systemic barriers, lack access to educational opportunities, or experience discrimination that affects their academic journey. Mentors can play a crucial role in advocating for equitable resources, providing guidance on navigating challenges, and fostering a supportive environment that acknowledges and addresses the cultural impact on academic expectations and goals within the mentoring relationship (Duckworth and Maxwell, 2015).

Conflict resolution

Cultural differences in approaches to conflict resolution, feedback, and decision-making can impact how challenges are addressed within the mentor-mentee relationship. Awareness of these cultural nuances can help mentors navigate conflicts constructively and maintain a positive mentoring environment.

This is a crucial aspect of mentoring relationships in education, and culture plays a significant role in shaping how conflicts are perceived, managed, and resolved between mentors and mentees. Different cultural backgrounds bring diverse approaches to conflict resolution, communication styles, and conflict management strategies.

Cultural conflict styles

Cultures vary in their preferred conflict resolution styles, ranging from direct and confrontational to indirect and harmonious approaches. Some cultures may view disagreements or conflicts as opportunities for open debate and problem-solving, while others may prioritise harmony, saving face, and avoiding confrontation. These cultural differences can influence how conflicts are addressed and resolved within the mentoring relationship (Hansman, 2002).

Communication patterns

Cultural norms around communication, assertiveness, and expression of emotions can influence how conflicts are communicated and perceived. Mentors and mentees from different cultural backgrounds may have distinct communication patterns that impact their conflict resolution strategies and the effectiveness of communication during disagreements.

A staff development session activity for prospective mentors

Scenario Task: Cultural Miscommunication and Resolution for Prospective Mentors Scenario: Chloe is assigned to mentor Anika, a trainee teacher from a different cultural background. During their initial meeting, Chloe notices that Anika avoids making direct eye contact and speaks softly. Chloe interprets this as a lack of confidence and engagement in the mentoring process. However, Anika comes from a culture where direct eye contact is considered disrespectful and speaking softly is a sign of respect.

Give the group the scenario and ask them to discuss the following questions in pairs:

1 Why do you think Chloe interpreted Anika's quietness in this way?
2 What could be the impact of making these assumptions on the mentoring relationship?
3 What steps should Chloe take to manage these potential issues?

Some hints to a resolution

1 Reflect on Assumptions: Chloe might reflect on her initial interpretation of Anika's behaviour and consider how cultural differences may have influenced her perceptions. Encourage self-awareness and examination of biases.
2 Seek Understanding: Chloe could engage Anika in a conversation about cultural norms and communication styles in her background. Encourage open dialogue to understand Anika's perspective and communication preferences.
3 Adapt Communication Style: She could adapt her communication style by being more attentive to nonverbal cues and respecting Anika's cultural norms. Practice active listening and validate Anika's communication preferences.
4 Establish Clear Communication Guidelines: Chloe might collaboratively establish clear communication guidelines with Anika to ensure mutual understanding and respect in their mentoring relationship.
5 Reflect and Adjust: After implementing the resolved strategies, Chloe could reflect on the effectiveness of the new communication approach and its impact on the mentoring dynamic.

Power dynamics and hierarchical structures

Cultural values related to power distance and hierarchy can influence how conflicts are addressed within the mentoring relationship. In cultures with high power distance, mentees may be less inclined to challenge or express disagreement with mentors, leading to potential conflicts being overlooked or unresolved. Mentors need to be aware of these cultural dynamics and adapt their conflict resolution strategies accordingly to ensure that conflicts are addressed openly, constructively, and equitably in the mentoring relationship (Hansman, 2002).

Scenario: 'Power Dynamic Issue Related to Culture in a Mentoring Relationship'.
Background: Maria, a seasoned mentor, has been matched with Ahmed, a mentee from a different cultural background. As they work together, Maria notices a power dynamic issue emerging that is rooted in cultural differences.
Scenario: During their mentoring sessions, Maria and Ahmed often discuss Ahmed's career goals, aspirations, and challenges. However, Maria unintentionally starts to dominate the conversations, steer the direction of the discussions, and offer advice without soliciting Ahmed's input or perspective. Ahmed, who comes from a cultural background that values respect for authority figures and deference to elders, hesitates to assert himself or express his own opinions, feeling compelled to comply with Maria's guidance and suggestions.

As the mentoring relationship progresses, Maria notices that Ahmed appears hesitant, reserved, and passive during their interactions. Despite her efforts to encourage Ahmed to share his thoughts, goals, and concerns openly, he remains reluctant and deferential, deferring to Maria's expertise and authority in their discussions. Maria also realises that some of her assumptions about Ahmed's needs, preferences, and learning style may stem from cultural biases and stereotypes rather than a genuine understanding of Ahmed's unique background and experiences.

Reflecting on the situation, Maria recognises the power imbalance that has emerged in their mentoring relationship due to cultural differences in communication styles, hierarchical structures, and deference to authority. She acknowledges the need to take a more collaborative and inclusive approach, actively listen to Ahmed's perspective, and create a safe space for him to engage authentically and assert his autonomy within the mentoring relationship. By addressing the power dynamic issue related to culture, Maria aims to foster mutual respect, empowerment, and trust in their mentoring interactions.

Questions

Why did the relationship between them begin to break down?
Which of Maria's assumptions about her mentee seemed to be creating the biggest barriers between them?
What kind of impact do you think this was having upon Ahmed's development as a teacher?
What kind of practical changes would you put in place to support Ahmed's development if you were his mentor?
How would you assess the effectiveness of these changes over time?

Personal and collective orientations

The emphasis on individuality versus collectivism in different cultures can also impact conflict resolution. Cultures that value collective harmony and group cohesion may prioritise consensus-building and compromise in conflict resolution, while individualistic cultures may focus on assertiveness and individual rights. Mentors and mentees need to navigate these cultural orientations in conflict resolution to foster understanding, respect, and positive outcomes in the mentoring relationship (Johnson-Bailey and Cervero, 2002).

Mentorship approaches

Respect for diversity

Culturally responsive mentorship involves recognising, respecting, and valuing the diversity of cultural backgrounds, traditions, values, and beliefs within the mentor-mentee relationship. By embracing cultural differences and fostering inclusivity, mentors can create a nurturing and inclusive learning environment that supports the mentee's academic growth and personal development. These can include the following:

- Listen actively and empathetically

Mentors should actively listen to their mentee's perspectives, experiences, and challenges with an open mind. Showing empathy and understanding towards their mentee's cultural context can foster trust and communication.

- Acknowledging the unique cultural background of their mentees

By recognising and valuing diverse perspectives, mentors create an inclusive space where mentees feel understood and appreciated.

- Capitalising on their mentees' cultural strengths, values, and experiences to enhance their learning and personal growth.

For instance, mentors can encourage mentees to draw upon their cultural heritage, language skills, or community networks to explore new opportunities, overcome challenges, and develop leadership qualities.

- Building trust and rapport

This trust-based relationship allows mentees to be more open, responsive, and receptive to guidance and feedback from their mentors (Johnson-Bailey and Cervero, 2002).

- Addressing cultural barriers

Mentors can help them navigate cultural barriers, biases, and stereotypes that may impact their educational journey. This can help to empower mentees to overcome obstacles, build resilience, and thrive academically and personally (Marshall *et al.*, 2022).

- Avoiding assumptions and stereotypes

Mentors should refrain from making assumptions or generalisations based on their mentee's cultural identity. Avoiding stereotypes and approaching each mentee as an individual can help prevent bias and misinterpretation.

Stereotyped thinking can have negative repercussions on mentoring relationships in education by perpetuating biases, hindering communication, eroding trust, and limiting the potential for mutual learning and growth. Mentors and mentees bring their own preconceived notions, assumptions, and stereotypes based on factors such as race, gender, ethnicity, or socio-economic background (Woodcock *et al.*, 2022).

Unconscious bias

Unconscious biases rooted in stereotypes can manifest in subtle ways that negatively impact mentoring relationships. These biases may influence mentors' decisions on allocations of resources, opportunities, or feedback, leading to inequitable outcomes for mentees.

Unconscious biases held by mentors in education can significantly impact their decisions regarding the allocation of resources, opportunities, and support for their mentees. These biases, which are often rooted in stereotypes, prejudices, and ingrained beliefs, can shape mentors' perceptions, judgements, and actions in ways that may perpetuate inequalities, hinder academic progress, and limit the potential for student success (Davies and Crozier (2006).

For example, a mentor with biases towards certain ethnic groups may unconsciously favour students who align with their own cultural norms or values when providing resources, such as access to extracurricular activities, specialised learning materials, or networking opportunities. This preferential treatment can result in unequal distribution of resources and opportunities, disadvantaging students who do not fit the mentor's biased mould (Young, Haffejee and Corsun, 2017).

Moreover, unconscious biases can also impact mentors' perceptions of mentees' abilities, potential, and needs, leading to inaccurate assessments and misguided resource allocations. For instance, a mentor with implicit biases about gender roles may underestimate the leadership capabilities of female students, thereby overlooking their potential for leadership development opportunities or career advancement resources.

Unconscious biases can significantly influence how mentors in education provide feedback to their mentees, shaping the tone, content, and effectiveness of their guidance. These biases, which often stem from deeply ingrained stereotypes, prejudices, and assumptions, can impact mentors' perceptions of their mentees' skills, abilities, and potential for growth. As a result, unconscious biases can lead to skewed evaluations, unfair judgements, and differential treatment in the feedback process (Osipov, Ziyatdinova and Irismetova, 2020).

One way in which unconscious biases can affect feedback provision is through the lens of perceived competence. Mentors may unknowingly hold biases based on factors such as race, gender, socio-economic status, or cultural background, leading them to assess their mentees' performance through a distorted or narrow perspective (Javier *et al.*, 2022).

Additionally, unconscious biases can influence the language and tone used in feedback delivery. Mentors may unknowingly use language that reflects their biases, such as using more critical or dismissive language when providing feedback to mentees from underrepresented groups. This can create a hostile or discouraging feedback environment, undermining mentees' confidence, motivation, and sense of belonging (Cobb-Roberts *et al.*, 2017).

Unconscious biases self-test

1: How can mentors become aware of their unconscious biases when mentoring others?

A. By taking unconscious bias training courses
B. By ignoring their biases and focusing solely on their mentees
C. By relying on their gut feelings and instincts
D. By assuming that they have no biases

2: What can be the potential impact of mentors' unconscious biases on their mentees?

A. Positive reinforcement and growth opportunities
B. Enhanced self-esteem and confidence
C. Limited access to opportunities and biased evaluation
D. Increased trust and effective communication

3: What strategies can mentors employ to mitigate the influence of their unconscious biases?

A. Trusting their initial impressions and assumptions
B. Engaging in self-reflection and seeking diverse perspectives
C. Relying on stereotypes to make quick judgements
D. Assigning mentees based on personal preferences

4: Why is it important for mentors to challenge their unconscious biases?

A. Unconscious biases have no impact on mentoring relationships.
B. Unconscious biases can perpetuate inequalities and hinder growth.
C. Unconscious biases lead to stronger mentor-mentee connections.
D. Unconscious biases should be embraced and celebrated.

5: How can mentors create an inclusive and bias-free mentoring environment?

A. By only mentoring individuals who share their background and experiences
B. By recognising and embracing their biases without addressing them
C. By actively seeking diverse mentees and promoting equal opportunities
D. By relying solely on their expertise and professional achievements

6: What is the potential consequence of mentors failing to address their unconscious biases?

A. Enhanced learning and development opportunities for mentees
B. Creation of a supportive and inclusive mentoring environment
C. Reinforcement of stereotypes and discrimination
D. Strengthened mentor-mentee relationships

7: How can mentors ensure fair and unbiased performance evaluations for their mentees?

A. By relying on their gut feelings and initial impressions
B. By setting unrealistic expectations and standards
C. By using objective criteria and avoiding personal biases
D. By comparing mentees to their own achievements and progress

8: How can mentors actively challenge their unconscious biases during mentoring sessions?

A. By avoiding difficult conversations and uncomfortable topics
B. By regularly seeking feedback from their mentees
C. By enforcing their own opinions and values on mentees
D. By prioritising their own needs and goals over their mentees'

9: What role does self-awareness play in addressing mentors' unconscious biases?

A. Self-awareness has no impact on unconscious biases.
B. Self-awareness helps mentors justify their biases.
C. Self-awareness allows mentors to recognise and challenge their biases.
D. Self-awareness leads to a stronger bond between mentors and mentees.

10: How can mentors advocate for diversity and inclusion in their mentoring relationships?

A. By avoiding mentees from diverse backgrounds
B. By promoting equal opportunities and addressing biases
C. By prioritising their own personal preferences and biases
D. By excluding diverse perspectives from the mentoring process

The answers

1. Answer: A. By taking unconscious bias training courses
2. Answer: C. Limited access to opportunities and biased evaluation
3. Answer: B. Engaging in self-reflection and seeking diverse perspectives
4. Answer: B. Unconscious biases can perpetuate inequalities and hinder growth.
5. Answer: C. By actively seeking diverse mentees and promoting equal opportunities
6. Answer: C. Reinforcement of stereotypes and discrimination
7. Answer: C. By using objective criteria and avoiding personal biases
8. Answer: B. By regularly seeking feedback from their mentees
9. Answer: C. Self-awareness allows mentors to recognise and challenge their biases.
10. B. By promoting equal opportunities and addressing biases

Case Study Task: 'Exploring Unconscious Bias in Mentoring Relationships'

Objective: The purpose of this case study task is to provide mentors with an opportunity to reflect on their own unconscious biases and examine how these biases may influence their mentoring interactions with students.

Scenario: You are a mentor in an educational programme, working with a diverse group of students from various cultural backgrounds. One of your mentees, Sarah, has been struggling academically and seeking guidance on improving her performance. During a recent mentoring session, you noticed that you provided more critical feedback to Sarah compared to other mentees who are performing similarly. Reflecting on this interaction, you realise that Sarah's cultural background differs from your own, and you may have unconsciously held biases that influenced your feedback.

Task: Reflect on the following questions and consider how your unconscious biases may have impacted your mentoring relationship with Sarah:

1 What assumptions or stereotypes might you hold about students from different cultural backgrounds? How might these biases influence your perceptions of their abilities and performance?
2 How did your feedback to Sarah compare to feedback provided to other mentees in similar situations? Were there differences in tone, content, or level of criticism?
3 In what ways did your unconscious biases manifest in your interactions with Sarah, and how might they have affected her motivation, self-esteem, or willingness to seek help?
4 How can you become more aware of your unconscious biases and mitigate their impact on your mentoring relationships moving forward? Reflect on strategies for fostering a more inclusive and equitable mentoring environment for all students.

Mentoring and neurodiversity

The understanding of neurodiversity is grounded in several theoretical frameworks that shape the perception of neurological differences and diversity in the human population. Some key theoretical underpinnings of neurodiversity include the following.

Social model of disability

The social model of disability is a theoretical framework that views disability as a result of societal barriers, discrimination, and exclusion rather than as an inherent limitation of an individual's impairment. The social model of disability posits that disability is not solely a result of an individual's impairment but is also influenced by societal barriers, attitudes, and structures. In the context of neurodiversity, this model shifts the focus from viewing neurological differences as deficits to recognising them as part of the natural variation of human cognition and behaviour. The main characteristics of the social model of disability include (Goering, 2015):

- Focus on Social Context

  The social model emphasises that disability is not solely a result of an individual's impairment or medical condition but is shaped by the physical, attitudinal, and social barriers present in society.

- Distinction Between Impairment and Disability

It distinguishes between impairment (the physical, sensory, cognitive, or emotional differences a person may have) and disability (the limitations and disadvantages imposed by society on individuals with impairments).

- Emphasis on Structural Barriers

It highlights the role of structural and environmental barriers, such as physical obstacles, lack of accessibility, discriminatory practices, and social attitudes, in creating disabling conditions for individuals with impairments and advocates for the recognition of disability rights, equal opportunities, and social inclusion for all individuals, regardless of their impairments (Cope and Remington, 2022).

- Shift in Perspective

It promotes a shifting in focus from the individual's impairment to the social and environmental factors that create disabling conditions, challenging traditional medical models of disability and promoting a more inclusive and rights-based approach to understanding and addressing disability (2022).

- Neurodiversity Paradigm

The neurodiversity paradigm asserts that neurological differences, such as autism, ADHD, dyslexia, and other conditions, are valuable variations of the human brain rather than disorders or deficiencies. This perspective emphasises the strengths, talents, and unique perspectives that neurodivergent individuals bring to society. It is a perspective that challenges traditional views of neurological differences, such as autism, ADHD, dyslexia, and other conditions, by reframing them as natural variations of human neurocognition rather than disorders or deficits (Hamilton and Petty, 2023). The characteristics of the Neurodiversity Paradigm include the following.

Respect for neurological diversity

It recognises and respects the diverse ways in which individuals' brains function and process information. It acknowledges that neurodivergent individuals have unique strengths, talents, and perspectives to offer. It promotes the acceptance and celebration of neurodivergent identities and encourages individuals to embrace their neurocognitive differences as integral aspects of their identities rather than something to be fixed or cured (Jaarsma and Welin, 2012).

Emphasis on accommodation and inclusion

It advocates for creating environments that accommodate the needs and preferences of neurodivergent individuals. This includes promoting accessibility, providing support services, and fostering opportunities for inclusion and participation (Mirfin-Veitch, Jalota and Schmidt, 2020).

Challenging medical pathologisation

It reframes neurodivergence as a natural variation within the human population and critiques the pathologisation of neurological differences and challenges the notion that these differences represent disorders or deficits that need to be cured.

Advocacy for neurodivergent rights

It promotes social acceptance, equal opportunities, and respect for the diversity of human neurocognition and emphasises the rights of neurodivergent individuals to self-advocate, access accommodations, and participate fully in society. It also embraces the idea that individuals have the right to self-identify and define their own neurocognitive identities, whether it be as autistic, ADHD, dyslexic, or any other neurodivergent trait or condition (Fernandes, 2019).

Autonomy and agency

It values the autonomy and agency of neurodivergent individuals, recognising their right to make decisions about their own lives and experiences, and fosters a sense of community and connection among neurodivergent individuals, providing opportunities for mutual support, shared experiences, and collective advocacy efforts. It also recognises the intersection of neurodivergence with other aspects of identity, such as race, gender, sexuality, and socio-economic status, and advocates for inclusive and intersectional approaches to identity and self-advocacy (Heng, Quinlivan and du Plessis, 2019).

> **Intersectionality self-reflective task for prospective mentor teachers**
>
> Step 1: Understanding Intersectionality
> Reflect on your own social identities (e.g. race, gender, socio-economic status, sexual orientation) and how they intersect to shape your experiences and perspectives.

Step 2: Recognising Privilege and Marginalisation
   Identify areas where you hold privilege and how this may impact your interactions with trainee teachers from diverse backgrounds. Consider the systemic barriers that marginalised individuals face in the education system.

Step 3: Cultural Competence
   Assess your cultural competence and awareness of diverse perspectives. Reflect on how your background and experiences may influence your mentoring approach and communication style with trainee teachers.

Step 4: Addressing Bias
   Examine unconscious biases that may affect your perceptions and interactions with trainee teachers. Consider how power dynamics and stereotypes can impact your mentoring relationships.

Step 5: Creating an Inclusive Environment
   Reflect on strategies to create an inclusive and supportive mentoring environment for trainee teachers of all backgrounds. Consider how your intersectional awareness can enhance mentorship effectiveness.

Step 6: Action Plan
   Develop an action plan outlining concrete steps you can take to foster a more inclusive and equitable mentoring experience for trainee teachers. Set goals for ongoing reflection and growth in intersectional awareness as a mentor.

Neurodiversity and mentoring

Mentoring a trainee who is mentoring a neurodiverse mentee

Mentoring a neurodiverse trainee teacher can present unique challenges for mentors due to differences in processing styles, sensory sensitivities, communication preferences, and social interaction norms. Mentors may struggle with understanding and accommodating these differences, leading to barriers in effective mentorship. One key reason is the lack of awareness and training on neurodiversity among mentors, which can result in misconceptions, biases, and limited knowledge about how to support neurodiverse individuals effectively (Ravet, 2017).

They may find it challenging to recognise and interpret the behaviours, needs, and preferences of neurodiverse trainee teachers. This lack of understanding can lead to misinterpretations, frustration, and feelings of inadequacy in the mentorship relationship. Additionally, mentors may struggle with adapting their communication style, providing appropriate support, and creating an inclusive environment that caters to the unique strengths and challenges of neurodiverse individuals (Livingston, Hargitai and Shah, 2024).

They may also face difficulties in addressing sensory sensitivities and processing differences that can impact the trainee teacher's learning and engagement. Creating accommodations, modifying teaching strategies, and providing tailored feedback requires a high level of flexibility, patience, and adaptability on the part of the mentor. Failure to address these needs effectively can result in decreased confidence, motivation, and progress for the neurodiverse trainee teacher (Young, Haffejee and Corsun, 2017).

A mentor could also encounter challenges in navigating social interaction norms and building rapport with mentees. Differences in social cues, nonverbal communication, and social dynamics can create misunderstandings, conflicts, and disconnect in the mentorship relationship. Mentors will need to develop cultural competence, empathy, and active listening skills to foster a supportive and inclusive mentorship environment for neurodiverse trainee teachers (Sewell and Park, 2021).

Ways to develop the support of neurodiverse trainees

These could include the following suggestions (Sewell and Park, 2021).

Increase awareness and understanding

Potential mentors can educate themselves about neurodiversity, including different neurodevelopmental conditions, sensory sensitivities, processing styles, communication preferences, and social interaction norms. This knowledge can help mentors better understand and support neurodiverse trainee teachers.

Foster an inclusive and supportive environment

Mentors can create an inclusive and supportive environment by promoting acceptance, empathy, and respect for neurodiverse individuals. Encouraging open communication, providing accommodations, and recognising diverse strengths can help trainee teachers feel valued and supported in their learning and growth (Ravet, 2017).

Adapt communication and feedback

Mentors should adapt their communication style to meet the needs of neurodiverse trainee teachers, such as providing clear instructions, using visual aids, giving structured feedback, and allowing extra processing time. If they are flexible and patient in their communication approach, mentors can facilitate effective learning and development for neurodiverse individuals.

Provide structured support and resources

Mentors can offer structured support and resources to help neurodiverse trainee teachers navigate challenges, build skills, and achieve their goals. This may include access to assistive technologies, additional training opportunities, and mentoring sessions focused on specific areas of growth or improvement (Lambe, 2007).

Encourage self-advocacy and development

Mentors should empower neurodiverse trainee teachers to advocate for their needs, communicate their preferences, and take ownership of their professional development. When they facilitate the development of self-awareness, self-confidence, and self-advocacy skills, mentors can help trainee teachers thrive in their teaching roles and succeed in their career paths (2007).

Mentors who are neurodiverse

Neurodiverse mentors can bring a range of unique strengths and perspectives to their role, enhancing the mentorship experience in a college setting (Cope and Remington, 2022):

1 Diverse Problem-Solving Approaches
   Neurodiverse individuals often have unique problem-solving skills and alternative perspectives, allowing them to approach challenges in creative and innovative ways (Sewell and Park, 2021).
2 Attention to Detail
   Many neurodiverse individuals exhibit a strong attention to detail and a keen focus on specific tasks, which can benefit trainee teachers in lesson planning, assessment, and instructional design. Neurodiverse mentors may also excel in analysing data, patterns, and information, enabling them to provide insightful feedback and guidance to trainee teachers on their teaching practices (Cope and Remington, 2022).
3 Passion and Dedication
   Neurodiverse individuals often demonstrate intense passion and dedication in their work, showing a deep commitment to supporting and nurturing the growth of trainee teachers. According to Anet:

> Some of my mentees never mention the problems they are having in their placement because of the needs with their university tutors because they are afraid of appearing being unable to cope so they ask me to step in as a go between.

4 Empathy and Understanding
   Neurodiverse mentors may have a heightened sense of empathy and understanding towards the challenges and struggles faced by trainee teachers, especially those who are also neurodiverse, fostering a supportive and inclusive mentorship relationship (Mirfin-Veitch, Jalota and Schmidt, 2020). According to Angela and Marius:

> I have mentored several trainees with Dyslexia over the past five years and I think that for the most part my own dyslexia has helped me to understand their problems on a day-to-day basis and to provide effective support on the PGCE course.
>
> (Angela)

> I think that a big plus (of being neurodiverse) is that I don't have to hesitate when I raise the issues about their needs with my mentees, nor do I feel embarrassed or patronising.
>
> (Marius)

Here are some of the main obstacles they may face:

1 Lack of Understanding and Awareness
   Colleagues and trainee teachers may have limited understanding of neurodiversity, leading to misconceptions, stigma, and discrimination against neurodiverse individuals (Milton, 2012). For example:

> I applied to be a mentor on the course for four years running and never even got an interview. I think they turned me down because of my autism. It was only when they were really desperate last year in my college and couldn't find any one else that they that they gave me a chance.
>
> (Clementina)

> I found it really hard to support some of my trainees' learning needs as well as battle against some of the prejudices of my colleagues who used to make comments about the competency of my trainees and ... who sometimes used to present obstacles in my way.
>
> (Caroline)

2 Communication Challenges
   These could include some of the following:

> In the first instance, a neurodiverse mentor who has a different processing style, such as needing more time to process information or preferring

visual aids for comprehension, may struggle to keep up with the fast-paced nature of mentorship meetings or workshops. This could lead to misunderstandings, missed cues, or feelings of being overwhelmed, hindering effective communication and collaboration with trainee teachers.

(Lambe and Bones, 2006)

It is also possible that a neurodiverse mentor who is sensitive to certain sensory stimuli, such as loud noises, bright lights, or strong aromas, may find it challenging to focus and engage in mentorship sessions held in environments with overwhelming sensory input. This could result in discomfort, distraction, or difficulties in conveying information clearly, impeding effective mentorship interactions (Mirfin-Veitch, Jalota and Schmidt, 2020).

Someone who struggles with social interaction norms, such as understanding nonverbal cues, interpreting facial expressions, or navigating complex social dynamics, may face difficulties in building rapport, establishing trust, and maintaining positive relationships with trainee teachers. This could lead to misunderstandings, miscommunications, or conflicts, affecting the effectiveness of mentorship (Jaarsma and Welin, 2012).

There may also be communication differences as a neurodiverse mentor who communicates in a direct, literal, or detailed manner may have challenges in interpreting and responding to subtle nuances, implicit cues, or abstract concepts conveyed by trainee teachers. This mismatch in communication styles could result in misinterpretations, misalignments, or breakdowns in communication, hampering effective mentorship interactions (Milton, 2012).

In addition, a neurodiverse mentor who experiences difficulties in executive functioning skills, such as organisation, planning, time management, or task prioritisation, may struggle to coordinate mentoring activities, provide timely feedback, or meet deadlines effectively. This could lead to inconsistencies, delays, or disorganisation in mentorship processes, impacting the quality and outcomes of mentorship (Mirfin-Veitch, Jalota and Schmidt, 2020)

3 Work Environment and Supports

The college environment may not be adequately designed or supportive of neurodiverse individuals, lacking accommodations such as flexible schedules, sensory-friendly spaces, or resource accessibility:

> Sometimes I really felt between a rock and a hard place as I had to work hard to make reasonable adjustments to meet my mentees' own needs whilst struggling against the constraints of the system to meet my own needs.
>
> (Angela)

4. Bias and Stereotyping

Neurodiverse mentors may face bias, stereotyping, or unconscious discrimination based on misconceptions about their abilities, leading to limited opportunities for professional growth and recognition (Robinson and Hobson, 2017).

> My ex-line manager used to put me off from applying to be a mentor because she said that the universities wouldn't be keen on a mentor with a disability mentoring student with disabilities.
>
> (Lianne)

5. Mental Health and Well-being

The stress and demands of mentoring in a college setting may exacerbate mental health challenges often associated with neurodiversity, such as anxiety, burnout, or sensory overload. According to Margaret:

> I struggle checking my mentees' PowerPoints for spelling and grammar, but I never get enough time to look at them properly because my own preparation for classes gets in the way.

6. Professional Development Opportunities

Limited access to tailored professional development programmes or resources specifically catered to neurodiverse educators may hinder their growth and advancement in their mentoring roles (Marshall *et al.*, 2020):

> I received quite a lot of mentoring training over the two years but in spite of the fact that there were at least five of us out of 20 that had learning needs, there was no real attempt to cater for them. We were just left to our own devices really.
>
> (Joshua)

Self-reflection task

If you were asked to support a new mentor who was neurodiverse, how would you support their development within the following areas.

Communication Issues	How you could support someone with this difficulty
Processing Styles	
Sensory Sensitivities	
Social Interaction Norms	
Communication Differences	
Executive Functioning Challenges	

References

Blake-Beard, S. (2009) 'Mentoring as a bridge to understanding cultural difference', *Adult Learning*, 20, pp. 14–18. doi:10.1177/104515950902000104.

Cobb-Roberts, D., Esnard, T., Unterreiner, A., Agosto, V., Karanxha, Z., Beck, M. and Wu, K. (2017) *Race, gender and mentoring in higher education*. SAGE Publications Ltd. doi:10.4135/9781526402011.

Cope, R. and Remington, A (2022) 'The strengths and abilities of autistic people in the workplace', *Autism Adulthood 2022*, 4(1), pp. 22–31.

Davies, J. and Crozier, G. (2006) 'Tackling diversity in ITE: unpacking the issues', *Race Equality Teaching*, 24, pp. 18–21. doi:10.18546/RET.24.3.06.

Duckworth, V. and Maxwell, B. (2015) 'Extending the mentor role in initial teacher education: embracing social justice', *International Journal of Mentoring and Coaching in Education*, 4(1), pp. 4–20.

Fernandes, L. (2019) Is initial teacher education (ITE) based on the capabilities approach likely to foster inclusion for autistic learners in the further education sector? *Teacher Education Advancement Network Journal*, 11(1), pp. 46–56.

Garner, P. (2003) 'Pretzel only policy? Inclusion and the real world of initial teacher education', *British Journal of Special Education*, 27, pp. 111–116. doi:10.1111/1467-8527.00172.

Goering, S. (2015) 'Rethinking disability: the social model of disability and chronic disease', *Current Reviews in Musculoskeletal Medicine*, 8(2), pp. 134–8. doi:10.1007/s12178-015-9273-z.

Hamilton, L.G. and Petty, S. (2023) 'Compassionate pedagogy for neurodiversity in higher education: a conceptual analysis', *Frontiers in Psychology*, 14, p. 1093290. doi: 10.3389/fpsyg.2023.1093290. Erratum in: *Frontiers in Psychology*, 14, p. 1345256. doi: 10.3389/fpsyg.2023.1345256.

Hansman, C.A. (2002) 'Diversity and power in mentoring relationships'. Semanticscholar.org/paper/Diversity-and-Power-in-Mentoring-Relationships-Hansman/7b5dc3ca15cca442ee1c5b850e0c6003d3db7b6b

Heng, L., Quinlivan, K. and du Plessis, R. (2019) 'Exploring the creation of a new initial teacher education (ITE) programme underpinned by inclusion', *International Journal of Inclusive Education*, 23(10), pp. 1017–1031. doi:10.1080/13603116.2019.1625454.

Jaarsma, P. and Welin, S. (2012) 'Autism as a natural human variation: reflections on the claims of the neurodiversity movement', *Health Care Analysis 2012*, 20(1), pp. 20–30.

Javier, D., Solis, L.G., Paul, M.F., Thompson, E.L., Maynard, G., Latif, Z., Stinson, K., Ahmed, T. and Vishwanatha, J.K. (2022) Implementation of an unconscious bias course for the National Research Mentoring Network. *BMC Medical Education*, 22(1), p. 391.

Johnson-Bailey, J. and Cervero, R. (2002). 'Cross-Cultural Mentoring As a Context for Learning', *New Directions for Adult and Continuing Education*, 10(96), pp. 15–26.

Johnson-Bailey, J. and Cervero, R.M. (2004) 'Mentoring in black and white: the intricacies of cross-cultural mentoring', *Mentoring & Tutoring: Partnership in Learning*, 12(1), pp. 7–21. doi:10.1080/1361126042000183075.

Lambe, J. (2007) 'Student teachers, special educational needs and inclusion education: reviewing the potential for problem-based, e-learning pedagogy to support practice', *Journal of Education for Teaching*, 33(3), pp. 359–377. doi:10.1080/02607470701450551.

Lambe, J. and Bones, R. (2006) 'Student teachers' attitudes to inclusion: implications for initial teacher education in Northern Ireland', *International Journal of Inclusive Education*, 10, pp. 511–527. doi:10.1080/13603110500173225.

Livingston, L.A., Hargitai, L.D. and Shah, P. (2024) 'The double empathy problem: a derivation chain analysis and cautionary note', *Psychological Review*, 2024. doi:10.1037/rev0000468.

Marshall, A.G., Brady, L.J., Palavicino-Maggio, C.B., Neikirk, K., Vue, Z., Beasley, H.K., Garza-Lopez, E., Murray, S.A., Martinez, D., Shuler, H.D. and Spencer, E.C. (2020) The importance of mentors and how to handle more than one mentor. *Pathogens and Disease*, 80(1), pp. 1–6.

Milton, D.E.M. (2012) 'On The ontological status of autism: the "double empathy problem"', *Disability and Society*, 27(6), pp. 883–887.

Mirfin-Veitch, B., Jalota, N. and Schmidt, L. (2020) 'Responding to neurodiversity in the education context: an integrative literature review', *Donald Beasley Institute*, 56.

Osipov, P., Ziyatdinova, J. and Irismetova, I. (2020) Mentoring across cultures and professions: approaches and methods. doi:10.1007/978-3-030-40271-6_76.

Ravet, J. (2017) '"But how do I teach them?": autism & initial teacher education (ITE)', *International Journal of Inclusive Education*, 22(7), pp. 714–733. doi:10.1080/13603116.2017.1412505.

Robinson, C. and Hobson, A. (2017) Mentor education and development in the Further Education sector in England. https://www.brighton.ac.uk/education-research-centre/research-projects/mentor-education-and-development-in-the-further-education-sector-in-england.aspx.Licence:Unspecified.

Sewell, A. and Park, J. (2021) 'A three-factor model of educational practice considerations for teaching neurodiverse learners from a strengths-based perspective', *Support for Learning*, 36(4), pp. 678–694.

Singh, P. (2022) The role of body language in cross cultural communication. *IJRTI*, 7(5). https://ijrti.org/papers/IJRTI2205150.pdf.

Tyrer, C. (2023) 'Untangling the complexity of mentoring feedback practices in post-compulsory initial teacher education in the UK', *Journal of Further and Higher Education*, 47(1), pp. 31–44. doi:10.1080/0309877X.2022.2088271.

Woodcock, S., Sharma, U., Subban, P. and Hitches, E. (2022) 'Teacher self-efficacy and inclusive education practices: rethinking teachers' engagement with inclusive practices', *Teaching and Teacher Education*, 117, p. 103802. doi:10.1016/j.tate.2022.103802.

Young, C., Haffejee, B. and Corsun, D. (2017) 'Developing cultural intelligence and empathy through diversified mentoring relationships', *Journal of Management Education*, 42, 105256291771068. doi:10.1177/1052562917710687.

Chapter 11

Approaches to failure and repairing mentoring relationships

The importance of professional boundaries in the mentoring relationship

Boundaries are crucial in the education mentoring relationship to establish a professional and respectful dynamic between the mentor and mentee. This is because of some of the following factors:

Professionalism

> Boundaries help maintain a professional relationship between them ensuring that interactions and discussions remain focused on the mentee's professional growth and development. This prevents the relationship from becoming overly personal or crossing professional boundaries (Ambrosetti and Dekkers, 2010).

Objectivity

> Boundaries support the mentor in providing objective and unbiased feedback and guidance. By maintaining appropriate boundaries, the mentor can offer constructive criticism and support without personal biases or conflicts of interest.

Trust and Confidentiality

> Establishing clear boundaries builds trust between them. When mentees feel confident that their conversations and concerns will be kept confidential, they are more likely to be open and honest, enabling deeper learning and growth (2010).

Respect

> Boundaries demonstrate respect for each other's roles, responsibilities, and boundaries. Both parties have distinct professional roles, and setting boundaries helps ensure that these roles are respected and upheld (Eller, Lev and Feurer, 2014).

Maintain Professional Boundaries

> Boundaries help both parties maintain appropriate relationships and avoid potential ethical or legal issues. It ensures that interactions remain within the professional context and do not cross into personal or inappropriate territory (2010).

Mentor's Well-being

Boundaries also protect the mentor's well-being by defining the limits of their involvement and responsibilities. It helps prevent mentor burnout and ensures that the mentor can maintain a healthy work-life balance.

Boundaries and the evaluation process

Boundaries are essential in the evaluation processes involved in mentoring in education to maintain fairness, objectivity, and professionalism. They help to ensure the following:

- Fairness and impartiality

    Boundaries ensure that the evaluation process is fair and impartial. By establishing clear boundaries, the evaluator can approach the evaluation with objectivity and avoid any personal biases or preferences that may influence the assessment.
- Consistency and standardisation

    Boundaries help maintain consistency and standardisation in the evaluation process. Clear boundaries provide a framework and guidelines for assessing the mentee's performance based on predetermined criteria, ensuring that all mentees are evaluated using the same standards (Rhodes, Liang and Spencer, 2009).
- Professionalism and ethical conduct

    Boundaries uphold professionalism and ethical conduct in the evaluation process. By setting clear expectations, boundaries ensure that the evaluator maintains confidentiality, respects the mentee's privacy, and avoids any conflicts of interest or inappropriate behaviours.
- Trust and confidentiality

    Establishing boundaries builds trust between the evaluator and the mentee. When mentees trust that the evaluation process will be conducted with integrity and confidentiality, they are more likely to be open and honest, providing accurate information for evaluation purposes.
- Clear expectations

    Boundaries help define the expectations and parameters of the evaluation process. This clarity enables the mentee to understand the evaluation criteria and expectations, allowing them to focus on meeting those standards (Chase, Chin and Oppezzo, 2009).
- Professional growth

    Boundaries support the mentee's professional growth by providing constructive feedback and guidance within the evaluation process. Clear boundaries ensure that the evaluation is focused on the mentee's development and improvement, helping them identify areas of strength and areas for further growth.

> **Self-reflection activity**
>
> Rachel is observing Ana's teaching on a regular basis as part of their mentoring relationship. However, they have developed a personal friendship outside of the mentoring context. Ana is not performing well in the classroom, and during the observation feedback sessions, Rachel finds it challenging to separate her personal feelings for Anne from her objective assessment of her performance and tends to overlook some of the issues with her teaching in the summative feedback and has over graded her in her assessment. Ana's university tutor also has observed her and feels that her teaching is not progressing because of this.
>
> What would you advise Rachel to do under these circumstances?
>
> Have you ever been in a similar situation with one of your mentees? How did you handle it?

Integrity and the mentoring relationship

Integrity in assessment refers to the adherence to principles of honesty, fairness, and ethical conduct throughout the assessment process. It encompasses the values, behaviours, and practices that ensure the validity, reliability, and credibility of assessments in educational settings.

At its core, integrity in assessment means that assessments are conducted with the utmost sincerity and transparency. It involves ensuring that the assessment tasks are designed to measure what they intend to measure, aligning with the learning objectives or standards being assessed. Assessments should be valid, accurately reflecting the knowledge, skills, and abilities of the individuals being assessed (Chase, Chin and Oppezzo, 2009).

It also entails providing equal opportunities for all learners to demonstrate their abilities, without any form of discrimination or bias. Assessments should be fair, free from any influence that may disadvantage certain individuals or groups. This includes offering reasonable accommodations for learners with disabilities or special needs.

It can necessitate the appropriate administration and scoring of assessments. The process should be consistent, reliable, and free from errors or misconduct. The confidentiality and privacy of assessment results should be respected, ensuring that personal information is protected (Hudson, 2013).

It can extend to the interpretation and use of assessment data. It entails using assessment results to inform educational decisions, such as identifying areas for improvement, providing feedback to learners, and informing instructional practices. The results should be used responsibly and ethically, avoiding any misuse or misrepresentation of data. Integrity in an educational context is underpinned by the following theories:

- Utilitarianism

    Utilitarianism is an ethical theory that emphasises the greatest overall good for the greatest number of people. In the context of evaluation in education, integrity is viewed through a utilitarian lens by prioritising the positive impact and value of evaluations. Evaluations should be conducted in a way that maximises benefits, such as improving educational programmes, enhancing student learning outcomes, and informing policy decisions.
- Fairness and Equity

    Theories of fairness and equity emphasise the importance of ensuring that evaluation processes are fair, unbiased, and equitable. This involves treating all individuals and groups with respect, avoiding discrimination or favouritism, and providing equal opportunities for participation and representation. Theories such as distributive justice and procedural justice contribute to the understanding of integrity in evaluation by focusing on the principles of fairness and equity.
- Constructivism

    Constructivism is an educational theory that emphasises the active construction of knowledge by individuals and the importance of context in learning. Applied to evaluation in education, constructivism highlights the need for evaluations to be contextually sensitive, recognising the diverse perspectives and experiences of stakeholders. It emphasises the importance of involving multiple perspectives, engaging stakeholders in the evaluation process, and valuing their input and contributions (Cox, 2005).

The importance of integrity within the evaluation process

Integrity is vital in the evaluation process that underpins a mentoring relationship for several reasons:

- Trust and Credibility

    Integrity in evaluation builds trust between the mentor and mentee. When the evaluation process is conducted with honesty and transparency, the mentee feels confident that their performance and progress are being assessed fairly and accurately. This trust is essential for maintaining a strong and effective mentoring relationship.
- Objective and Unbiased Assessment

    Integrity ensures that the evaluation process remains objective and unbiased. Evaluators must approach the assessment without personal biases or preferences, focusing solely on the mentee's performance and growth. This objectivity allows for a fair and accurate evaluation, providing valuable feedback and guidance.

- Professionalism and Ethical Conduct
    Conducting evaluations with integrity upholds professionalism and ethical conduct in the mentoring relationship. It ensures that the evaluator respects confidentiality, adheres to ethical guidelines, and avoids any conflicts of interest. This professionalism fosters a positive and respectful mentoring environment (Ganser, 1996).
- Growth and Development
    Integrity in evaluation supports the mentee's growth and development. By providing honest and constructive feedback, the evaluation process identifies areas of strength and areas for improvement. This feedback allows the mentee to reflect, set goals, and make progress in their professional journey.
- Accountability and Improvement
    Evaluations conducted with integrity hold both parties accountable for their roles and responsibilities. The evaluation process encourages both parties to reflect on their performance, identify areas for improvement, and take necessary actions. This accountability fosters a culture of continuous improvement and professional development (Chase, Chin and Oppezzo, 2009).
- Quality Assurance
    Integrity in evaluation ensures the quality and effectiveness of the mentoring relationship. By providing accurate and reliable assessments, the evaluation process helps mentors and mentees gauge the success of their collaboration. It allows for adjustments and improvements to be made, ultimately enhancing the overall mentoring experience (Deutsch and Spencer, 2009).

Some strategies for maintaining integrity in evaluation processes

Maintaining integrity in the evaluation process within a mentoring relationship requires the implementation of several practical strategies. Here are some central strategies for ensuring integrity in the evaluation process:

- Clear and transparent criteria
    Both parties need to establish clear evaluation criteria which can help to ensure that both parties understand the expectations and standards being assessed.
- Objective and standardised assessment tools
    Mentors could design objective and standardised assessment tools to minimise bias and subjectivity such as rubrics, checklists, rating scales, or other tools to provide a consistent framework for evaluating performance.
- Regular feedback and communication
    Open and regular communication between the mentor and mentee could be facilitated to provide ongoing feedback and timely adjustments, clarification, and support.

Confidentiality and privacy

Confidentiality and privacy should be established throughout the evaluation process, including protecting the personal information and assessment results of the mentee, ensuring that they are only shared with appropriate individuals for evaluation purposes.

- Avoiding conflicts of interest
  Be mindful of any potential conflicts of interest that may compromise the integrity of the evaluation process. This could include situations where the mentor has a personal or professional relationship with the mentee that could influence the assessment (Jones, 2000).
- Reflective practice and self-assessment
  Both the mentor and the mentee need to engage in reflective practice and self-assessment. This allows them to critically evaluate their own performance, identify areas for improvement, and take ownership of their professional growth.
- Continuous professional development
  Mentors need also to engage in continuous professional development, including training on evaluation techniques, ethical considerations, and best practices, which can help to ensure that they stay updated and knowledgeable about effective evaluation methods (Kupersmidt and Rhodes, 2014).
- Documentation and record-keeping
  Accurate and organised documentation of the evaluation process, including assessment results, feedback, and any discussions or decisions made, can help ensure transparency and accountability. Regular evaluation and feedback of the assessment process can identify areas for improvement.

Self-reflection activity

How do you maintain integrity in assessment in your role as a mentor? Complete the checklist box with suggestions for each category

Categories of strategy	Your examples of mentoring practice
Clear and Transparent Criteria Establish clear evaluation criteria. This ensures that both parties understand the expectations and standards being assessed	
Objective and Standardised Assessment Tools This can include rubrics, checklists, rating scales, or other tools that provide a consistent framework for evaluating performance	

(Continued)

Categories of strategy	Your examples of mentoring practice
Regular Feedback and Communication Foster open and regular communication between you and your mentee to provide ongoing feedback, ensuring that both parties are on the same page regarding the evaluation process	
Confidentiality and Privacy Establish and maintain confidentiality and privacy throughout the evaluation process. This includes protecting the personal information and assessment results of your mentee, ensuring that they are only shared with appropriate individuals for evaluation purposes	
Avoiding Conflicts of Interest Be mindful of any potential conflicts of interest that may compromise the integrity of the evaluation process. This could include situations where you have a personal or professional relationship with the mentee that could influence the assessment	
Reflective Practice and Self-Assessment Engage in reflective practice and self-assessment and encourage your mentee to do the same. This allows you to critically evaluate your own performances, identify areas for improvement, and take ownership of your professional growth	
Documentation and Record-Keeping Maintain accurate and organised documentation of the evaluation process, including assessment results, feedback, and any discussions or decisions made. This helps ensure transparency and accountability	
Regular Evaluation of the Evaluation Process Periodically review and evaluate the evaluation process itself to identify areas for improvement. Solicit feedback from your mentees to gather insights and make necessary adjustments to enhance the integrity of the process	
Continuous Professional Development Engage in continuous professional development, including training on evaluation techniques, ethical considerations, and best practices. This will ensure that you stay updated and knowledgeable about effective evaluation methods	

Why things can go wrong in the mentoring relationship

- Power relationships

    Mentors, in the traditional sense of the term, are usually people in leadership roles or are people whom the mentee aspires to be like (Cox, 2005). However, research suggests that mentees may have more negative than positive experiences in this type of relationship (Eby *et al.*, 2000).

    In their study of negative mentoring experiences, they found that mentor skills (or lack of them) and personality mismatches were the main causes of negativity in traditional mentoring relationships (Ambrosetti and Dekkers, 2010). As power exists with the mentor, the mentee may be unwilling to question institutional practices or the mentor for fear of fracturing the relationship or affecting the mentor's evaluation of their progress

- Role clashes

    In addition, the mentor's dual role as confidant and assessor to the mentee can be a catalyst for further relationship tensions (Ganser, 1996).

- Expectation differences

    Sometimes this can be the result of a misunderstanding between mentor and mentee. Here is a mentee's account of what she felt when she was given a new class to teach for the first time:

    > I got the feeling that she expected me to know everything and be able to ... but what it turned out to be is I misinterpreted it... The reason I think I misinterpreted her is because I went through a bit of a panic where I thought I don't have the knowledge to do this, I don't know what I'm doing.

    > So I went into a bit of a panic but he sat me down and she said that you know you need to build your confidence, you're not expected to know everything. She made that clear to me and this is your time to learn. So she was very comforting. She had faith in me if that makes any sense.

- Mentor not understanding the reality of a mentee's life

    Connected to the issue of diverse expectations, some coordinators reported instances where mentors were not familiar with the life experiences of adult trainee teacher's living and the variety of intersectional pressures they could be under (Niehoff, 2006).

- Micro-management

    This can create tension in the relationship as it can impact upon a mentee's self-confidence and erode the level of trust between mentor and mentee. Facilitating a supportive, risk-taking environment is essential for both mentors and mentees as it builds confidence and develops independence. It's important that mentors encourage their mentees to step out of their comfort zones and try different approaches in class and to develop the resilience to believe that even if it fails, it's not reflective of their teaching (Hudson, 2013).

- Getting the balance right

    The role of effective mentors is not to force novices to adopt their view, but rather to reflect on alternative strategies and their implications for the trainee teacher's practice. The goal here is striking a balance between supporting and challenging the novice (Upson Bradbury, 2010). According to research, mentors who challenged mentees to think through possible solutions to problems and then decide on solutions were much more valuable than merely being told what to do (Hayes, 2001).
- Changed circumstances or commitments

    The success of the relationship can be influenced by unexpected happenings in the wider contexts of the lives of the mentor or trainee not always directly related to the programme features or the mentoring relationship.
- Understanding the developmental level of the mentee

    Mentors must be able to recognise the developmental level of the mentee and operate within their Zone of Proximal Development to gradually push the mentee in the direction of independent teaching practices. Some mentees may not be developmentally ready to benefit from generating all ideas independently and may therefore require more direct advice (Upson Bradbury, 2010). When a mentor ignores the former, this can lead to undue pressure being placed on the mentee and tension within the mentoring relationship.
- Incompatible expectations

    For instance, trainees may want their mentor to walk them through the internship application process through weekly meetings, while the mentor envisions a once-a-month appointment to discuss future research and career goals (Martin and Sifers, 2012).

- Conflicting views of teaching strategies

Conflicting views over teaching strategies can significantly impact a mentoring relationship in several ways:

Communication Breakdown

   They can lead to breakdowns in communication between the mentor and the mentee. When they have opposing perspectives, it becomes challenging to effectively communicate and understand each other's viewpoints. This can impact the sharing of ideas, feedback, and constructive criticism.

Strained Trust and Rapport

   They can strain the trust and rapport between them. If the mentee feels that their ideas or approaches are consistently dismissed or criticised by the mentor, they may become hesitant to openly share their thoughts or seek guidance which can hinder their growth and development.

Reduced Collaboration and Support

They can also hinder collaboration and support within the mentoring relationship. If they cannot find common ground or compromise on teaching approaches, it becomes difficult to work together effectively. This can limit the opportunities for the mentee to learn from the mentor's expertise and benefit from their guidance (Freeman, 2008).

Frustration and Demotivation

They can lead to frustration and demotivation for both parties. Constant disagreement or lack of alignment can create a negative and discouraging atmosphere within the mentoring relationship. This can impact the mentee's enthusiasm, willingness to learn, and overall job satisfaction.

> **A self-reflective scenario**
>
> You have just observed your mentee taking a class and a classroom management issue arose that you felt they handled badly. You have given them advice on this area of their teaching many times and you feel that it has made no impact on their teaching practice. You ask the mentee to stay behind after the classroom has emptied and you sit down with your notebook open. You feel annoyed and frustrated by your mentee's performance.
>
> How do you handle your feedback?

> **A mentor's tip**
>
> 'I see my role is to help my mentee identify their weaknesses so that they can become their strengths and that's what we work on. I don't provide prescribed answers for her in her feedback. For example, one of the weaknesses I identified in an observation was her questioning, so I provided her with a few articles explaining different strategies and she was happy to trial them in her class and for me to observe her'.
>
> What are the strengths and weaknesses of this approach to mentor feedback?

According to Cherian (2007), the main factors that have a negative impact on the mentor-mentee relationship are

- Mentor-mentee communication difficulties or inability to make a connection
- Mentor intervention style
- Level of mentor expertise and skills

- Perceived lack of mentee motivation
- Poor mentor training and low confidence
- Unfulfilled expectations of the programme
- Mentee abandonment or mentor too busy
- Meeting time issues
- Inadequate or inappropriate programme support

> How common are these factors in your own institution?
> What provisions, if any, have been in place to manage some of these issues?

Mentoring and disciplinary action

There may be times when a mentor has to take disciplinary action against their mentee. These may arise due to their conduct, performance, or adherence to professional standards. These disciplinary issues can affect their progress in the programme and their future career as educators ().

Role-playing scenarios are an effective way to train ITE mentors on how to handle disciplinary matters involving trainee teachers. These scenarios can help mentors practice their communication, problem-solving, and conflict-resolution skills in a controlled environment. Here are three different role-play scenarios:

You might want to use these role-play scenarios involving potential disciplinary situations to help train new mentors:

Scenario 1: Unprofessional Behaviour

Background:

A trainee teacher, Abraham, has been observed making sarcastic remarks towards students and colleagues. This behaviour has been reported by several staff members and has also been noticed by the college principal. The mentor needs to address this issue with Alex.

Training objectives:

In groups of three, do the following:
Identify the unprofessional behaviour and discuss its impact
Provide constructive feedback
Develop a plan for improvement for the mentee

Play Script:

Mentor: Good morning, Alex. Thank you for meeting with me today.
Abraham: No problem. Is everything okay?
Mentor: I wanted to discuss some concerns that have been brought to my attention. Several staff members and the principal have noticed

Abraham:	that you've been making sarcastic remarks towards students and colleagues. Can you tell me a bit about what might be happening?
	I didn't realise it was a big deal. I thought I was just being funny.
Mentor:	I understand that you might not have intended to cause any harm, but sarcasm can sometimes be taken the wrong way and can affect the classroom environment and professional relationships. It's important to maintain a positive and professional demeanour at all times. How do you feel about that?
Abraham:	I guess I didn't think about it that way. I can see how it might be a problem.
Mentor:	I appreciate your understanding. Let's work together on developing strategies to improve this. How about we start with setting a goal to focus on positive communication? I can also observe a few of your classes and give you feedback on your interactions.
Abraham:	That sounds fair. I'll try to be more mindful of my comments.
Mentor:	Great. Let's schedule a follow-up meeting in a couple of weeks to review your progress. We're here to support you in becoming the best teacher you can be.

Group Question:

Which practical tips would you give Abraham in order to improve his positive communication?

Scenario 2: Attendance Issues

Background:

A trainee teacher, Janelle, has been frequently late to school and has missed several professional development sessions without prior notice. This has raised concerns among the college staff and has affected Janelle's performance and reliability. The mentor needs to address these attendance issues with Jamie.

Training Objectives:

In groups of three, do the following:
Address the attendance and punctuality issues
Understand the underlying reasons
Develop a plan to improve attendance and punctuality

Role-Play Script:

Mentor:	Hi Janelle, thanks for coming in today. How are you?
Janelle:	I'm okay, just a bit stressed with everything going on.
Mentor:	I understand. I wanted to talk to you about your attendance and punctuality. I've noticed you've been late several times and missed a few professional development sessions. Is everything alright?

Janelle: I've been having some personal issues at home, and it's been hard to manage everything.
Mentor: I'm sorry to hear that. It sounds like you're dealing with a lot right now. It's important to address these issues because consistent attendance and punctuality are crucial for your development and for maintaining a professional standard. How can we help you manage this better?
Janelle: I could use some help with planning my schedule better. Maybe some tips on time management?
Mentor: Absolutely. Let's work on a plan together. We can start by identifying the main challenges you're facing and then look at some strategies to help you manage your time more effectively. We can also set up regular check-ins to see how you're doing. Does that sound good?
Janelle: Yes, that would be really helpful. Thank you.
Mentor: Great. We'll get through this together. Let's make sure we set some clear goals and take it step by step.

Group task

Design a checklist of different time management strategies that Janelle could use in order to deal with her time management issues

Scenario 3: Inadequate Lesson Preparation

Background:

A trainee teacher, Tayler, has been consistently underprepared for lessons, resulting in poor classroom management and ineffective teaching. This has been observed by both the mentor and the classroom teacher. The mentor needs to address Tayler's lack of preparation and help develop a plan for improvement.

Training Objectives:

In groups of three, do the following:

- Address the issue of inadequate lesson preparation
- Provide constructive feedback and support
- Develop a structured plan to improve lesson planning and delivery

Role-Play Script:

Mentor: Hi Tayler, thanks for meeting with me. How are you doing today?
Tayler: I'm doing alright. What's up?
Mentor: I wanted to discuss some observations regarding your lesson preparation. It seems like you've been struggling to prepare adequately for your classes, which has impacted your classroom management and teaching effectiveness. Can you tell me more about your current preparation process?

Tayler: I've been trying to keep up, but I'm finding it hard to plan everything in detail with all the other responsibilities.

Mentor: I understand that it can be overwhelming. Effective lesson preparation is essential for successful teaching. Let's look at how we can make this process more manageable for you. Can you walk me through your typical planning routine?

Tayler: I know this sounds really bad, but I have to put my children to bed first and I usually try to plan the night before, but sometimes I run out of time and end up winging it.

Mentor: Planning last minute can be really challenging. How about we work on a more structured approach? We can start with creating a weekly planning schedule that allows you to prepare in advance. I can also share some resources and templates that might help streamline your planning process.

Tayler: That sounds helpful. I could definitely use some structure and resources.

Mentor: Great. Let's set some specific goals for your lesson planning and have regular check-ins to review your progress and adjust as needed. We're here to support you every step of the way.

Tayler: I appreciate that. I'll definitely put in the effort to improve.

Group question

Design a structured weekly planning schedule for Tayler and provide some ideas for lesson planning that will help them spend less time on planning.

How to repair broken mentoring relationships?

Repairing a broken mentoring relationship can be challenging, but it is possible with effort and open communication. Every mentoring relationship is unique, and the process of repairing a broken relationship will vary depending on the specific circumstances (Kobayashi, 2024).

Reflect on the situation

A mentor should take time to reflect on the factors that may have contributed to the breakdown of the mentoring relationship. They should consider their own actions, communication style, and any misunderstandings or conflicts that may have occurred (Baskin and Enright, 2004).

Take responsibility

They might acknowledge and take responsibility for their role in the breakdown of the relationship and be honest with themselves about any mistakes or shortcomings and be prepared to apologise if necessary.

Initiate a conversation

It is important to reach out to their mentee and express their desire to repair the mentoring relationship and be prepared to listen to their perspective and be open to constructive feedback (Eby et al., 2008).

Active listening and communication

During meetings with their mentee, they should practice active listening by giving them full attention and seeking to understand their point of view. They should use 'I' statements to express their feelings and thoughts without blaming or accusing the other person.

Clarify expectations

It is also important to discuss and clarify expectations for the mentoring relationship moving forward. This includes defining goals, boundaries, and roles to ensure that both parties have a clear understanding of what they expect from each other (Enright and Human Development Study Group, 1991).

Establish trust

Rebuilding trust is crucial for repairing a broken mentoring relationship. Trust is built over time through consistent and honest behaviour. If the issues are complex or difficult to resolve, the mentor can consider involving a neutral third party, such as a supervisor or a trusted colleague, to mediate the conversation (McCullough, 2000).

Commit to growth and improvement

Both parties must be committed to personal growth and improvement to repair the mentoring relationship. This may involve reflecting on past mistakes, seeking professional development opportunities, and actively working on communication and collaboration skills (Worthington, 2005).

Regular check-ins

Regular check-ins to assess the progress of the repaired mentoring relationship can help. This allows both parties to provide feedback, address any concerns, and make necessary adjustments along the way (Parker and Pattenden, 2009).

Develop emotional intelligence skills (EI)

Here is a list of the key components of emotional intelligence. Rate yourself from One to Five (being strong) in each area and provide an example of how you will improve it.

Components of emotional intelligence	Rating	How will you improve this?
Self-awareness		
Self-management		
Social awareness		
Relationship management		

References

Ambrosetti, A. and Dekkers, J. (2010) 'The interconnectedness of the roles of mentors and mentees in preservice teacher education mentoring relationships', *Australian Journal of Teacher Education*, 35(6). doi:10.14221/ajte.2010v35n6.3.
Baskin, T.W. and Enright, R. (2004) 'Intervention studies of forgiveness: a meta-analysis', *Journal of Counseling and Development*, 82, pp. 79–90.
Chase, C.C., Chin, D.B., Oppezzo, M.A. et al. (2009) 'Teachable agents and the protégé effect: increasing the effort towards learning', *Journal of Science Education and Technology*, 18, pp. 334–352. doi:10.1007/s10956-009-9180-4.
Cherian, F. (2007) 'Learning to teach: teacher candidates reflect on the relational, conceptual and contextual influences of responsive mentorship', *Canadian Journal of Education*, 30(1), pp. 25–46.
Cox, E. (2005) 'For better, for worse: the matching process in formal mentoring schemes', *Mentoring and Tutoring: Partnership in Learning*, 13(3), pp. 403–414.
Deutsch, N.L. and Spencer, R. (2009) 'Capturing the magic: assessing the quality of youth mentoring relationships', *New Directions for Youth Development*, 121, pp. 47–70. doi:10.1002/yd.296.
Eby, L.T., Durley, J.R., Evans, S.C. and Ragins, B.R. (2008) 'Mentors' perceptions of negative mentoring experiences: scale development and nomological validation', *Journal of Applied Psychology*, 93, pp. 358–373. doi:10.1037/0021-9010.93.2.358.
Eby, L.T., McManus, S.E., Simon, S.A. and Russell, J.E. (2000). 'The protege's perspective regarding negative mentoring experiences: the development of a taxonomy', *Journal of Vocational Behavior*, 57(1), pp. 1–21.
Eller, L.S., Lev, E.L. and Feurer, A. (2014) 'Key components of an effective mentoring relationship: a qualitative study', *Nurse Education Today*, 34(5), pp. 815–820. doi:10.1016/j.nedt.2013.07.020.
Enright, R.D. and the Human Development Study Group (1991) 'The moral development of forgiveness', in Kurtines, W. and Gewirtz, J. (eds), *Handbook of moral behavior and development*, Vol. 1. Lawrence Erlbaum, pp. 123–152.
Freeman, H.R. (2008) *Mentoring is a two way street: an examination of mentor/mentee relationships in a pre-service, residency-based, teacher education program*. Boston College.
Ganser, T. (1996) 'Preparing mentors of beginning teachers: an overview for staff developers', *Journal of Staff Development*, 17(4), pp. 8–11.
Hayes, D. (2001) 'The impact of mentoring and tutoring on student primary teachers' achievements: A case study', *Mentoring and Tutoring*, 9(1), pp. 5–21.
Hudson, P. (2013) 'Developing and sustaining successful mentoring', *Journal of Relationships Research*, 4, pp. 1–10.
Jones, M. (2000) 'Trainee teachers' perceptions of school-based training in England and Germany with regard to their preparation to teaching, mentor support and assessment', *Mentoring and Tutoring*, 8(1), pp. 63–80.
Kobayashi, K. (2024) 'Interactive learning effects of preparing to teach and teaching: a meta-analytic approach', *Educational Psychology Review*, 36, pp. 26. doi:10.1007/s10648-024-09871-4.

Kupersmidt, J.B. and Rhodes, J.E. (2014) 'Mentor training', in Dubois, D. and Karcher, M. (eds.) *Handbook of youth mentoring.* 2nd edn. Sage, pp. 439–455.

Martin, S.M. and Sifers, S.K. (2012) 'An evaluation of factors leading to mentor satisfaction with the mentoring relationship', *Children and Youth Services Review*, 34, pp. 940–945. doi:10.1016/j.childyouth.2012.01.025.

McCullough, M.E., Pargament, K.I. and Thoresen, C.E. (Eds.) (2000) *Forgiveness: theory, research and practice.* Guilford Press.

Niehoff, B.P. (2006) 'Personality predictors of participation as a mentor', *Career Development International*, 11(4), pp. 321–333. doi:10.1108/13620430610672531.

Parker, R. and Pattenden, R. (2009) Strengthening and repairing relationships: addressing forgiveness and sacrifice in couples education and counselling. ARFB Briefing. Number 13. Core.ac.uk.

Rhodes, J., Liang, B. and Spencer, R. (2009) 'First do no harm: ethical principles for youth mentoring relationships', *Professional Psychology: Research and Practice*, 40, pp. 452–458. doi:10.1037/a0015073.

Upson Bradbury, L. (2010) 'Educative mentoring: promoting reform-based science teaching through mentoring relationships', *Science Education*, 94, 1049–1071.

Worthington, E.L. (ed.) (2005) *Handbook of forgiveness.* Routledge.

Chapter 12

Partnership models

Some of the key models found in post-compulsory education

One of the most common is the collaborative model in which colleges, schools, and providers work closely together on a regular basis, developing programmes collectively and integrating their individual strengths and qualities, such as Teaching School Alliances (TSAs) or Multi-Academy Trusts (MATs). Developing such skills and attributes through effective, collaborative partnerships can support the mentor in adapting to changing expectations (Aderibigbe, 2011).

Participatory partnership can offer mentors the chance to network and collaborate with other colleagues in their own and other colleges and schools and provide opportunities for mentors to share information and knowledge. This may be achieved through, for example, Local Education Authorities (LEAs) and Regional Partnerships, communities of practice and professional learning hubs, particularly in areas such as Science, Technology, Engineering, Arts, and Mathematics (STEAM), developed both formally and informally (this can prove to be particularly effective in supporting more isolated mentors working in a small college or school, for example) (Aderibigbe, 2011).

These types of partnerships can also be found where FE colleges are themselves ITE providers and either work internally in partnership with mentors or externally with other FE colleges. ITE partnerships in the post-compulsory sector can also be based on university-college partnerships in which universities collaborate with colleges to provide placements where trainee teachers can gain practical experience. Colleges offer real-world teaching environments, while universities provide academic support and resources. This can be combined with co-teaching models, which aim to allow trainee teachers to benefit from the expertise of both academic and practical perspectives (Mackie, 2020).

Relationships between placement mentors and course tutors

Strong relationships between placement mentors and course tutors are essential in ITE programmes. These relationships provide guidance, support, modelling, feedback, assessment, collaboration, and contextual understanding, which are critical for trainee teachers' professional development and success as educators. Collaborative efforts between mentors and tutors create a cohesive and comprehensive learning experience that integrates theory and practice in the classroom (Betlem, Clary and Jones, 2019). These relationships play a critical role in shaping the quality of teacher training and, consequently, the effectiveness of future educators.

Successful mentor and tutor relationships in Initial Teacher Education (ITE) are characterised by several central traits that collectively enhance the quality of teacher training. These characteristics ensure that student teachers receive comprehensive support and effective guidance throughout their training (Martin and Johnston, 2013).

- Open and effective communication
   Successful relationships are marked by frequent and open communication. Regular meetings, updates, and discussions help ensure that both mentors and tutors are aligned in their approach and expectations.
- Mutual respect and trust
   Both parties should respect each other's expertise and roles. Recognising the value that each brings to the table fosters a collaborative and supportive environment. Trust is foundational. When they trust each other, they can work more effectively together to support the student teacher and address any issues that arise.
- Common objectives
   Successful relationships are built on a shared understanding of the goals for the student teacher's development. They should work towards common objectives, ensuring consistency in guidance and expectations, and ensure that both parties are aligned with the ITE programme's standards and benchmarks helps maintain a coherent approach to teacher training (Lofthouse, 2018).
- Coordinated support
   Effective coordination in providing support ensures that the student teacher receives a balanced and comprehensive educational experience. Successful relationships are flexible and responsive to the evolving needs of the student teacher DFE (2025). Mentors and tutors should be willing to adapt their approaches to better support the student's development. Flexibility in problem-solving ensures that challenges do not hinder the student teacher's progress (Mackie, 2020; Manning and Hobson, 2017).
- Supportive and encouraging environment
   Providing emotional support and encouragement helps build the student teacher's confidence and resilience. A supportive environment fosters a

positive learning experience. Recognising and celebrating the achievements and milestones of the student teacher reinforces their progress and motivation (Oti, 2012).
- Clear roles and responsibilities

    Clarity in the roles and responsibilities helps avoid overlap and confusion. Understanding each other's contributions ensures a more effective partnership (Maxwell and Hobson, 2016). They should act as role models, demonstrating professional behaviour, effective teaching practices, and ethical standards.
- Feedback loops

    Regular and open communication between them allows for timely and constructive feedback. This helps student teachers quickly identify areas for improvement and celebrate their successes (Mellor, 2020).
- Joint insights

    Strong relationships ensure that the theoretical knowledge gained at the university is effectively integrated with practical experience in the classroom. This integration is crucial for the development of competent and confident teachers (Hobson *et al.*, 2016; Robinson and Hobson, 2017).
- Preparation for the world of work

    Through coordinated efforts, they can provide student teachers with a more extensive and realistic view of the teaching profession, preparing them for the challenges and rewards they will face in their careers (Betlem, Clary and Jones, 2019).
- Assessment and feedback collaboration

    Mentors and tutors collaborate in various ways to provide valuable feedback and assessment to trainee teachers, ensuring that the feedback is comprehensive, constructive, and conducive to the trainee's professional growth (Hindle, 2020).

Joint observations

Joint tutor and mentor observations of trainee teaching are crucial in ITE for several compelling reasons. These observations play a significant role in ensuring the comprehensive development of trainee teachers by providing a well-rounded perspective on their performance and growth (Shanks, 2017).

Effective joint tutor and mentor trainee teaching observations help ensure that the observations are meaningful, productive, and conducive to the professional growth of trainee teachers (Maxwell, 2014).

- Multiple perspectives

    Joint observations allow for the integration of different perspectives. Mentors bring practical classroom experience, while tutors provide academic and theoretical insights. This multifaceted view leads to a more comprehensive evaluation of the trainee's teaching abilities and can ensure that feedback is balanced, covering both practical execution and alignment with educational theories and methodologies (Brondyk and Searby, 2013; Martin and Johnston, 2013).

- Regular feedback meetings

   Holding regular, scheduled meetings to discuss the trainee's progress ensures that feedback is continuous and timely. Triangular meetings involving all three parties can help align feedback from both the practical and academic sides, ensuring consistency (Manning and Hobson, 2017).

- Alignment of assessment criteria

   Developing and using standardised assessment rubrics ensures that both mentors and tutors are evaluating trainee teachers based on the same criteria. Joint observations help ensure that both mentors and tutors are assessing trainee teachers against the same standards and criteria, promoting consistency and fairness in evaluations which can help both calibrate their judgements and ensure that their evaluations are aligned, reducing discrepancies and biases in assessment. This can be combined with participating in workshops together to calibrate assessment standards and ensure consistency in grading and feedback (Manning and Hobson, 2017).

- Shared documentation

   Using standardised feedback forms ensures that both mentors and tutors are assessing the trainee teachers against the same criteria. And regularly updating shared progress reports allows both mentors and tutors to track the trainee's development over time and adjust feedback accordingly (Stephens, 2024).

- Peer review and support

   Facilitating opportunities for trainee teachers to observe their peers and participate in peer review sessions can provide additional perspectives and feedback. In addition, mentors and tutors can review and discuss peer feedback to ensure it aligns with their own assessments and provides a comprehensive view (Hobson *et al.*, 2009). Sharing techniques and strategies for providing effective feedback ensures that both parties are equipped to support trainee teachers effectively.

- Action plans and goal setting

   Joint observations can help identify potential issues or areas of concern early in the trainee's development. Collaboratively creating individualised development plans for trainee teachers, with input from both mentors and tutors, can help to ensure that feedback is more targeted and actionable and setting specific, measurable goals for the trainee teacher and regularly reviewing progress towards these goals (Brondyk and Searby, 2013).

- Reflective practice

   Joint observations can encourage trainee teachers to engage in reflective practice and learn from their teaching experiences by considering feedback from multiple sources. This reflection is crucial for their professional growth and development (Martin and Johnston, 2013). Encouraging trainees to maintain reflective journals, which can be reviewed and discussed in meetings, also helps integrate feedback into their ongoing development (Betlem, Clary and Jones, 2019).

A checklist of ten ways mentors can build effective relationships with ITE tutors in ITE

Establish regular communication

- Schedule regular meetings (weekly/biweekly) to discuss student progress.
- Use multiple communication channels (email, phone calls, video conferences) to stay connected.
- Maintain open lines of communication for urgent matters.

Set clear goals and expectations

- Collaborate to define clear, achievable goals for student teachers.
- Ensure mutual understanding of roles and responsibilities.
- Align expectations regarding student teacher evaluations and outcomes.

Share resources and best practices

- Exchange teaching materials, strategies, and resources.
- Discuss and share successful mentoring and tutoring techniques.
- Provide access to professional development opportunities.

Provide consistent feedback

- Offer regular, constructive feedback on student teacher performance.
- Encourage university tutors to share their observations and insights.
- Create a feedback loop to continuously improve mentoring practices.

Foster collaborative planning

- Jointly plan student teacher activities and assignments.
- Coordinate lesson plans that integrate theoretical knowledge with practical application.
- Work together on developing comprehensive training schedules.

Engage in joint reflection

- Reflect together on the progress and development of student teachers.
- Discuss challenges and successes in mentoring and tutoring.
- Use reflective practices to refine and improve approaches.

Promote mutual respect and trust

- Show respect for each other's expertise and contributions.
- Build trust through reliability and professional integrity.
- Value and acknowledge each other's perspectives.

Encourage professional development

- Participate in joint professional development sessions.
- Share information about relevant workshops, seminars, and courses.
- Encourage continuous learning and improvement.

Align assessment practices

- Coordinate assessment methods and criteria for evaluating student teachers.
- Ensure consistency in grading and feedback.
- Discuss and agree on the documentation required for assessments.

Support and celebrate achievements

- Recognise and celebrate the successes of student teachers.
- Acknowledge each other's contributions to student development.
- Create a positive and encouraging environment for collaboration.

Reflective activity

Select four ways from the checklist and put together an action plan showing how you will achieve these tasks.

Ways in which Mentors Can Build Effective Relationships with University and ITE Tutors	How this can be achieved
Establish Regular Communication Set Clear Goals and Expectations Share Resources and Best Practices	

(Continued)

Ways in which Mentors Can Build Effective Relationships with University and ITE Tutors	How this can be achieved
Provide Consistent Feedback Foster Collaborative Planning Engage in Joint Reflection Promote Mutual Respect and Trust Encourage Professional Development Align Assessment Practices Support and Celebrate Achievements	

A checklist of advice for joint teaching observations

Clear objectives and criteria

Establish clear objectives for the observation

Both the mentor and tutor should agree on what specific aspects of teaching will be the focus, such as classroom management, instructional strategies, or student engagement, which should be contained within standardised criteria or rubrics for assessment to ensure consistency and fairness in evaluating the trainee's performance.

Joint planning sessions

Before the observation, mentors and tutors should meet to plan the observation. This includes discussing what to look for, how to document observations, and how to provide feedback, ensuring that the observation aligns with the trainee's learning goals and the overall ITE curriculum.

Pre-observation briefing

Conduct a pre-observation meeting with the trainee teacher to set the context, explain the observation process, and alleviate any concerns they might have. In addition, schedule a debrief session after the observation to discuss what was observed, provide feedback, and answer questions.

Constructive feedback

Specific and actionable

Provide feedback that is specific, actionable, and focused on improvement. Highlight both strengths and areas for development and balanced, offering praise for effective practices and constructive criticism for areas needing improvement.

Reflective practice

Prompt the trainee teacher to reflect on their own performance before providing feedback. This encourages self-assessment and critical thinking. In addition, mentors and tutors should also reflect on their observations and discuss their reflections with each other and the trainee.

Supportive environment

Create a supportive and encouraging atmosphere where the trainee teacher feels comfortable and valued, showing empathy and understanding towards the challenges faced by trainee teachers, and offering support to help them overcome these challenges.

Documentation and follow-up

Keep detailed records of the observations, including notes on specific incidents and examples of effective or ineffective practices, and develop a follow-up plan to address the areas for improvement identified during the observation. This may include additional training, resources, or further observations.

Professional development

Use the observations as opportunities for ongoing professional development for both the trainee and the mentors/tutors discussing new strategies, resources, and best practices.

Alignment with ITE standards

Ensure that the observations and feedback are aligned with the standards and benchmarks of the ITE programme using the observations to benchmark the trainee's progress against these standards, helping to track their development over time.

Mentor support for academic studies

Although the main role of the mentor is to support the student in their teaching practice in placement, they can also play a crucial role alongside their university or college tutor in supporting trainee students in their academic studies when on ITE programmes (Collison, 2004). For example, they can provide the following:

- Academic guidance and advice
  For example, they could assist in developing study plans that balance coursework, teaching practice, and personal commitments.

Creating a balanced study plan template for an ITE mentee involves organising their time effectively to accommodate coursework, teaching practice, and personal commitments. Here is a structured template that can help mentees manage their time efficiently and ensure they maintain a healthy balance:

1 **Daily Schedule**
   Day:
   Date:

Time	Activity/Task	Priority (High/Medium/Low)	Notes/Comments
6:00–7:00 AM	Personal Care/Exercise		
7:00–8:00 AM	Breakfast		
8:00–10:00 AM	Coursework Study (Subject/Topic)		
10:00–12:00 PM	Teaching Practice Preparation/Reflection		
12:00–1:00 PM	Lunch		
1:00–3:00 PM	Teaching Practice (Classroom/Observation)		
3:00–4:00 PM	Coursework Study (Assignments/Projects)		
4:00–6:00 PM	Personal Time/Rest		
6:00–7:00 PM	Dinner		
7:00–9:00 PM	Coursework Study (Reading/Research)		
9:00–10:00 PM	Personal Commitments (Family/Social Activities)		

2 **Monthly Goals**

Week	Academic Goals	Teaching Practice Goals	Personal Goals
Week 1			
Week 2			
Week 3			
Week 4			

3 **Task List and Deadlines**

Task/Assignment	Due Date	Status (Not Started/In Progress/Completed)	Notes/Comments

4 **Reflection and Adjustments**
   Weekly Reflection:

- What went well this week?
- What challenges did I face?
- How can I improve my time management next week?
- Any additional notes or thoughts?

Adjustments for Next Week:
Instructions for Use:

1 **Weekly Overview:** Fill in the weekly overview at the beginning of each week to map out major activities and commitments.
2 **Daily Schedule:** At the end of each day, plan the next day in detail, ensuring a balance between coursework, teaching practice, and personal time.
3 **Monthly Goals:** Set clear academic, teaching practice, and personal goals at the beginning of each month to stay focused and motivated.
4 **Task List and Deadlines:** Keep a running list of tasks and assignments with their deadlines, updating the status regularly to stay on track.
5 **Reflection and Adjustments:** Reflect on the week's activities, note successes and challenges, and make necessary adjustments to improve the following week.

Additional Tips:

- **Prioritse Tasks:** Focus on high-priority tasks first to ensure that the most important work is completed.
- **Be Flexible:** Allow for some flexibility in your schedule to accommodate unexpected events or changes.
- **Self-Care:** Make sure to include time for self-care and relaxation to avoid burnout.
- **Seek Support:** Reach out to your mentor for guidance and support whenever needed.

By following this structured study plan, ITE mentees can effectively manage their time, ensuring they meet their academic requirements while also gaining valuable teaching experience and maintaining a healthy balance with their personal lives.

- Providing resources
    Recommended reading
    Mentors could suggest relevant books, articles, and research papers that can deepen students' understanding of key concepts and also provide access to teaching materials, lesson plans, and other resources that can be used for

both academic assignments and practical teaching (Crooks, London, and Snelson, 2021).
- Tutoring and academic support

    They can provide guidance on how to approach and complete academic assignments, including structuring essays, developing arguments, and referencing sources, and review drafts of assignments and provide constructive feedback to help improve the quality of work before submission (Maxwell, 2014).
- Reflection

    Mentors can encourage students to maintain reflective journals where they can critically analyse their learning experiences and teaching practice and facilitate discussions that prompt students to reflect on their academic progress, challenges, and areas for improvement (Garbett, Orrock, and Smith, 2013). They can also share personal experiences and insights from their own academic and professional journey to provide relatable examples and inspiration (Tedder and Lawy, 2009).
- Professional development

    Mentors could also play a role in encouraging the participation of their mentees in academic workshops, seminars, and conferences that can enhance their knowledge and skills and facilitate networking with other professionals in the field, including attending events and joining professional organisations (Goldshaft and Sjølie, 2024).

Relationship issues between tutor and mentor

The mentor-tutor relationship in ITE is crucial for the development and success of trainee teachers. However, there are several ways this relationship can break down, potentially impacting the quality of support and guidance provided to the trainee.

- Infrequent communication

    If they do not communicate regularly, misunderstandings and misalignments in goals and expectations can occur which can lead to missed messages and a lack of clarity. This lack of collaboration and failure to set common goals for the trainee can result in a disjointed approach to their development (Tedder and Lawy, 2009).
- Inconsistent feedback

    Without coordination, mentors and tutors might focus on different aspects of the trainee's performance, leading to inconsistent guidance, and the contradictory feedback can confuse the trainee and undermine their confidence (Robinson and Hobson, 2017).
- Power struggles

    These can create a tense atmosphere and hinder the trainee's progress. They can also be caused by a lack of mutual respect which can lead to

undermining each other's authority and expertise. Allowing personal conflicts to influence the professional relationship can also detract from the focus on the trainee's development (Martin and Johnston, 2013).
- Differing educational philosophies

    Differing educational philosophies and teaching methodologies can lead to disagreements on how best to support the trainee. Thus, resistance from either party to adapt or consider alternative approaches can create a rigid and unproductive environment (Manning and Hobson, 2017).
- Failure to set clear boundaries

    Unclear boundaries between the roles of mentor and tutor can lead to overlapping responsibilities and confusion and cause friction and diminish the effectiveness of the support provided. This could also impact professionalism which could erode trust and respect (Martin and Johnston, 2013).
- Lack of training and reflection

    Inadequate training for mentors and tutors on how to work together can lead to misunderstandings and inefficiencies. Not engaging in regular reflection on the effectiveness of their collaboration can prevent mentors and tutors from identifying and addressing issues (Jones, Tones and Foulkes, 2019).

Resolve some of the major conflicts that can occur between you and the tutor by completing the table below.

Issues of conflict between mentors and tutors	Ways to resolve them
Infrequent communication	
Misalignment of goals	
Power struggles	
Differing educational philosophies	
Failure to set clear boundaries	
Personal conflicts	
Professional issues	
Fragmented support systems	
Neglecting the mentee's individual needs	
Failure to reflect	

Collaboration with placement colleagues

Collaboration and cooperation with colleagues in ITE placement settings are fundamental to providing a holistic and consistent approach to mentorship. This collaborative effort enhances the trainee's learning experience, supports their professional growth, and ensures that they receive comprehensive and aligned guidance (Maxwell and Hobson, 2016).

By working together, mentors and colleagues create a supportive, effective, and cohesive environment that benefits everyone involved. They can be essential for ensuring a holistic and consistent approach to mentorship (Goldshaft and Sjølie, 2024; Hindle, 2020; Hobson *et al.*, 2012). For example:

- Shared expertise

  When mentors collaborate with colleagues, they can pool their collective expertise and experiences. This can provide a richer and more comprehensive support system for the trainee teacher as different colleagues can bring diverse perspectives and teaching styles, which can help the trainee teacher develop a more well-rounded approach to teaching (Lejonberg, Elstad and Christophersen, 2015).
- Consistency in guidance

  Working together can help establish and maintain standardised expectations and practices within the placement setting, ensuring that the trainee has a clear understanding of what is expected (Robinson and Hobson, 2017).
- Holistic development

  Collaboration allows for comprehensive feedback that can address all of the main development areas. Colleagues from different roles (e.g., subject teachers, support staff, administrators) can provide whole institution insights that help the trainee understand the broader school ecosystem and their role within it (Hankey, 2004).
- Enhanced problem-solving

  According to research by Mackie (2020), addressing issues as a team spreads the responsibility and ensures that the trainee receives well-rounded support and guidance.
- Professional growth for mentors

  Mentors also benefit from collaboration as they can learn from each other's experiences, strategies, and approaches. This professional growth enhances their own mentoring skills. In addition, engaging in regular discussions and reflections with colleagues helps mentors refine their practice and stay updated on best practices in mentoring and teaching (Shanks, 2017).
- Supportive environment

  Collaboration can foster a sense of community and support among staff, creating a positive and encouraging environment for both mentors and trainees based on a network of colleagues to share experiences and provide emotional support can prevent burnout and maintain morale (Willy, 2023).
- Consistent monitoring and assessment

  A collaborative approach can allow for more effective monitoring of the trainee's progress (Hobson and Malderez, 2013). Colleagues can share observations and assessments, which are balanced and fair, reducing the risk of bias and providing a more complete picture of the trainee's development (Manning and Hobson, 2017).

- Resource sharing
    Collaborating with colleagues allows for the sharing of resources, such as teaching materials, lesson plans, and professional development opportunities. This enriches the trainee's learning experience and can also lead to more efficient use of available materials and support, benefiting both trainees and the placement setting (Hobson *et al.*, 2015, 2016).

Partnerships between the subject specialist mentor and the pastoral mentor

Over the past few years, the Department of Education has introduced the role of a Pastoral Mentor into PCET ITE programmes to complement that of the Subject Specialist Mentor. While the latter focuses on helping trainees develop their teaching practice, the former aims to provide personal, emotional, and professional guidance to ensure trainees' holistic well-being and development (Hobson, 2016). A partnership between a Subject Specialist Mentor and a Pastoral Mentor can be crucial for the comprehensive development of trainee teachers. This partnership ensures that trainee teachers receive both academic and personal support, helping them to become well-rounded professionals. It should be characterised by the following:

- Integration of pastoral and academic support
    Working in tandem, mentors can work towards a whole-person approach that recognises the interconnectedness of personal and professional growth, leading to more effective mentorship. In addition, integrating pastoral and academic support can help to ensure that the trainee's personal well-being and professional skills development are addressed simultaneously (Jones, Tones and Foulkes, 2019).
- Collaborative goal setting
    Both mentors should collaborate to set shared goals for the trainee's development, ensuring that academic and personal growth are aligned. Tailoring the development plan to meet the trainee's individualised needs and strengths can help address their unique challenges and aspirations (Lejonberg, Elstad and Christophersen, 2015).
- Consistent feedback
    They should provide coordinated and consistent and holistic feedback that encompasses both subject-specific and personal development aspects which can ensure that the trainee receives a balanced perspective and avoids contradictory advice and helps the mentee understand their progress and areas for improvement (Duckworth and Maxwell, 2015).
- Professional respect
    This could be centred on a shared vision and core values such as integrity, empathy, and dedication for the trainee's success and professional growth (Mackie, 2020).

- Regular check-ins

    Consistent check-ins and follow-ups help track the trainee's progress and address issues promptly, which can build trust and help ensure that the mentee feels supported throughout their training. Hence, when conflicts or challenges arise, both mentors can work together to find constructive solutions that prioritise the trainee's best interests (Ingleby, 2014).

Reflective activity

Complete the table with some of your own ideas on how you can manage any potential relationship issues with another mentor.

Potential barriers	*Ways in which they can be managed*	*Your examples*
Lack of clear roles and responsibilities Ambiguity about the specific roles and responsibilities of each mentor can lead to confusion, overlap, or gaps in support	For example: Develop a written agreement or framework that outlines the specific areas each mentor will cover and share this with the trainee	
Poor communication Ineffective or infrequent communication between mentors can result in missed opportunities for collaboration and support	Utilise multiple communication channels (e.g., email, face-to-face meetings, virtual meetings) to ensure open and consistent and scheduled ongoing dialogue	
Conflicting advice Trainees may receive contradictory advice from their mentors, leading to confusion and inconsistency in their development	Coordinate feedback and advice through joint meetings or collaborative planning sessions. Ensure that both mentors provide a unified and consistent message to the trainee by documenting each meeting with the mentee and making these available to both mentors	
Differing priorities Subject mentors may prioritise academic achievement, while pastoral mentors focus on personal well-being, leading to potential conflicts in prioritising the trainee's needs	It is important to set shared objectives that encompass both academic and personal development. Also, to regularly revisit and adjust these goals to ensure they remain aligned, involving the mentee in the process throughout	

(Continued)

Potential barriers	Ways in which they can be managed	Your examples
Time constraints Busy schedules and heavy workloads can limit the time mentors have to collaborate effectively	Schedule dedicated time for mentoring activities and collaboration, meeting for short periods and often if need be.	
Lack of training and professional development Mentors may lack the necessary training and skills to effectively fulfil their roles, particularly in understanding the complementary aspects of academic and pastoral support	Institutions or ITE providers could hold ongoing professional development and training for mentors to enhance their mentoring skills and understanding of both academic and pastoral support. They could also encourage mentors to attend workshops, seminars, and training sessions	
Resistance to collaboration Some mentors may prefer to work independently or may be resistant to collaborative approaches	Encourage team-building activities and create opportunities for mentors to build trust and rapport with each other Highlight successes	
Inconsistent feedback mechanisms Inconsistent or unstructured feedback can hinder the trainee's ability to receive comprehensive and constructive guidance	Develop and implement a structured feedback mechanism that includes regular, coordinated feedback sessions using standardised forms or templates to ensure consistency in feedback	
Different approaches to mentoring Variations in mentoring styles and approaches can create confusion for the trainee There can also be misunderstandings about the specific contributions and expertise of each mentor which can potentially lead to underutilisation of their skills	Institutions should provide opportunities for mentors to observe each other's mentoring practices and learn from each other. CPD should also be provided in different styles of mentoring	
Personal or personality differences These can impede their ability to work together effectively.	Meetings can help to address personal differences using open communication and conflict resolution strategies Mediation could also help to encourage mentors to focus on their shared goal of supporting the trainee's development	

Managing the four-way relationship between two mentors, tutor, and mentee is crucial for providing comprehensive support and fostering the mentee's development. Here are some strategies to effectively manage this relationship. Complete the table below with examples of how these can be achieved.

Strategies to manage the relationship	Your examples of how this can be achieved
Establishing clear roles and responsibilities amongst all three parties	
Fostering open and regular communication amongst all three parties	
Developing systematic collaborative goal setting	
Organising opportunities for consistent and coordinated formative and summative feedback	
Creating a supportive and safe environment where the mentee feels comfortable expressing concerns, asking questions, and seeking guidance	
Encouraging reflective practice amongst all three parties to share insights and develop practice	
Monitoring and evaluating the progress of the mentee in a collaborative process	
Implementing an evaluation framework to assess the effectiveness of the mentoring relationship and identify areas for improvement	

References

Aderibigbe, S.A. (2011) 'Exploring collaborative mentoring relationships between teachers and student teachers', *TEAN Journal*, 3(1). Available at: http://bit.ly/xMlqKB (Accessed 05 September 2011).

Betlem, E., Clary, D. and Jones, M. (2019) 'Mentoring the mentor: professional development through a school-university partnership', *Asia-Pacific Journal of Teacher Education*, 47(4), pp. 327–346.

Brondyk, S. and Searby, L. (2013) 'Best practices in mentoring: complexities and possibilities', *International Journal of Mentoring and Coaching in Education*, 2(3), pp. 189–203.

Collison, J. (2004) 'Mentoring: realising the true potential of school-based ITE', in *Primary teacher education*. Routledge, pp. 177–185.

Crooks, V., London, L. and Snelson, H. (2021) '"Singing from the same hymn-sheet": exploring school-based mentors' perceptions of the role of HEI subject tutors in ITE partnerships', *TEAN Journal*, 13(1), pp. 3–16.

Department for Education (DFE) (2025) Expectations for the delivery of initial teacher education for FE. https://www.gov.uk/government/publications/further-education-initial-teacher-education/expectations-for-the-delivery-of-initial-teacher-education-for-fe.

Duckworth, V. and Maxwell, B. (2015) 'Extending the mentor role in initial teacher education: embracing social justice', *International Journal of Mentoring and Coaching in Education*, 4(1), pp. 4–20.

Garbett, G., Orrock, D. and Smith, R. (2013) 'Culture clash: mentoring student literacy educators in a marketised and instrumentalist further education policyscape', *Research in Post-Compulsory Education*, 18(3), pp. 239–56. doi:10.1080/13596748.2013.819258.

Goldshaft, B. and Sjølie, E. (2024) Creating communicative learning spaces in initial teacher education (ITE) with observation-grounded co-mentoring practices. *Professional Development in Education*, 6, pp. 1–18.

Hankey, J. (2004) 'The good, the bad and other considerations: reflections on mentoring trainee teachers in post-compulsory education', *Research in Post-Compulsory Education*, 9(3), pp. 389–400. doi:10.1080/13596740400200185.

Hindle, G.L. (2020) A study on the changing role of the mentor in school-led initial teacher education (Doctoral dissertation, Manchester Metropolitan University).

Hobson, A.J. (2016) 'Judgementoring and how to avert it: introducing ONSIDE mentoring for beginning teachers', *International Journal of Mentoring and Coaching in Education*, 5(2), pp. 87–110.

Hobson, A.J., Ashby, P., Malderez, A. and Tomlinson, P. D. (2009) 'Mentoring beginning teachers: what we know and what we don't', *Teaching and Teacher Education*, 25(1), pp. 207–216.

Hobson, A.J., Castanheira, P., Doyle, K., Csigás, Z. and Clutterbuck, D. (2016) The mentoring across professions (MaP) project: what can teacher mentoring learn from international good practice in employee mentoring and coaching? London: Gatsby Charitable Foundation. Available at: http://www.gatsby.org.uk/uploads/education/reports/pdf/mentoring-across-the-professionsfinal300816.pdf.

Hobson, A.J. and Malderez, A. (2013). 'Judgementoring and other threats to realizing the potential of school-based mentoring in teacher education', *International Journal of Mentoring and Coaching in Education*, 2(2), pp. 89–108.

Hobson, A.J., Maxwell, B., Stevens, A., Doyle, K. and Malderez, A. (2015) *Mentoring and coaching for teachers in the further education and skills sector in England: Full report*. Gatsby Charitable Foundation. Available at: http://www.gatsby.org.uk/uploads/education/reports/pdf/mentoring-fullreport.pdf.

Hobson, A.J., McIntyre, J., Ashby, P., Hayward, V., Stevens, A. and Malderez, A. (2012) The nature, impact and potential of external mentoring for teachers of physics and other subjects in England: full report. Available at: http://www.gatsby.org.uk/~/media/Files/Education/Gatsby%20%20Impact%20of%20Mentoring.

Ingleby, E. (2014) 'Developing reflective practice or judging teaching performance? The implications for mentor training', *Research in Post-Compulsory Education*, 19(1), pp. 18–32. doi:10.1080/13596748.2014.872917.

Jones, L., Tones, S. and Foulkes, G. (2019) 'Exploring learning conversations between mentors and associate teachers in initial teacher education', *International Journal of Mentoring and Coaching in Education*, 8(2), pp. 120–133.

Lejonberg, E., Elstad, E. and Christophersen, K. (2015) 'Mentor education: challenging mentors' beliefs about mentoring', *International Journal of Mentoring and Coaching in Education*, 4(2), pp. 142–158.

Lofthouse, R.M. (2018) 'Re-imagining mentoring as a dynamic hub in the transformation of initial teacher education: the role of mentors and teacher educators', *International Journal of Mentoring and Coaching in Education*, 7(3), pp. 248–260.

Mackie, L. (2020) 'Understandings of mentoring in school placement settings within the context of initial teacher education in Scotland: dimensions of collaboration and power', *Journal of Education for Teaching*, 46(3), pp. 263–280.

Manning, C. and Hobson, A.J. (2017) 'Judgemental and developmental mentoring in further education initial teacher education in England: mentor and mentee perspectives', *Research in Post-Compulsory Education*, 22(4), pp. 574–595.

Martin, A.M. and Johnston, M.P. (2013) 'Mentoring through partnerships', *Knowledge Quest*, 41(4), p. 6.

Maxwell, B. (2014) 'Improving workplace learning of lifelong learning sector trainee teachers in the UK', *Journal of Further and Higher Education*, 38(3), pp. 377–399.

Maxwell, B. and Hobson, A.J. (2016) Re-examining the 'architecture' for teacher mentoring in the further education and skills sector in England. Keynote symposium paper presented at the Annual Conference of the British Educational Research Association (BERA), University of Leeds, 13–15 September 2016.

Mellor, P. (2020) 'Working with your mentor', in *A practical guide to teaching physical education in the secondary school*. Routledge, pp. 287–304.

Oti, J. (2012) 'Mentoring and coaching in further education', in Fletcher, S. and Mullen, C. (eds.) *The SAGE handbook of mentoring and coaching in education*. SAGE, pp. 59–73.*

Robinson, C. and Hobson, A. (2017) Mentor education and development in the Further Education sector in England. https://www.brighton.ac.uk/education-research-centre/research-projects/mentor-education-and-development-in-the-further-education-sector-in-england.aspx.

Shanks, R. (2017) 'Mentoring beginning teachers: professional learning for mentees and mentors', *International Journal of Mentoring and Coaching in Education*, 6(3), pp. 158–163.

Stephens, G. (2024) Bridging the gap: an investigation into Initial Teacher Education Partnerships using a "Teachers Teaching Teachers" model [PhD Thesis]. Australian Catholic University. doi:10.26199/acu.909wv.

Tedder, M. and Lawy, R. (2009) 'The pursuit of "excellence": mentoring in further education initial teacher training in England', *Journal of Vocational Education and Training*, 61(4), pp. 413–429.

Willy, T. (2023) Lived experiences of teacher mentors; the importance of context and partnership in mentoring arrangements in the English school system (Doctoral dissertation, UCL (University College London)).

Chapter 13

Conclusion

The essence of effective mentorship in teacher education

In the dynamic and challenging world of education, the role of a mentor is indispensable. A good mentor possesses a unique blend of characteristics and fulfils critical roles and responsibilities that are essential in nurturing and supporting trainee teachers. These mentors are not just advisers but are the guiding lights that shape the future of education by moulding the educators of tomorrow (Eklin, 2006).

At the heart of effective mentorship lies a deep sense of empathy. A good mentor understands the complexities and anxieties that trainee teachers face and offers a compassionate ear and thoughtful guidance. Patience is another cornerstone, as mentors must allow mentees to grow at their own pace, making room for mistakes and learning opportunities (Irby et al., 2020). The ability to communicate clearly and effectively is paramount, ensuring that feedback is constructive, actionable, and encouraging.

Trustworthiness and reliability are also crucial characteristics. Trainee teachers must feel confident that their mentor is a dependable source of support who respects confidentiality and stands by their side through challenges (Iredale, 2015). Additionally, a good mentor demonstrates a commitment to continuous learning and professional development, modelling the importance of lifelong learning for their mentees.

The main roles and responsibilities of a mentor in supporting trainee teachers are multifaceted. Firstly, mentors serve as role models, exemplifying professional behaviour, ethical standards, and effective teaching practices. They provide a safe and supportive environment where trainees can observe, practice, and refine their skills. Through regular and structured feedback, mentors help trainees identify their strengths and areas for improvement, guiding them towards achieving their professional goals (Daresh, 2002).

They also play the role of facilitators, helping trainees navigate the complexities of the institutional environment, understand institutional policies, and build relationships with colleagues and students. They encourage reflective practice (Portner, 2008), prompting trainees to critically analyse their experiences and develop a deeper understanding of their teaching practices.

Mentors advocate for their mentees, ensuring they have access to necessary resources and opportunities for growth. They foster resilience and adaptability, preparing trainees to handle the inevitable challenges of the teaching profession with confidence and poise (Carroll, Owens and Langston, 2021).

The importance of reflective practice as a mentor

Reflective practice is a cornerstone of effective mentoring in Initial Teacher Education (ITE). It involves the continuous process of self-examination and evaluation of one's own teaching and mentoring practices. Reflective practice is crucial for mentors in ITE because it

- enhances professional growth and development
  It can help mentors gain a deeper understanding of their own strengths, weaknesses, and areas for improvement. This self-awareness is essential for personal and professional growth and by regularly reflecting on their mentoring practices, they can identify what works well and what doesn't, leading to ongoing refinement and enhancement of their skills (Gravells and Wallace, 2007).
- improves effectiveness
  It can enable them to adapt their approach to meet the individual needs of trainee teachers. Understanding what each trainee requires allows for more personalised and effective support, and in turn reflecting on the feedback from trainees and their progress helps them to adjust their strategies to better support the trainees' development (Beattie *et al.*, 2025).
- promotes a culture of reflection
  Mentors who engage in reflective practice model this important skill for their mentees, demonstrating its value and encouraging them to adopt similar practices in their teaching and help develop the habit of self-reflection, which is essential for their long-term professional development and effectiveness as teachers (Sempowicz and Hudson, 2012).
- enhances problem-solving skills
  According to Pelissier (2020), reflective practice encourages mentors to think critically about their experiences and challenges, and this can lead to better problem-solving abilities and more innovative solutions. Reflecting on past experiences can also provide insights that inform future decisions, making them more adept at handling complex situations.
- supports emotional well-being
  It can allow mentors to process their experiences, including challenges and successes, which can reduce stress and prevent burnout by providing a constructive outlet for managing emotions and also build resilience and develop coping strategies for future challenges (Klasen and Clutterbuck, 2002).

- enhances communication and relationships

    Dominguez and Hager (2013) suggest that it can help them to become more aware of their communication styles and how they interact with trainees, which can lead to more effective and empathetic communication and build stronger, more supportive relationships with their trainees.
- aligns with educational standards and best practices

    Engaging in reflective practice can help mentors stay in alignment with current educational standards and best practices, ensuring that they provide high-quality support to trainee teachers.

    Reflective practice also fosters a sense of accountability, as mentors continuously evaluate and improve their practices in line with professional expectations which can instil a mindset of lifelong learning which can help them to ensure that their mentoring practices remain relevant and effective (Angelique, Kyle and Taylor, 2002).

The central ethical issues that a mentor may face in their role and the importance of maintaining ethical boundaries

Maintaining ethical boundaries within mentoring relationships is crucial for several reasons, as these boundaries help ensure the integrity, effectiveness, and professionalism of the mentoring process.

The mentor-mentee relationship can become too personal or overly friendly, which can blur professional lines. Ethical boundaries can help clarify the roles and responsibilities of both the mentor and the mentee. This clarity ensures that the relationship remains focused on professional development and learning objectives, and therefore mentors can provide objective, unbiased guidance and support, which is essential for the mentee's growth and development (Kemmis *et al.*, 2014).

Adhering to ethical boundaries also can foster a safe and respectful environment where mentees feel comfortable sharing their challenges and seeking advice. They can also help to ensure that mentors respect their autonomy and individual agency allowing them to make their own decisions and learn from their experiences (Horn and Metler-Armijo, 2010).

Ethical boundaries can help prevent dual relationships where the mentor and mentee have multiple overlapping roles (e.g., mentor and friend). Such relationships can lead to conflicts of interest and compromise the mentoring process, and thus, by avoiding conflicts of interest, mentors can remain impartial and focused on the mentee's best interests, rather than being influenced by personal relationships or external factors (Aderibigbe *et al.*, 2022).

They can help to protect sensitive information shared by them, and this confidentiality is crucial for building trust and encouraging open communication. This is a legal and ethical requirement in professional settings and violating this can have serious repercussions for both the mentor and the organisation.

Dilemmas can occur and then it can be necessary to disclose information, especially if it involves potential harm to the mentee or others (Ragins, 1989).

Mentors serve as role models for their mentees. By adhering to ethical boundaries, they demonstrate the importance of ethical behaviour and integrity, which helps them to understand the importance of making ethical decisions and navigating complex ethical dilemmas in their professional lives and which sets a positive example for the mentee to follow (Hobson *et al.*, 2015).

Mentoring relationships often involve a power dynamic where the mentor has more experience, knowledge, or authority. Ethical boundaries help prevent the exploitation or abuse of this power differential and help to ensure that mentees are treated fairly and with respect, without being subjected to favouritism, discrimination, or manipulation (Mullen and Lick, 1999). By adhering to ethical boundaries, mentors can protect their own professional integrity and reputation, ensuring that they can continue to provide effective and ethical guidance to others.

There can be issues surrounding fair assessment and providing unbiased feedback and assessments of the mentee's performance without letting personal opinions or relationships affect judgements which can involve the importance of recognising and managing any unconscious biases that may influence interactions and evaluations (Mullen and Lick, 1999).

Thus, it is important for a mentor to strike a balance between being empathetic and supportive while maintaining professional detachment to ensure objective guidance. Managing personal emotions and preventing burnout from being too emotionally invested in the mentee's experiences and challenges becomes imperative according to Dominguez and Hager (2013).

It is vital for mentors to recognise and respect cultural, linguistic, and individual differences among mentees and provide equitable support and also to address and challenge any prejudices or discriminatory behaviours within the mentoring environment (Norley, 2017).

It can be problematic for a mentor to balance institutional policies and requirements with the individual needs and circumstances of the mentee and advocate for their needs within institutional constraints without compromising professional integrity. This can often mean making ethical decisions that prioritise the welfare and development of the mentee, even in complex or ambiguous situations and also being accountable for the guidance provided and its impact on their professional growth (Allen, Eby and Lentz, 2006).

The importance of adapting strategies to meet the needs of mentees who have diverse needs

Adapting approaches and strategies to meet the diverse needs of trainee teachers is crucial for mentors in ITE programmes. Daresh (2002) suggests that this adaptability can help to ensure that all trainee teachers receive the support and guidance necessary for their professional growth and development, leading to a more effective and inclusive teaching workforce.

Trainee teachers come from varied backgrounds, with different experiences, learning strategies, and strengths. Some may have extensive prior experience in education, while others might be new to the field. By recognising and acknowledging these differences, mentors can tailor their support to match the individual needs of each trainee (Beattie *et al.*, 2014). This personalised approach can help trainees build on their strengths and address their specific challenges, leading to more effective learning and professional development (Stahl, Sharplin and Kehrwald, 2017).

A one-size-fits-all approach to mentoring can inadvertently disadvantage some trainees, particularly those from underrepresented or marginalised groups. By adapting their strategies, mentors can help to ensure that all trainees have equal opportunities to succeed. This commitment to inclusivity and equity not only benefits the trainees but also fosters a more diverse and representative teaching profession. It encourages a broader range of perspectives and experiences in the classroom, which can enhance the learning environment for students (Niklasson, 2018).

When mentors adapt their approaches to suit the needs of individual trainees, it demonstrates a genuine interest in their development. This personalised attention can significantly enhance the trainees' engagement and motivation. Mentees are more likely to be invested in their learning and committed to their professional growth when they feel valued and understood (Hansman, 2002). This increased motivation can lead to better outcomes in their training and future teaching careers.

Niklasson (2018) suggests that adapting mentoring strategies also encourages trainees to become reflective practitioners. By modelling flexibility and responsiveness, mentors show them the importance of being adaptable and reflective in their own teaching practices. This skill is crucial for teachers, who must continuously assess and adjust their methods to meet the diverse needs of their students. Through this process, trainees learn to be more self-aware, critical, and innovative in their approach to teaching (Horn and Metler-Armijo, 2010).

The central barriers that can impede effective mentoring schemes in institutions

Mentoring schemes in educational institutions have the potential to significantly enhance the professional development of teachers, students, and other staff members (Iredale, 2015). However, various barriers can impede the effectiveness of these mentoring programmes. Recognising and addressing these barriers is crucial for the success of mentoring initiatives.

- Indifferent institutional culture and support

    If the institution does not actively support and prioritise mentoring programmes, it can lead to a lack of resources, recognition, and encouragement for participants, and in some institutions, there may be resistance to

new mentoring initiatives due to entrenched practices or scepticism about their value (Allen, Eby and Lentz, 2006).
- Institutional resource limitations

    Limited funding can restrict the availability of resources, training, and support necessary for a robust mentoring programme, and in addition, a shortage of experienced mentors can lead to overburdening and inadequate support for mentees (Stahl, Sharplin and Kehrwald, 2017).
- Insufficient training and support

    Mentors may not receive proper training on how to mentor effectively, leading to a lack of confidence and skills in providing meaningful support. Mentors and mentees may need continuous support and resources to navigate challenges and develop their mentoring relationship effectively (Cope, 2024).
- Lack of clear institutional goals and structure

    Without clear institutional goals and objectives, mentoring programmes can lack direction and purpose, making it difficult to measure progress and success. This lack of structured processes and guidelines can result in inconsistent mentoring experiences and varying levels of support (Iredale, 2015).
- Lack of evaluation and feedback processes

    Without proper assessment mechanisms, it can be difficult to assess the effectiveness of the mentoring programme and identify areas for improvement. Regular feedback from both parties is crucial for continuous improvement. A lack of structured feedback processes can impede the programme's growth (Cope, 2024).
- Weak institutional diversity and inclusivity policies

    A lack of diversity in mentor-mentee pairings can limit the perspectives and experiences shared, reducing the richness of the mentoring experience. Therefore, ensuring equitable access to mentoring opportunities for all individuals, regardless of their background, is essential for a truly inclusive programme (Carroll and Barnes, 2015).
- Heavy institutional workloads

    Both parties often have demanding schedules, making it challenging to find regular, dedicated time for mentoring sessions. Insufficient time allocated for mentoring activities can limit the depth and quality of the interactions, reducing the overall effectiveness of the programme (2015).
- Problems with institutional confidentiality policies

    Building trust is essential for effective mentoring. Concerns about confidentiality and the potential misuse of shared information can hinder open communication. This can have several adverse impacts on the potential success of a mentoring culture (Norley, 2017). For example, if mentees are not confident that their conversations will remain confidential, they may be reluctant to share personal challenges, concerns, or seek advice. This limits the depth and effectiveness of the mentoring relationship, and without this trust, interactions between mentors and mentees may remain superficial, preventing meaningful dialogue and genuine support (Ragins, 1989).

Potential mentees may also be hesitant to participate in the mentoring programme if they perceive that confidentiality is not adequately maintained. This can lead to lower involvement and engagement rates. They may choose to withdraw from the programme if they experience breaches of confidentiality, undermining the programme's continuity and success (Hobson *et al.*, 2015).

Breaches of confidentiality can harm the institution's reputation, making it appear unreliable and untrustworthy in managing sensitive information. Therefore, the effectiveness and credibility of the mentoring programme, and by extension, the institution, can be questioned if confidentiality and trust are compromised (Klasen and Clutterbuck, 2002). This can have the overall effect of compromising the mentoring programme as participants may not feel safe and supported in the mentoring environment.

Self-reflection exercise

What can you do to help build a successful mentoring culture in your workplace? Complete the table.

Central institutional barriers to the effectiveness of mentoring	*Strategies to manage them*
Indifferent institutional culture and support	
Institutional resource limitations	
Insufficient training and support	
Lack of clear institutional goals and structure	
Lack of evaluation and feedback processes	
Weak institutional diversity and inclusivity policies	
Heavy institutional workloads	
Problems with institutional confidentiality policies	

Conclusion

In conclusion, I hope this book has shown that mentoring in post-compulsory education stands as a pivotal element in fostering a robust educational ecosystem. Its impact extends far beyond the immediate benefits of guidance and support for mentees; it cultivates a culture of continuous professional development, reflective practice, and collaborative growth. Effective mentoring empowers educators at all stages of their careers, from novice teachers honing their craft to experienced practitioners seeking to refine their skills. This culture of mentorship not only enhances teaching quality but also promotes higher job satisfaction, reducing turnover rates and fostering institutional stability.

Through personalised support and constructive feedback, mentoring helps educators navigate the complexities of modern teaching, adapt to diverse student needs, and implement innovative pedagogical strategies. In addition, a well-structured mentoring programme contributes to the broader educational community by nurturing leaders who are committed to lifelong learning and the advancement of the profession (Klasen and Clutterbuck, 2002).

As teachers grow and succeed, their positive impact ripples outwards, enriching the learning experiences of countless students. Thus, embedding effective mentoring practices within institutions is not merely an investment in individuals but a strategic imperative that elevates the entire educational landscape, ensuring sustainable, high-quality education for future generations.

References

Aderibigbe, S.A., Holland, E., Marusic, I. and Shanks, R. (2022) 'A comparative study of barriers to mentoring student and new teachers', *Mentoring & Tutoring: partnership in Learning*, 30(3), pp. 355–376.

Allen, T., Eby, L. and Lentz, E. (2006) 'The relationship between formal mentoring program characteristics and perceived program effectiveness', *Personnel Psychology*, 59, pp. 125–153. doi:10.1111/j.1744-6570.2006.00747.x.

Angelique, H., Kyle, K. and Taylor, E. (2002) 'Mentors and muses: new strategies for academic success', *Innovative Higher Education*, 26, pp. 195–209. doi:10.1023/A:1017968906264.

Beattie, R.S., Kim, S., Hagen, M.S., Egan, T.M., Ellinger, A.D. and Hamlin, R.G. (2014) 'Managerial coaching: a review of the empirical literature and development of a model to guide future practice', *Human Resources*, 16, pp. 184–201.

Beatty, C.C. and Guthrie, K.L. (2025) '7 Leadership learning and college student leadership development', *The Routledge handbook on postsecondary student success*. Routledge.

Carroll, H.C., Owens, J. and Langston, J. (2021) *The school mentor's guide: how to mentor new and beginning teachers*. SAGE Publications, Limited.

Carroll, M.A. and Barnes, E.F. (2015) 'Strategies for enhancing diverse mentoring relationships in STEM fields', *International Journal of Evidence-Based Coaching and Mentoring*, 13(1), pp. 58–69.

Cope, M. (2024) *Seven Cs of coaching*. Routledge.

Daresh, J.C. (2002) *Teachers mentoring teachers: a practical approach to helping new and experienced staff*. Corwin Press.

Dominguez, N. and Hager, M. (2013) 'Mentoring frameworks: synthesis and critique', *International Journal of Mentoring and Coaching in Education*. doi:10.1108/IJMCE-03-2013-0014.

Eklin, J. (2006) 'A review of mentoring relationships: formation, function, benefits, and dysfunction', *Otago Management Graduate Review*, 4, pp. 11–23.

Gravells, J. and Wallace, S. (2007) *Mentoring in the lifelong learning sector*. SAGE Publications, Limited.

Hansman, C.A. (2002). 'Diversity and power in mentoring relationships', *Critical Perspectives on Mentoring: Trends and Issues*, 3, pp. 39–48.

Hobson, A.J., Maxwell, B., Stevens, A., Doyle, K. and Malderez, A. (2015) *Mentoring and coaching for teachers in the further education and skills sector in England: full report*. Education Research Centre, University of Brighton Centre for Education and Inclusion Research, Sheffield Hallam University.

Horn, P.J. and Metler-Armijo, K. (2010) *Toolkit for mentor practice*. Corwin Press.

Irby, B.J., Boswell, L.J., Searby, F.R., Kochan, F. and Garza R. (2020) *The Wiley international handbook of mentoring*. John Wiley & Sons.

Iredale, A. (2015) In pursuit of professional knowledge and practice: some experiences of lifelong learning sector trainee teachers in England 2008-10. Doctoral thesis, University of Huddersfield. available at http://eprints.hud.ac.uk/id/eprint/26227.

Kemmis, S., Heikkinen, H., Fransson, G., Aspfors, J. and Edwards-Groves, C. (2014) 'Mentoring of new teachers as a contested practice: supervision, support and collaborative self-development', *Teaching and Teacher Education*, 43, pp. 154–164. doi:10.1016/j.tate.2014.07.001.

Klasen, N. and Clutterbuck, D. (2002) *Implementing mentoring schemes, a practical guide to successful programs.* Butterworth-Heinemann.

Mullen, C.A. and Lick, D.W. (eds.) (1999) *New directions in mentoring: creating a culture of synergy.* Taylor & Francis Group.

Niklasson, L., (2018) 'Mentors in Initial Teacher Education-initiatives for professional development', *Journal of Arts and Humanities*, 7(8), pp. 11–22.

Norley, K. (2017) 'Mentoring teacher trainees of mathematics for ESL learners in post-compulsory education', *International Journal of Mentoring and Coaching in Education*, 6(1), pp. 64–77.

Pelissier, C. (2020) *Support in education.* John Wiley and Sons.

Portner, H. (2008) *Mentoring new teachers.* Corwin Press.

Ragins, B.R. (1989) 'Barriers to mentoring: the female manager's dilemma', *Human Relations*, 42(1), pp. 1–22.

Sempowicz, T. and Hudson, P. (2012) 'Mentoring preservice teachers' reflective practices to produce teaching outcomes', *International Journal of Evidence Based Coaching and Mentoring*, 10(2), pp. 52–64.

Stahl, G., Sharplin, E. and Kehrwald, B. (2017) *Real-time coaching and pre-service teacher education.* Springer.

Index

academic studies 246–249
accommodation 213, 215, 218, 224
accountability 171, 179; and improvement 226; and progress monitoring 179
action-reflection model 64–65, 66
active listening 236
advocacy: for neurodivergent rights 213; self-advocacy 213, 216
agency 71, 213, 260
Aguirre-Garzón, E.A. 121
Alnajjar, K. 113
American Institute for Research (AIR) 45
anxiety reduction 140
appreciative feedback approach 180–181; strengths of 182; weaknesses of 182
appreciative inquiry (AI) 71–74; Anticipatory Principle 73; Constructionist Principle 72; phases of 73–74; Poetic Principle 72; Positive Principle 72; Principle of Simultaneity 72
apprenticeship model of mentoring 59–60
Astall, C. 48
autonomy 60, 96, 205, 213; and agency 213; and learning in partnership models 7
awareness 47, 65–69, 90, 123, 203, 215

Bachkirova, T. 94
barriers: to effective feedback 187–188; impeding effective mentoring schemes in institutions 262–264
Bateson, G. 67
Bell, J. 127
Bereiter, C. 121
Beyene, T. 51

bias/prejudice 43, 207–211
Bird, M. 121
Blinkert, J. 72
body language 201
boundaries and evaluation process 223
Bronfenbrenner, U. 67
Burn, K. 115, 121

career mentor **35**
career support theories 9–10
cheerleader mentor **34**
Cheng, T.L. 33
Clancy, A.L. 72
Classroom Assessment Scoring System (CLASS) 146
classroom environment and atmosphere 145
classroom management 144
CLEAR model 87–89; limitations 88; mindful listening group practice 88–89; overview 87
Clutterbuck, D. 96, 99
coaching 78; defined 11; integrating mentoring and 80; and mentoring 10–11; *vs.* mentoring 78–79; models and mentoring 81–82
coaching mentor **34**
COACH model 89–91, 95; limitations 90; overview 89–90; self-reflection activity 91
collaboration: mentor recruitment in education 41–42; with placement colleagues 250–252; shared decision-making 41; weaknesses of using 42
collaborative mentoring workshop 63–64
colleague peer mentor **35**
Colley, H. 106

communication 236; adapting 215–216; direct 201; egalitarian 201; hierarchical 201; indirect 201; nonverbal 201–202; patterns 203; styles 188, 200; verbal 200–201
Community of Practice (COP) 62
confidence building 140
confidentiality 16, 189, 222–224, 227
confirmation bias 164–165
conflict resolution 203
connecting mentor **34**
constructive feedback 245–246
constructivism 225
content mentor **33**
Cooperrider, D.L. 71
co-planning: benefits for mentee 118–119; benefits for mentor 117–118; benefits of 117–119; developing teaching resources 129–132; enhanced learning experience 118; enhanced professional growth 117; importance of 123–124; importance of questioning 126–127; increased confidence 118; increased job satisfaction 118; mentee's scheme of work design 127–129; professional development 118; rubrics 124–126; self-reflection 118; skill development 118; stages of 119–121; *see also* lesson planning; supporting planning
co-regulation 61–62
co-teaching 132–133
course tutors 240–241
Cox, E. 94
critical feedback 175
critical friend *vs.* pastoral supporter 101–102
critiquing, challenging mentor **35**
cultivation stage of mentoring 12
cultural and diversity factors 188
cultural bias 166
cultural capital 9
cultural conflict styles 203
cultural iceberg exercise 202
cultural perceptions of success 202
customisation 180

Dantzler, M. 47
DeNisi, A. 170
design phase, appreciative inquiry 73
destiny phase, appreciative inquiry 73–74
developmental mentoring 25

developmental theories: Kegan's Developmental Stages 8–9; Levinson's Life Stage Theory 8; mentoring with 8–10
differentiation 120, 128, 130, 144, 145, 146
direct communication 201
directive feedback approach 180; strengths of 181; weaknesses of 181
directive mentoring relationship 49
direct observation of tasks 187
disciplinary action 232–236
discovery phase, appreciative inquiry 73
dream phase, appreciative inquiry 73
Duckworth, V. 27

Eaton, A. 47
ecological systems theory 97
education: aspirations 202–203; mentoring in 23–25
Education and Training Foundation (ETF) 26
effective mentorship in teacher education 258–259
egalitarian communication 201
emotional intelligence skills (EI) 236–237
emotional reactions 188
employee development 6
encouragement 171, 179
equity 199, 225, 262
ethical boundaries: central ethical issues faced by mentors 260–261; maintaining 170–195; mentor feedback, approaches to 170–195; and mentor feedback 170–195
ethical conduct 226
evaluative feedback approach 180; strengths of 181–182; weaknesses of 181–182
Everatt, J. 48
expectations/goals 202
external partnerships 40–41

face to face feedback 184–185
face work theory 175
fairness 61, 166, 223–225
feedback: adapting 215–216; communication styles 188; cultural and diversity factors 188; emotional reactions 188; Feedback 173; Feedforward 173–174; Feed up 173;

lack of direct observation of tasks 187; lack of specificity 188; lack of trust 188; organising successful session 189–190; and reflection 145; time constraints 188
Feedforward 173–174
Feed up 173
Fisher-Ari, T.R. 47
Flanders Interaction Analysis Categories (FIAC) 146
flash mentoring 16–17
Fletcher, J. 48
follow-me 133–134; active learning 133; building trust and rapport 134; demonstrating best practices 133; immediate feedback 133; real-time observation 133
formal mentoring programmes 11, 13–14
formative observations 143
Fulton, L.A. 48
Furlong, J. 65

gestures 29, 201
goal, reality, options, and will (GROW) 184–185
goals and objectives: availability/commitment 50–51; mentees 50–51; and mentees 54; mentors 50–51; and mentors 54
Goffman, Erving 175
GROW model: checklist of guide questions when using 83–84; Health Action Process Approach (HAPA) 84; limitations 82–83; overview 81–82
growth 171; and development 226; promoting 178
Guedes, B.A.M. 96

Hackworth, J.M. 33
Hadwin, A. 61
Hagger, H. 115, 121
Halo and the Horn effects 165–166
Hargreaves, A. 65
harmonious relationship 108
Hattie, J. 170, 172–173
Hawthorne effect 161–163
Health Action Process Approach (HAPA) 84
hierarchical communication 201
hierarchical structures 205
Hobson, A. 6, 25

imbalance of influence 52
improved performance 6
inclusion 199, 213
inclusive and supportive environment 215
inclusive mentoring relationships 200–204; communication patterns 203; conflict resolution 203; cultural conflict styles 203; cultural perceptions of success 202; educational aspirations 202–203; expectations and goals 202; mentor cultural awareness and sensitivity 200; nonverbal communication 201–202; support systems and resources 203; verbal communication 200–201
incompatible personal histories and dispositions 52–53
indirect communication 201
informal mentoring 14–15
Ingleby, E. 101
in-house recruitment 38–40
Initial Teacher Education (ITE) 29–30, 240, 243–244, 259
initiation stage of mentoring 11
institutional culture 39, 41
institutions 262–264
instructional strategies 144
integrity and mentoring relationship 224–226
interactive relationship 49
International Comparison Analysis of Learning and Teaching (ICALT) 146
intersectionality self-reflective task for prospective mentor teachers 213–214
ITE tutors 243–244

Jacobi, M. 13
Järvelä, S. 61
joint planning sessions 245
judgemental mentoring 25
judgements 101

Kardos, S.M. 51
Kilburg, G. 61
Kleiner, A. 135
Kluger, A.N. 170
knowledge transfer 6
Kochan, F. 107, 108
Kram, K.E. 11, 96
Kvale, S. 59

lack of specificity 188
lack of trust 188
Lai, Y.-L. 94–95
language nuances 200–201
Lave, J. 62
Lawy, R. 101, 104
learning 178–179
learning outcomes 144, 178
learning partnership: mentoring as 7–8
Legitimate Peripheral Participation (LPP) 120
Lejonberg, E. 61
lesson planning 115; case study 123; characteristics of 115; for mentor 117; self-reflection scenario exercise 126; supported by mentors 118–119; for trainee teacher 115–116; *see also* co-planning
line managers as mentors 48
listening and feedback 201–202

Malderez, A. 25
managerialism 101
Mathematical Quality of Instruction framework (MQI) 146
Maxwell, B. 27
Maynard, T. 65
McDowall, A. 94–95
McHenry, L.K. 95
medical pathologisation 213
mentees: availability/commitment 50–51; benefits of mentoring 5; collaboration 41–42; with diverse needs 261–262; external partnerships 40–41; goals and objectives 50–51; importance of adapting strategies to meet needs of 261–262; in-house recruitment 38–40; matching 50–52; mismatches between mentor 51–52; neurodiverse 214–215; power relationships between mentors and 52–54; recruitment and selection of 38–44; relationship with mentors 23–24; role clarity 53–54; selection by 42–43; self-evaluation prompts for 172; strengths of 42–43; transitioning 54–55; weaknesses of 43
mentor(s) 94–110; attitudes about their mentees 104–105; attitudes and dispositions 45; availability/ commitment 50–51; barriers to effective recruitment and selection of 47–48; benefits of mentoring 5; collaboration 41–42; cultural awareness and sensitivity 200; cultural barriers 108–110; and cultural factors 107–108; defined 4, 24; external partnerships 40–41; goals and objectives 50–51; importance of reflective practice as 259–260; in-house recruitment 38–40; lesson planning for 117; line managers as 48; matching 50–52; mentor and mentee roles 100–102; mentoring relationships 95–96; mentoring relationship theories 97–99; mentoring skills and attributes 94–95; mentors' attitudes about their mentees 104–105; mismatches between mentees 51–52; neurodiverse 216–219; outcomes 104, **106**; power relationships 103–104; power relationships and mentoring 103–104; power relationships between mentees and 52–54; recruitment and selection of 38–44; relationships and reflection 102–103; relationship with mentee 23–24; role clarity 53–54; selection 44–46; self-reflection 102–103; self-reflection activity 99–100, **102**, 105–107, 110; self-reflective question 102; staff development session activity for prospective 204; stages of mentoring 96–97; subjectivity and bias 164–166; support for academic studies 246–249; training exercise for mentors and mentees 106–107; tutor and 249–250
mentor and mentee roles 100–102; confusion of differing models 101; critical friend *vs.* pastoral supporter 101–102; lack of understanding of programme content 100–101; managerialism, judgements, and mentoring 101; responsibilities of mentoring 101
mentor feedback: accountability 179; aligning teaching practices 178; approaches to 170–195; barriers to effective feedback 187–188; clarity and focus 179; critical feedback using face work theory 175; customisation and personalisation 180; effective verbal observation feedback 190–192; enhancing learning outcomes 178;

face to face feedback 184–185; four levels of feedback 170; given 177–180; Hattie and Timperley 172–173; main phases of feedback 173–174; and maintaining ethical boundaries 170–195; mentorship and support 179; motivation and accountability 179; oral feedback 193–194; Pendleton's 'Feedback Sandwich' 186–187; phases of 176–177; preparedness and confidence 178; progress monitoring 179; promoting reflection and growth 178; reflection and learning 178–179; reflection and self-awareness 179; self-reflection activity 176; self-reflection task 183–184, 195; self-reflective activity 183; situation, behaviour, impact (SBI) 185–186; some obstacles to effective 174–175; some preconditions for 172–173; successful feedback session 189–190; for trainee teacher 171–172; using online feedback 194–195; validation and encouragement 179; written observation feedback 192–194

mentoring 199; apprenticeship model of 59–60; and coaching 10–11, 78–79; and coaching models 81–82; community of practice 59; conceptions of 1, 53; definitions of 1–2, 10–11; with developmental theories 8–10; and disciplinary action 232–236; and disciplinary issues 29–33; in education 23–25; generic benefits of 5; integrating coaching and 80; as a learning partnership 7–8; learning through imitation 60; and neurodiversity 211; neurodiversity and 214–215; professional identity 60; as a psychosocial support system 6–7; quality of product 60; and reflection 65–67; relationships 48–49; and relationships 61–62; stages and categories of 11–13; trainee who is mentoring neurodiverse mentee 214–215; in workforce as a whole 2–5

mentoring relationships: active listening and communication 236; approaches to failure and repairing 222–237; clarify expectations 236; confidentiality and privacy 227; emotional intelligence skills (EI) 236–237; establish trust 236; growth and improvement 236; initiate a conversation 236; and integrity 224–226; integrity in evaluation processes 226; mentoring and disciplinary action 232–236; professional boundaries in 222–224; reflect on the situation 235; regular check-ins 236; self-reflection activity 227–228; taking responsibility 235; things going wrong in 229–232

mentorship 179; approaches 206–207; respect for diversity 206–207
mentor training exercise 202
Mezirow, J. 8
Miller, M. 61
monitoring 179
Most Knowledgeable Other (MKO) concept 113
motivation 179
Mullen, C.A. 17
Multi-Academy Trusts (MATs) 239
Mutton, T. 115, 121

networking events 43
neurodivergent rights 213
neurodiverse mentee 214–215
neurodiverse mentors 216–219
neurodiverse trainees: adapt communication and feedback 215–216; fostering inclusive and supportive environment 215; increase awareness and understanding 215; self-advocacy and development 216; structured support and resources 216; ways to develop support of 215–216
neurodiversity 211; and mentoring 214–215
neurological diversity 212
Nielsen, K. 59
nonverbal communication 201–202
novice-oriented cultures 51

Objective and Unbiased Assessment 225
observations and feedback 139–167; importance 139–140; mentee for teaching observation 140–141; overview 139; qualitative approaches 145–146, 148–160; quantitative approaches 144–145, 146–148; self-reflection 141; self-reflection exercise

166–167; summative and formative approaches 142–143; validity/reliability 161–166
OFSTED criteria for teaching observations 159–160
O'Leary 191
online feedback 194–195
ONSIDE mentoring 26–28, **29**
oral feedback 193–194
Orem, S.L. 72
OSCAR model 85–87, 95; limitations 86; overview 85–86; stages of **86–87**

Panchal, S. 84
partnership models 239–255; collaboration with placement colleagues 250–252; joint observations 241–244; joint teaching observations 245–246; mentor support for academic studies 246–249; placement mentors and course tutors 240–241; post-compulsory education 239; reflective activity 244–245; subject specialist mentor and pastoral mentor 252–255; tutor and mentor 249–250
Pascarelli, J.T. 107
pastoral mentor 252–255
Pedagogical Content Knowledge (PCK) 120
pedagogical philosophy 55
Peer Collaborative Mentoring (PCM) 61
peer mentoring 15
Peer Mentor support 62–63
Pendleton's 'Feedback Sandwich' 186–187
personal and collective orientations 206
personalisation 145, 180
personal space and proximity 201
placement mentors 240–241
post-compulsory education 239
Powell, C. 120
power dynamics 205
power relationships 103–104
practice theory 65–66
pre-observation briefing 245
preparedness and confidence 178
privacy 227
professional boundaries in mentoring relationship 222–224
professional culture 51

professional development 118, 140, 149, 171, 246, 249; accountability and growth 171; trainee teacher 171; validation and encouragement 171
professional growth 42
professional identity 60
professionalism 65, 222, 226
progress monitoring 179
psychosocial support system: counselling 7; mentoring as 6–7; role modelling 6–7; social integration and networking 7
Pylman, S. 117, 124–125, 127

quality assurance 226

reciprocity, importance of 113–115
redefinition stage of mentoring 12–13
reflection 178–179; and professional growth 146; promoting 178
relationship dynamics, of mentor-mentee 54
relationships: directive mentoring 49; interactive 49; issues between tutor and mentor 249–250; and mentoring 61–62; responsive mentoring 48; unequal power 52
representativeness of teaching observation 163–164
respect and value cultural differences 200
respect for diversity 206–207
respect for neurological diversity 212
responsive mentoring relationship 48
reverse-follow-me 134–135; active participation 134; peer learning 134–135; reflection and feedback 134; skill development 135
reverse mentoring 17–18
Riddell, P. 84
Roth, G. 135
rubrics 124–126; clarity and consistency 124; collaboration and communication 125; formative assessment 124; prompt checklist 125; skill development 124

Saariaho, E. 62
Scandura, T.A. 25
Schön, D.A. 133–134
Schunk, D.H. 17
Schwille, S.A. 115

Science, Technology, Engineering, Arts, and Mathematics (STEAM) 239
selection by mentee 42–43
self-advocacy 213, 216
self-awareness 179
self-evaluation prompts for the mentee 172
self-reflection 46
self-reflection activity 176, 183, 227–228
self-reflection exercise 264
self-reflection task 183–184, 195, 219
self-reflective questions 177
semi-structured observations 152–156
separation stage of mentoring 12
shared decision-making 41
situation, behaviour, impact (SBI) 185–186
Snyder, W.M. 66
social capital 9
social capital theory 98–99
social cognitive career theory (SCCT) 97
social desirability 105
social exchange theory 98
social explanatory models **105**
socialisation 9
social model of disability 211–214
social theories 9, 10
social utility 105
Srivastva, S. 71
staff development session activity for prospective mentors 204
stages of mentoring 96–97
Stevenson, J. 107
student engagement 144
student engagement and interaction 145
subject specialist mentor 252–255
succession planning 6
summative observations 142–143
supporting planning: benefits of co-planning a lesson 117–119; concurrent 122; co-teaching 132–133; developing teaching resources 129–132; differentiating instruction 132; ensuring accessibility 131; follow-me 133–134; identifying resource needs 131; importance of co-planning 123–124; importance of questioning 126–127; importance of reciprocity 113–115; integrating technology 131; lack of experience 130; lack of knowledge of learning levels 131; lesson planning 115; lesson planning with mentor 117; mentee's scheme of work design 127–129; mentor and mentee joint reflection exercise 136; and observing classroom practice 113–136; promoting sustainability 132; providing feedback 131; reverse-follow-me 134–135; sourcing materials 131; stages of co-planning lesson 119–121; team-teaching 135–136; Think Alouds 121–123; time constraints 130; uncertainty about student needs 130; using rubrics 124–126; *see also* co-planning
support systems and resources 203
systemic mentoring (SM) 67–71; developing approaches to 69–71; and questioning 68–69

Taylor, E. 8
teacher education 258–259
teaching identity 55
teaching practices 178
Teaching School Alliances (TSAs) 239
teaching strategies and approaches 145
team mentoring 16
team-teaching 135–136; building trust and rapport 136; immediate feedback 135; professional growth 135; shared expertise 135
Tedder, M. 101, 104
Think Alouds 121–123; benefits of 122–123; retrospective/reflective 122–123
time constraints 188
time management 144
Timperley, H. 170, 172–173
trainee teacher: improvement and reflection 171; mentor feedback important for 171–172; professional development 171
transformational mentoring 25–26
transformative feedback approach 181; strengths of 182; weaknesses of 182
tutors: ITE 243–244; and mentor 249–250

Unconditional Positive Regard (UPR) 95
unconscious bias 207–211
understanding 215
unequal power relationships 52
unprofessional behaviour 30–31

unstructured teaching observations 156–159
Utilitarianism 225

validation 171, 179
verbal communication 200–201
verbal observation feedback 190–192
verbal teaching observation feedback: strengths of 194; weaknesses of 194
veteran-oriented cultures 51
virtual mentoring 18–19
Vygotsky, L.S. 113

Wang, J. 48
Weasmer, J. 66
Wenger, E. 62
Wexler, L.J. 114
Whitmore, J. 81
Williams, E.A. 25
Woods, A.M. 66
workshops 43
written observation feedback 192–194
written teaching observation feedback: strengths of 193; weaknesses of 193

For Product Safety Concerns and Information please contact our EU
representative GPSR@taylorandfrancis.com
Taylor & Francis Verlag GmbH, Kaufingerstraße 24, 80331 München, Germany

www.ingramcontent.com/pod-product-compliance
Lightning Source LLC
Chambersburg PA
CBHW051606230426
43668CB00013B/1998